JUNGLE GREEN
& RUGBY

MEMOIRS OF A COMMON SOLDIER

C W (TASI) WOODARD

To order additional copies of this book, contact:
Xlibris
AU TFN: 1 800 844 927 (Toll Free inside Australia)
AU Local: 02 8310 8187 (+61 2 8310 8187 from outside Australia)
www.xlibris.com.au
Orders@Xlibris.com.au

ISBN:	Softcover	978-1-6698-8770-6
	Hardcover	978-1-6698-8772-0
	EBook	978-1-6698-8771 -3

Library of Congress Control Number: 2022905973

Print information available on the last page

Rev. date: 02/27/2023

ABOUT THE AUTHOR

The author's family heritage is traced back to convict stock with the mother's side Irish and the father's English.

Tasi was born on a remote Bass Strait Island at the end of the great depression and before the initiation of World War Two. With little schooling he virtually lived off the land, never experienced electricity or even riding in a car for the first ten years of his life. This period existed mainly in dairy farming along with many other requirements, with his father and two elder siblings.

His family's military history details ten members, which involved service in World War One and World War Two. Tasi's military service covered almost twenty-six years during both times of peace and warfare, with six years of service in southeast Asia, Malaysia, and Viet Nam.

The author's post-military service included involvement in the 100th anniversary (2018) of the battles on the Western Front with a presentation to the Mayor of Montbrehain, France (the village reclaimed in General Monash's last conflict of World War One utilising the Australian Imperial Forces), Dawn Services at both Gallipoli, Turkey and Villers Bretonneux, France which upon invitation, included a wreath-laying ceremony at Menin Gate, Ypres Belgium on behalf of Australia.

Tasi's rugby career extended over forty years, in both service and civilian capacity. The book details the many stories of his involvement as a player, captain, and captain/coach of local and representative military rugby in both the northern and southern hemispheres. This then transpired into a tenure of involvement within the Queensland Rugby Union.

Tasi shares the creation and his Australian involvement with the development of the Veterans and Golden Oldies Rugby movement up to an international level.

The travelling experience of the author covers six continents with much of it being rugby-related though also covers numerous other sporting experiences. It involves some of the world's great and renowned sporting identities with Tasi being entertained by some.

This book is factual, historical, political, sporting, humorous and sad, and reaches out to an age group from the 1930s into the twenty-first century.

The author is at home on the Sunshine Coast, Queensland Australia. Along with his military medals, Tasi was awarded the Australian Sports Medal in the year 2000 (struck to commemorate the new millennium) for his dedication and achievements in rugby.

BY THE AUTHOR

Retired and following several years of urging by my son Norman, I finally put pen to paper to tell my story. I produced the detail and Norman collated a large volume of work. After having the manuscript appraised by qualified personnel, it was suggested that the merited content would be better served in two books.

With their advice duly followed the first book printed was *'Queensland Women in Rugby. The First Two Years 1996 - 1997'* to coincide with the 25th anniversary (2021) of this outstanding team. My original intention was to produce a book of their achievements to gift to them at the anniversary function.

This second book *'Jungle Green and Rugby'* unfolds my memoirs, in particular, a lifetime of military and sporting history, and to date, I am eighty-three years of age and still going strong.

Many readers will be able to relate to their past family military history, their own military engagement or similar sporting involvements, and perhaps in some cases, all of these scenarios. In any event, I trust you enjoy the book.

—m—

ACKNOWLEDGEMENT

It can be difficult being a soldier's wife and even more trying, once that military man has retired. It too can be said that a wife of an active, sporting person in both a playing and administrative capacity can be challenging. So when one is both a soldier and also participates in a sporting environment, which exceeds forty years it requires someone special to support, encourage and cheer their journey. To that, I gratefully thank my wonderful wife Ailsa.

I would also like to thank Heather Duniam (nee Woodard) from Bruny Island, Tasmania, for her pursuing the family history of the Woodwards'/Woodards' tracing back before 1770 in the borough of Chesterfield Derbyshire, England. This exercise took Heather several years including research into the archives of early Van Diemans Land (Tasmanian) history.

To my last auntie, Rosie Barnes from King Island, Tasmania, and past Barnes generations are to be recognised and thanked for information regarding their lineage, which was traced back to County Galway, Ireland in the early 1800s. Without their input, the family heritage on both sides of my family could not have been documented in this book.

Along with the photographs that I have taken and the family members and friends who have gifted such items, I wish to acknowledge the sources of materials that helped to mould this book to ensure its integrity and enhance the readers' experience.

All images and editorials are public and were kindly made available by the following sources with no restrictions or no known restrictions. Attributions have been identified where appropriate and every care was taken to gain permission as required.

Sources:

Australian War Memorial
Free World Maps
National Archives of Australia
National Library of Australia
Public Domain – The United States. Central Intelligence Agency
The Public Information Network Group
Wikimedia Commons

I also wish to thank Gary McKay for his advice with regards to the manuscript, subsequent book layout, and images from his book; Gary McKay and Graeme Nicholas, Jungle Tracks, Australian Armour In Vietnam, Allen & Unwin, 2001, Australia.

Finally, I wish to acknowledge the time and expertise Norman has contributed towards the compilation of this book and allowing this story to be told.

—ɱ—

DISCLAIMER

"During my almost twenty-six years of military service I have never kept a diary so some dates mentioned during this time may not be accurate, however, the contents are factual.

Historically before my time and during my time, the narrative of my memoirs expressed within the text is, to me being of sound mind, and the contributors' best knowledge, accurate."

Tasi Woodard.

INTRODUCTION

They say that you cannot take it with you to the grave however when someone leaves this place, they do take with them so much in the way of the many memories and stories of their life experiences. I discussed this with my son Norman a long time ago. *"I believe everyone has a story,"* I shared with him. He has stated that this is one of the many quotes from me that has always lived with him.

I was always going to join the army and I loved my sport. My life is perhaps unique to most Australians and further to this, no one had any bearing over me. So my self-directed future was decided whenever I felt the time or opportunity presented itself.

The greatest impact on my life was the twenty-six years of military service in the Australian Regular Army while rugby was at the heart of the sporting side, with forty-one years dedicated to the many facets of the great game. Even to this day, I am frequently in touch with associated reunions and social activities within both the military and rugby worlds.

I was enjoying retirement, keeping healthy in a gymnasium and swimming regime with fishing as an added activity, while Norman chanted, *"You need to tell your story. You have an articulate mind with clear memories of what has transpired in your life. As you have witnessed with people, in time this can, unfortunately, leave us."*

After constant urging from him, I did put pen to paper. It seemed difficult at the beginning, though I found that once started and the more I wrote, the more I recalled and upon reflection and timelines, I found so many moments, people, subjects and events that needed to be mentioned. This led to a body of works that manuscript assessors suggested that there were two books within this story … and so this is the second book.

At the time of writing, I am still enjoying retirement with everything it has to offer and believe everyone does have a story to tell. This is usually lost when they pass so I suggest that it should be catalogued in some way, shape or form as I am glad to have been pushed to tell mine, which ironically now completes another chapter of my life.

CONTENTS

About The Author...iii

By The Author v

Acknowledgement..vii

Disclaimer...ix

Introduction...xi

Chapter 1   Origin and Family Heritage 1

Chapter 2   King Island 7

Chapter 3   1939 – 1956 10

Chapter 4   A Brief Family Military History 22

Chapter 5   Military History of 61106 WOODARD C W 42

             Glossary Of Terms And Acronyms 63

Chapter 6   Military Oddities 78

Chapter 7   Post-Military Service Events 119

Chapter 8   My Rugby Career 136

Chapter 9   Veterans and Golden Oldies Rugby 158

Chapter 10 My Sporting Career 181

Chapter 11 Sporting Oddities 189

Chapter 12 Seeing Australia 233

In Conclusion 263

Twenty-Fifth Anniversary 265

Bibliography 269

ONE

ORIGIN AND FAMILY HERITAGE

I Came From Convict Stock

In the past, three family members from different lineage traced my family and proved on all accounts from my father's and mother's ancestry, that we came from convict stock.

A brief history of convict exportation from 1787 to 1853.

Family heritage on my father's side can be dated before 1770 in the Borough of Chesterfield, Derbyshire, England.

From the marriage of John and Sarah Woodward, son Peter was baptised on the 25th of November 1770. William Woodward was born on the 13th of April 1806 to parents Peter Woodward and Anne Harrison. William was convicted of stealing a watch in 1828 and sentenced to Van Diemen's Land for seven years. He was transported by the vessel Prince Regent arriving in 1830.

William was released as recorded on the 22nd of October 1835 and was followed on the 17th of September 1836 by the issue of a Free Certificate No. 403, which allowed him from then on to be a free man.

William Woodward and his spouse Elizabeth Taylor had thirteen children and among them (tenth born) was Catherine (Fanny) Woodward; born 22nd November 1855. It is not known when she moved to Victoria however, she had a son out of wedlock in 1873 and retained the surname of Woodward (George William); being my grandfather.

George William was reared and married in Victoria then moved to Tasmania, where most of his family was born, which included my father, Harold Raymond. When marrying, George William, being semi-illiterate signed his wedding certificate deleting the second 'w' of his surname. Thus, the change of surname … Woodward to Woodard.

—⅏—

A family tree on my grandfather's side from the marriage of George William (now) Woodard and Mary Alice Jane (nee Dellaca) in its simplicity follows; the children from the marriage were:

George William (Junior)
Ivy married Archie
Myrtle child death
Walter child death
Doris married Weller
William Henry
Harold Raymond
Norman Francis
Alice married Young
Enid married Groom

I do not know what order Myrtle and Walter were born though both died in Victoria at an early age.

The following family photograph was taken at a time when George William (Snr) and his first-born George William (Jnr) were both absent due to World War One service.

Standing (left to right): William and Doris
Centre (left to right): Norman, Ivy, Alice, Mother and Harold
Front: Enid.

The children from the marriage of my father Harold Raymond Woodard and Enid Elvie (nee Barnes) on King Island, Tasmania in 1934 were:

Veronica married Keen – deceased 2017
Richard George – deceased 2000
Clifford Walter
Rhonda married Porteous
Mary Alice married Burns
Elaine married Blizzard
Maxine married Cartledge
Noelene married Pickett

The children from my marriage Clifford Walter Woodard and Barbara Mary (nee Worth) in Sydney, New South Wales in 1959 were:

Norman Clifford
Eric Alan

My marriage to Barbara broke down and we were divorced in 1972. I remarried in 1975 to Ailsa Marie (nee Richards).

Above are photographs of my father during various stages of his life from 1908 to 1985.

The family heritage on my mother's side can be traced back to 1830 in County Galway, Ireland when my great-great grandfather, William Conely was born. By the time he reached the age of nineteen he was convicted of sheep stealing (a hanging offence) and fighting and was sentenced to Van Diemen's Land (VDL) penal colony in Hobart, Tasmania. William was exported on the brig Blenheim under the stewardship of Captain Watson in 1849. This was four years before the cessation of convict exportation, which saw one hundred and sixty-two thousand convicted men and women sent to the colony between 1787 and 1853.

Following up to four years of convict labour in which he became an outstanding carpenter, William was given his freedom. He moved to Cape Barren Island, Tasmania, married, and had a son in 1854 named John Conely who would become my great grandfather. Is not known when John Conley left Cape Barren Island and moved to King Island, Tasmania. He married on King Island and had a daughter Grace Maud Conely (my grandmother) who in turn married Richard George Barnes in 1904. The marriage of my grandmother produced eleven children (the eighth born being my mother Enid) as follows:

Thelma Irene married Petterson
Lilyas Lavinia married Summers
Richard Charles
Eric Anthony
Phillis Jean married Scott
Dulcie Joyce died aged five
Richard Leonard
Enid Elvie married Woodard
Gwendoline Edna married Mathewson
Clifford Keith
Desmond Frank

My great grandfather John Conely died on King Island in 1902.

My Great Grandfather's grave is at Bell Hill, Currie, King Island Tasmania.
The inscription reads: In Loving Memory of John Conely
Died 19th August 1902 Aged 48 Years
"I HEARD THE VOICE OF JESUS SAY COME UNTO ME AND REST."

My grandparents on my mother's side
Richard George Barnes and Grace Maud Barnes (nee Conely).

Early images of my Mother Enid Elvie Barnes, King Island.

TWO

KING ISLAND

My Island of Birth

King Island is situated at the western entrance of Bass Strait, while a slightly larger island, Flinders Island is located at the eastern entrance of the Bass Strait both north of Tasmania and south of Victoria. Both islands are part of the state of Tasmania. King Island is a low-lying island some sixty-four kilometres long and twenty-five kilometres wide. It straddles one-third of the western entrance of the Bass Strait being ninety kilometres from Cape Otway in Victoria and a similar distance from the northwest coast of Tasmania.

Recorded history discloses that the island was discovered in 1798 by Captain Reed in the thirty-ton schooner *Martha*. The name was given to the island by Captain Black after Governor King of New South Wales when in 1801 he visited the island in the brig *Harbinger*. There was no indication of Aboriginal occupation on King Island.

In its earliest days, the island gained a worldwide reputation for the vast numbers of sea elephants and seals. This brought ships from all parts of the world with China as the main market for skins. It is recorded that Captain Campbell of the *Snow Harrington* killed six hundred sea elephants and four thousand three hundred seals, principally at New Year Island off the northwest coast of King Island. Because of this onslaught, no sea elephants and very few seals are seen around the coast today.

Shipping Disasters:

In early history, many trading vessels would sail under South Africa across the Indian Ocean en route to the spice islands (Dutch East Indies, now Indonesia). Many of these vessels were caught in the winds of the *roaring forties*, swept under Australia into the Bass Strait then come to grief on the rugged west coast of King Island.

Recorded shipwrecks around King Island are sixty-three dating from 1801 with the loss of seven hundred and thirty-six lives, the worst in 1845 with the wreck of the *Cataraqui* losing four hundred lives. The *Cataraqui* was a convict ship that also carried quite a few marines on board. The ship's destination was Queensland and was supposed to sail under Van Diemen's Land (Tasmania) and then proceed north up the Australian east coast to Queensland.

As the ship was running weeks late the captain to make up time elected to bypass Van Diemen's Land and cut through the Bass Strait resulting in being wrecked on the west coast of the island losing all. Another big loss was the *British Admiral* in 1874 losing seventy-nine lives.

Mining:

Scheelite, a tungsten ore was discovered in the southern end of the island (Grassy) in 1911 and the discovery led to the growth of a world-famous industry. Tungsten is an agent for hardening steel and was a precious metal during the World Wars as it prolonged the life of all weaponry barrels from rifles up to artillery and the huge naval ship barrels. My father never served in uniform during WWII as he became a worker in essential services being the foreman on the King Island wharf overseeing the export of this extremely precious metal during the time of war. At the cessation of the war, he elected to go back to dairy farming. The scheelite mine was eventually closed in the early 1970s following the Viet Nam War.

Timber:

King Island was once wooded with fine stands of gums and blackwoods, but early milling and a series of severe forest fires removed these. It is understood that even as late as the 1960s there was evidence to show that trees of around three hundred feet or more had not been uncommon.

In the undeveloped regions around the island, the rate of regrowth has been good with gums and blackwoods again reaching fair proportions in places.

A Unique Harvest:

The wealth of the seas around King Island has given it a unique and rich harvest being the collection and processing of wave-cast bull kelp from the island's coastline. After an uncertain start, King Islanders found that kelp harvesting was an extremely rewarding though rugged way of life.

In the first months of operations in 1975 kelp industries only exported thirty-five tonnes of processed kelp; production for the year 1976 was seven hundred and seventy-five tonnes.

Since 1989 the annual tonnage of dried kelp is around three thousand five hundred tonnes. Brown seaweeds such as bull kelp are rich in salts and derivatives of alginic acid. These alginates are used in over thirteen hundred products around the world. Besides a nutrient gel used in medical research, you probably eat, drink or wear some of these products every day perhaps in ice cream, beer or cosmetics.

Pastures:

King Island has been recognised as one of the best and safest grass-growing areas in Australia, with year-round growth. These factors with the island's temperate climate lend themselves admirably to dairying and raising quality beef, fat lambs and wool. Both King Island beef and its wool have high reputations.

From a fairly chequered past the King Island Dairy has become economically viable and with entrepreneurial skills has lifted the dairy to a world-class producer of specialty cheeses.

The modern dairy factory is designed to cope with increased production in all lines. For example, the capability now exists to produce one thousand kilograms per day of the famous King Island Brie cheese. The newly introduced Creme Fraiche lines have gained wide acceptance, particularly in restaurants. The output of King Island Cheddar cheeses is approximately one hundred and twenty tonnes per annum, but the capability is two tonnes per day. Mozzarella cheese is produced from low-fat milk after the milk has been separated. Employing about twenty-five people, King Island Dairy is another success story.

Hunting and Fishing:

King Island has been described as a sportsman's paradise in the past, and although the native game has been considerably reduced there are still seasons for the shooting of wallabies, pheasants and wild ducks. The seas are abundant with fish and fishing for them is popular from either the beaches, rocks or boats. Mutton birds are always considered a great delicacy by many, and this season is also looked forward to with great anticipation. Crayfish and abalone are fished commercially in the seas around King Island.

So concludes a brief outline of the place of my birth on the 31st of May 1939 at the Cottage Hospital, Currie, King Island.

THREE

1939 – 1956

I was a pre-World War II baby though only just, being born in May 1939 with the war erupting later in the year. Born on King Island, I was the third child of the marriage at the birthplace of my mother (nee Barnes) who was the eighth born of a large family of eleven.

My first home was a dairy farm called The Man Trap though I never lived there long before we moved to another dairy farm called The Grooms. I can recall some early life incidents at The Grooms with the first being a very embarrassing situation.

As with all houses on King Island and possibly throughout Australia at the time, all toilets were outdoor dunnies erected some distance from the house. Now being toilet trained, on this occasion I visited the dunny and lifted the toilet lid, climbed up onto the seat and planted myself over the pan. However, by not supporting myself as well as I should, fell through the hole where I became stuck up to the back of my knees and armpits. No matter how I struggled I just could not prise myself out of this very embarrassing situation. Even at that early age, no one liked being laughed at. I realised my predicament could not be resolved without assistance, so I started shouting for help. Fortunately, my father was not far away attending the large vegetable garden and heard my pleas and came to my assistance without ridicule or laughter, thankfully … perhaps later.

This early photo was probably taken at the property The Man Trap with me on the left, elder brother Richard and first-born Veronica nursing a cousin.

10

Another early life recollection was that my paternal grandmother living in Tasmania was coming to visit us on King Island. We did not possess a motor vehicle; however, my father was picked up in an old utility to take him to the King Island airport to collect his mother. My mother and three children eagerly awaited the arrival of our grandmother and when they arrived, the driver and my father were in the ute cabin with the grandmother sitting in a rocking chair on the back tray of the ute along with her suitcase, on reflection in later years, a very comical arrangement. My grandmother died in Tasmania in 1946 so this incident occurred in the early forties during the war years.

Every second weekend I looked forward to the arrival of our Uncle Sam Massie. Not really an uncle however that is how we related to him. I never saw him arrive except on foot along the sandy dirt road that ran past our property, always accompanied by a sugar bag carried on his back. Now the contents of the sugar bag were what I looked forward to rather than the presence of Uncle Sam Massie. He always arrived with the contents of the sugar bag full of fruit including oranges, apples, some stone fruit and a bunch of bananas. It was my first introduction to bananas which had become my favourite fruit and almost eighty years later, it still is. Thank you, Uncle Sam Massie.

It was at this property that I witnessed for the first and only time the extraction of timber by a bullock team. My father and his father-in-law (my Grandfather Richard Barnes) with a team of six huge powerful bullocks hitched to a large, long wagon full of logs, and hauled the timber from the bush out to a gravel road. My grandfather with not a whip but a long rigid tea tree stick with a stout cord attached drove the bullock team. They were individually named, and I am sure they all knew their names as he yelled at them constantly and they obeyed his commands. It was an operation I shall never forget.

The iconic bullock team hauling logs.

My schooling began at The Grooms somewhere between the age of four and a half and five years old. As The Grooms was quite isolated with just a two-track sandy road between the property and the main gravel road, we three rode an old, quite docile horse out to the gravel road, perhaps a mile or more, where the horse was put in a paddock and we would be picked up by a school bus and let off after school. My sister the eldest would ride on the front of the horse operating the reins, my elder brother in the middle and I being seated on the rear end of our transport. This ceased on our move from *The Grooms* to a property close to the main island town of Currie and opposite the King Island racecourse. Here a whole change of life took place. My father was given the job of foreman at the King Island Wharf, a position that kept him from serving in World War II as he was considered an essential service worker. Our new home was a bicycle ride for my father to work, he never in his lifetime owned a motor vehicle.

It was during this period my father, who was a fishing companion to boat owner Cliff Day, started taking me to sea and introduced me to cray fishing with pots in the rich harvesting grounds on the west coast of King Island. It was not long after this introduction that led me to understand another education about catching food.

Shearwaters, locally known as mutton birds are the world's longest migrating birds. They would arrive annually from Siberia to claim a burrow in the vast sandhills on the north coast of King Island, lay their eggs and hatch their young. Once born the parent birds would go to sea at dawn and return at dusk to feed their young. As the chicks grew, they became extremely fat from the food stores they were being given, and at this point, all fishing would cease and the annual mutton bird season would commence. We would capture the young birds from their burrows, oil and clean their bodies, salt them down in eighteen-gallon beer barrel kegs then seal the container ready for export. We would spend many days and nights living in that environment catching mutton birds. My greatest memory of such adventure from the whole season was after dark and when the catching had ceased, was sitting around an open fire with a stick through the bird, patiently cooking it to eat it there and then. I could live on mutton birds.

It was at this location that I earned my first money. King Island was and still is inundated with wallabies and kangaroos and having no predators, their population is rife. Having no electricity on the island and wallaby meat being so prolific it was our main source of meat. I can recall my father walking out the back door with his 22 Repeater rifle and shooting the wallaby from within the backyard. A meat safe hung from the ceiling indoors, metal with small ventilation holes held leftover meat for several days – flyproof.

My father taught me how to skin a wallaby, lay the wallaby on its back and run a sharp-pointed pocketknife down the length of the inside tail, up both inner hind legs, followed by the length of the wallaby from hindquarters up to the neck, around the neck followed by stripping the skin from the tail and hindquarters then pulling the body away from the skin. The skin was pegged out and allowed to dry. For my efforts, I was paid ninepence a skin from a dealer who dealt in cattle skins. *"How easy was this?"* I thought. Our property was quite large with most of it covered in both scrub and timber. It was low set from the rear of the house and the land was mostly damp, which in turn showed up quite plainly wallaby imprints and runs. My Father taught me how to make *springer snares* out of tea trees which were very flexible and strong. So I would search out heavily used wallaby runs, then set a snare and was trapping wallabies daily. We had plenty of meat (hindquarters only used for consumption) and I was making money from the skins. Such was I so into the enterprise,

I would be up just after dawn checking my snares, skinning wallabies all before breakfast then off to school. My mother had a large hand-operated mixer clamped to one end of the table. She spent time mincing wallaby meat and mixed with chopped onions, shredded carrots and other vegetables she would make up the finest patties (rissoles), not forgetting we consumed plenty of wallaby tail and vegetable soup.

I may add here that at school once a week, the Commonwealth Bank would receive the pupil's money and record the deposit in our bank book. By the time we shifted back to dairy farming I had more than five pounds and in the mid-forties, five pounds was a great deal of money, which was all from selling wallaby skins.

Even though wallaby was our main source of meat, we did supplement it with beef, lamb and pork from the local butcher in Currie. We had a jersey cow on our property, a particularly good milker that supplied us with ample milk and of course many free-range fowls with eggs aplenty.

I can always remember my father no matter where he lived always had a large vegetable garden full of a variety of vegetables, more than we could consume. A large fence was built around the house and garden to keep the wallabies out of the garden. Uncle Sam Massie still arrived regularly with a sugar bag of fruit and departed with a selection of vegetables on his back. Having no electricity our lighting consisted of pressure lamps and candles with a wood chip heater for hot water. We had a large wood heap with my brother and myself responsible for the supply of stove and fireplace wood as we both had an axe. Veronica, the eldest, was taught how to milk the cow and the supply of milk was her responsibility.

An event to recall while living here was my fifth birthday, and not because it was my birthday. I remember my mother giving me a hug and a kiss because upon reaching the age of five in 1944, I now possessed a ration card. I felt so proud that I was contributing to the family's welfare.

Veronica the eldest was sent home from school with measles and of course my brother and I were not allowed to attend school until we also went through the process. This also occurred later with chickenpox. We always assumed that all children went through the measles/chickenpox process and cannot understand why now it is regarded as a serious health condition. We never heard, in our time, of anyone dying from these infectious diseases. At this location, I now had another two sisters.

Schooling at the King Island State School (Currie) was enjoyable more for the fact that the lunchtime was taken up by the boys in playing *Aussie Rules* and it was always Collingwood versus The Rest. I could never understand why half of the school supported Collingwood however, the contest always continued until the bell sounded out for our return to classes. At home, we had a large battery-operated wireless with an extremely high, long outside aerial, and on Saturdays, my brother and I would sit next to it and listen to the direct broadcast from Melbourne of the Victorian Football League matches. My brother Richard (Dick) was a Collingwood supporter, myself one of The Rest.

While at this property a DC-3 (propeller-driven airliner) crashed while attempting to land at the King Island Airport. I am uncertain if the aircraft was arriving from Tasmania or the mainland, however, word soon spread and we were picked up in a vehicle and transported to the crash site.

I was too young to realise the severity of this occurrence, to me it was just an unusual sight and I believe all aboard were killed. Little did I know at the time that in the future, while in uniform, I was to be exposed to two horrific aircraft incidents both being military aircraft.

My brother and I were responsible to carry the contents from the *dunny* down to the swamp area, digging a hole and burying the waste, which was not a pleasant chore, however, it became our responsibility and part of life's required education.

It was whilst living at this property just outside Currie, my father unknowingly greatly assisted me in another part of my education which to this day still aids me in my retirement. My father was a great cribbage player and being a very patient person persevered with us three elders in learning to play crib. I more than my two elder siblings took to cribbage, and to this day I still enjoy a game. Assisting in my education? This game taught me counting so at school I eventually was the smart one in mental arithmetic and arithmetic in general. Whether addition, multiplication, division or subtraction, especially in those days when the currency consisted of farthings, halfpennies, pennies, threepences, sixpences, shillings, two-shilling pieces, ten-shilling notes and pounds and it helped a great deal. Generations since the mid-sixties can be pleased with the introduction of the decimal system not only in currency but also in weights and measures, for the sheer simplicity of accounting.

This mode of life continued until the cessation of World War II, then it was back to dairy farming at a place called *The Dell* at Loorana, consisting of two hundred acres and sixty milking cows, being mid-island on the western side of King Island. Our place of residence was sold and the move some five miles north thus initiated a change of lifestyle.

Me with a cousin, Shirley Mathewson. The photograph was taken in 1945.

JUNGLE GREEN & RUGBY

I can remember walking our Jersey cow from one property to The Dell her new home to mix with some sixty other milking cows, although she always remained our favourite. This was probably in 1946 as I was now seven, and our lives altered dramatically. My father would have the cows in the milking shed by 4:00 AM, and we three elders would be up at 4:30 and down to the shed to assist in the milking. When completed it was off with the gumboots, wash, have breakfast then off to school. On arriving home from school by bus it was get changed, on with the gumboots and down to the dairy where the cows were waiting to be milked for the afternoon session. As any dairy farmer will tell, you this takes place 365 days of the year, however virtually being bred into this routine we were happy with our way of life. At the time our property adjoined the butter factory at Loorana, so our milk was separated on-site and the cream went to the butter factory via a factory pickup truck, which did the rounds of the island dairy farmers. Some years later the butter factory was transformed into a cheese factory, however this was well after we departed King Island.

Living on this property had its advantages with Porky Creek running through it so we had no water problems, apart from the effort of pumping it up to the dairy. All residences on King Island relied on rain tank water and it was fortunate that King Island did have a reliable annual rainfall. Along with the fowls we brought up from our previous property, turkeys, geese and ducks were introduced so we were never short of poultry and eggs. My father, brother and I erected pig pens with timber from the heavily wooded creek, so the separated milk (whey) added with wheat became the prime source of food for the pigs as nothing goes to waste on the farm. We made our butter with many hours spent on a hand-operated churn for this production of food.

As mentioned, the property was heavily timbered all along the creek line, large enough for posts and droppers in the erection of fences and a huge woodpile to supply a large kitchen stove, lounge room fire and a woodchip heater, for hot water. It remained my and Dick's responsibility to keep a well-stocked woodpile.

We also had two horses on this property, a flighty young horse called Chessy and an old ex-racehorse called Lord Raglan. Through these horses we three elders became quite good riders, especially the eldest Veronica.

Occasionally my father would shoot a wallaby, hang it and let it mature over a few days preparing it for bait, then with the horses loaded with crayfish pots (just a circular tea tree hoop with netting, a cross-section of rope tied across it) the bait was tied in the centre of the cross-section of rope and lowered into deep and still seawater rock pools. The west coast of King Island is extremely rugged with large rock formations along its coastline. The sea would crash into these rocks and in many places, gaps allowed the water to enter these rock pools. The nets were set for some two hours throughout these areas and then retrieved with numerous crayfish (lobsters) in them. We would return to the farm with potato bags full of crayfish, not forgetting we young ones would collect a bucketful of periwinkles so upon arriving home, we would boil them and then extract the meat from the shell with a needle. The crayfish were also boiled and then left to hang by the tail on the fence to drain. I will forever remember my best meals, sitting in front of a large lounge room fire, and eating crayfish with vinegar and pepper. We always had available to us a healthy diet and lifestyle while we lived on the farms in the locations we were.

It was about this time that our father gave my brother Dick and me, after a very thorough education in safety factors with firearms, a single barrel twelve-gauge shotgun and his Browning repeater .22 rifle. It was not Dick's first initiation to a firearm, as at our previous property my father gave him a fountain pen for his birthday. Dick took it to school and swapped it for an air rifle and soon after a noticeably short ownership, shot his sister Veronica in the arse with it - therefore no air rifle or fountain pen.

Our property and other farms surrounding it had numerous lagoons on them, thus wild duck was added to our menu. King Island was also populated with English pheasants which were introduced by the early settlers and through having no predators they multiplied very quickly. I can also recall the first pheasant I shot on the wing, which was added to the menu as it was consumed that evening.

—m—

My father came from a large family of ten children who still lived in Tasmania being mostly farmers and timber millers. So it was off to Tasmania for my first holiday, in 1948 aged nine to stay at three dairy farms, one at Stowport, outside Burnie with the other two at Upper Natone, inland from Burnie. Two of these farms were occupied by my father's sisters Enid and Doris, and the other by his brother Harry. So here I was with a pound in my pocket, put on a DC-3 aircraft on King Island, and was met at Wynyard Airport by my uncle and auntie, who owned the dairy farm at Stowport. I neither knew of electricity nor had seen it in operation, so the most intriguing part of this stay was that I could stand at a door, click a switch and have a light come on in the ceiling. ceiling. I was overawed as it was just beyond my comprehension. I believe I tried every switch in the dwelling before moving on and yes, the result was the same.

Another first occurred when my auntie took me shopping in Burnie. I spent the whole duration on the side of the Bass Highway leaning over a barrier looking down onto the train station, watching a steam engine, shunting carriages back and forth, which was another unbelievable occurrence at the time.

Before moving on, my uncle drove us to Launceston to meet up with my mother's sister. The approach to Launceston along the Bass Highway is elevated to the city and I thought when approaching and looking down at all the lights, it must have been the biggest city in the world ... nothing could be bigger. Was I getting educated?

From Stowport I was taken to my uncle's farm at Upper Natone where I had a short stay then several miles away to my Auntie Doris's family farm. There are no idle hands on dairy farms and since I had experience in these matters, I went to work. Three occurrences remain in my memory from this visit. One was that I spent Christmas there and received a pocketknife as a Christmas present. Secondly, my Auntie Doris gave birth on the homestead and after three days, she was back working in the dairy. Women nowadays can have three to six months off plus extras upon giving birth. How times changed over the years. My third memory was that my uncle had acres of potatoes to dig. Potato digging was done manually with diggers each starting at one end of the paddock and moving along hundreds of metres of a row turning around and commencing on a new row. Next came a crew to pick up and bag the potatoes, and when full, sew up the bag with a huge needle, to be collected by a tractor towing a trailer and then to the shed for brief storage before exporting. Now leftover from the bagging of export potatoes were the small potatoes called chats.

My uncle told me, *"You pick up and bag the chats and I will give you 9d (ninepence) a bag."* Now, these chats are kept for local consumption being too small for export, so many must be collected to fill a bag.

At the end of the day, my uncle asked me, *"How many bags of chats have you picked up?"*

I told him, *"Nine."*

He looked at me unbelievingly and as the bagged chats were still standing in the paddock he went up and counted them and on confirming my reply in turn gave me 6/9 (six shillings and ninepence). The next day we finished the digging early however earning me another 3/3 (three shillings and threepence) as my uncle rounded my pay to 12/- (twelve shillings). So, it was off home to King Island via Wynyard Airport and an adventure not to forget, seeing for the first time, electricity, train engines at work along with seeing the biggest city in the world – Launceston.

My dad was overwhelmed giving me a £1 (one pound) note for spending money when I left and upon my return giving him back £1.12.00 (one pound twelve shillings). I was the first child in the family to leave the place of our birth.

For several years we enjoyed the farm life and living off the land. When we killed a pig, we would share it with the neighbours and when they slew a beast, we would in return receive a share. Once a year my father would plant an acre of potatoes and upon maturity, the neighbours would turn up to assist in the digging and take a couple of bags home with them - community living.

It was just before the fifties that unknown to us children my father started to have health problems. Such was his health deterioration that the medical assistance required was unavailable on King Island so he was flown to Launceston where treatment on a larger scale was available. He was found to have an ulcerated stomach, which should have been treated at a much earlier stage, so he was to be operated on immediately. Following his surgery and rehabilitation in Launceston, changes in our dairy farming operations altered dramatically.

Veronica and Dick wished to continue their schooling, while as I was not that keen on going to school, was to remain at home to carry out all the basic dairy chores. Fortunately, we had a particularly good cattle dog called Mick and when let off the chain and at the command of *"Go way back"* would bolt and within half an hour would have all the cows in the cow yard. Following a headcount if one or more was missing it was *"Go way back"* and he would return with the missing cattle. After milking, my elder siblings would clean themselves up, have breakfast then off to catch the school bus, which left me to finalise the after-milking chores. This included finishing the separating of the milk and pulling the separator into pieces then washing them in firstly hot water with caustic soda, followed by hot water containing hydrochloric acid. The cow shed itself was cleaned thoroughly along with the buckets and other associated dairy equipment.

The cream was graded at the butter factory in classes of either Choice, First, Second, or Third grade and this would be acknowledged along with the monthly cheque. Even with our father's absence we never received that cheque for anything other than Choice cream. The higher the quality the more rewarding it was as I can recall our incoming cheques were always about £80 (eighty-pound) a month. Our mother would oversee the monetary side of things in the course of looking after a huge house, and by now the family had grown to six with another three sisters.

Following the dairy clean-up, I would then feed the pigs by carrying the separated milk with the wheat up to the pig pens to fill the troughs. I carried the milk from the dairy using a yoke, a frame fitting the neck and shoulders for carrying a pair of buckets with one at each end. Following pig feeding, I had to make sure the wood was chopped to service both our huge kitchen stove and fireplace. Dick would spend an hour or two on weekends chopping wood though it was very much my responsibility. Some days I would saddle the horse, grab the shotgun, ride to a lagoon, tie the horse up a little distance away and thread my way undetected through the surroundings and get two or three wild ducks. Mid-afternoon it was the time to unchain the dog Mick and pronounce *"Go way back"* to get the cows in for the late milking on the arrival of Veronica and Dick from school. The afternoon/evening milking session was not so laborious with all the three-tasking in. After the milking session, all three of us would move the heavy cream cans out for the morning factory pick-up. Milking, feeding pigs and general dairy work were much easier on the weekends with the three of us present, and when time allowed, I would follow Porky Creek right down to the ocean as I did love exploring.

My uncle Len Barnes would come, cut and bale the hay and we would stack it in the hay shed or if not bailed, make huge mounds of the mowed forage. Another uncle, Des, decided to plough acreage on the farm thus came my introduction to tractors and in this case, a Fordson Major. I would sit on the huge mudguard just to the side rear of my uncle during the ploughing and caught on quickly to the simplicity of driving a tractor. Under his guidance he let me operate the tractor and when he was satisfied with my capabilities, he would take several hours off and let me continue with the task. I was quite miffed when he again took over.

Relating to my father's health; I am not sure how long he was away but upon arriving home he had lost an obvious amount of weight, although I can never remember him being a big man. He explained that he had his whole stomach removed and the ends were sewn together. Having no stomach meant his only intake of food was milk arrowroot biscuits and milk. It used to go through him like a seagull, but he would have this little combination eight times a day, and in time his stomach did expand to eat regular meals.

Upon his return, my father could see that the farm was deteriorating, and instead of taking it easy and resting as ordered, he went about rectifying the issues that were beyond his eldest children's capabilities. We alone were just working on the milking and pig feeding aspects of dairy farming. For several weeks he overworked himself, busted his guts and was returned to Launceston under medical supervision. I do not know how long he was away, though, upon his return, he realised that continuing this lifestyle was beyond him. We had to leave the property and go to Tasmania where he was closer to medical assistance.

We departed in 1950, thus ending my first ten years of life, however giving me a huge mature outlook on life for one so young.

The eldest Veronica, stayed on King Island and went north, living and working on a dairy farm owned by our uncle Mr Fred Summers, who married my mother's sister, Lillian.

Richard (Dick) went to Tasmania, living and working on the farm at Upper Natone owned by dad's brother Harry. So was the disintegration of our family never to be reunited during our lifetime.

———*w*———

My father had organised a dairy farming job on a property at Sheffield in Tasmania belonging to a Mr Branningan. Sheffield, which is in central northern Tasmania, is the most miserable place I have ever lived in. It is situated at the foot of the Great Western Tiers and during the winter I witnessed water pipes bursting, went to school wearing three jumpers then walked home carrying them. I could not and still cannot handle wintery weather.

Mr Branningan saved me. One day he asked, *"Can you drive a tractor?"*

I informed him, *"I've operated a Fordson Major ploughing paddocks."*

"Come with me," he directed.

He took me into one of his large barns and said, *"Here's a tractor and trailer full of rabbit traps. Get rid of the rabbits on my farm."*

My eyes lit up. Here I was with a grey Ferguson tractor, trailer and a task. From snaring wallabies on King Island to trapping rabbits in Tasmania. No rabbits existed on King Island; however, one did not have to be smart to make this venture a success. The property had large growths of blackberries, applicable to much of the State and ideal for rabbits to make warrens.

I contacted the dealer in Sheffield who dealt in cattle skins. *"Do you take rabbit skins?"* I asked.

"Yes! 3d (threepence) each."

Here I was trapping again. I set traps around the numerous warrens on his large property, checking the traps early morning, skinning the kill, cleaning up and off to school, and then returning home to reset the traps. We became rabbit consumers in place of wallaby. Mother would bake three at a time enough to feed the family along with vegetables from the garden, virtually living off the land again. Of course, the rabbit meat was supplemented with the usual beef, pork and chicken. So, the rabbit trapping continued and the small income from skins kept me in pocket money.

I will mention here, that when Myxomatosis was introduced and I witnessed the ugly devastation it had on the rabbits, I could never eat one again.

Thankfully, we only spent one winter in Sheffield, as my father got a job on the Tasmanian Government Railway (TGR) as a ganger within the system. This was a mobile unit, which was moved around Tasmania for emergency and urgent repairs on any line within the State. The gang lived in railway carriages converted into mobile rolling homes and moved by train to any destination. We would see our father only every second weekend.

Leaving the farm in Sheffield I had made a huge dent in the rabbit population of Mr Branningan's farm. Now Latrobe is a much better place to live than Sheffield if one dislikes the cold, however there is little to do in Latrobe except go to school. I developed a large vegetable garden for family use and sold lettuce to the local shops for 3d (threepence) each.

Here our family fortune took another terrible turn. Our mother left home and went to work and live with her sister in Launceston. Our father got Veronica to leave King Island and come home to look after her five younger sisters still all of school age. I do not believe our stay at Latrobe lasted long and I do not know under what circumstances, however, we moved to Ulverstone. I started school once again at about twelve years old with this being my fourth school. I settled into sports gaining my Bronze Medal at the local surf club and representing my school in both cricket and Australian Rules against other schools along the Northwest Coast. I did get a paper delivery job for the West Ulverstone area, delivering *The Advocate* early morning before school. I did become a prefect within the Ulverstone High School, however, I did have a serious altercation with a teacher and I was threatened with expulsion.

Images of me transitioning from school into the real workforce at 14.

My father was still working for the TGR and found me a job as a cleaner down at Smithton in Circular Head, on the railway. This is where I got accustomed to cleaning, firing up and shunting, H&M and Garrett steam engines. So ended my schooling at thirteen and a half years and into the real workforce in 1953.

I was allocated a very cosy three-room cabin on-site at the railway property next to the engine sheds and a small rent was extracted from my pay on a fortnightly basis. This work was shift work sharing with another cleaner; one week 8:00 AM to 4:00 PM with the next week midnight to 8.00 AM. I grew a little tired of cleaning engines, shovelling tons of coal and drying out sand by heating (the sand was used in engines to assist in the traction of wheels on wet tracks). I had now worked in this capacity for one and a half years and the promotion to fireman now appeared a possibility too far.

I knew it was time to find a different job, so I ventured up to Launceston and found a rental with full board in Invermay, and a job at the flour millers Monds & Affleck. I was fifteen something going on sixteen years of age, and I knew this occupation was to be temporary as I did have a future planned. My job was humping bags of wheat. As trucks would come in, reversing to an unloading station I would throw those bags of wheat onto an escalator. I would be standing at the top of a stockpile of stacked wheat, grabbing a bag of wheat by the ear and bottom corner, and placing it across my shoulders to continue stockpiling. A bag of wheat weighs about one hundred and eighty pounds (approximately eighty-one kilos), I did not find this a heavy task and in later years I believed it benefited me in body mechanics and balance. Although lighter than the wheat in the years gone by, I can remember lifting the bags of potatoes when I was much younger. It is now against the law for workers to carry such weights, especially when considering the machinery that can easily accommodate the process today.

I had an income of £6.00 (six pounds) and paid £5.00 a week for board and meals. So at this rate, I was not going to save much money. This occupation lasted until the 31st of May 1956.

'You Bloody Beauty!!! Seventeen … I am off to join the Army'.

—ɯ—

FOUR

A BRIEF FAMILY MILITARY HISTORY

Family Military Medals
Top Bar – World War One.
Middle Bar – World War Two.
Bottom Bar – Malaysia and Viet Nam.

I, Clifford Walter (Tasi) Woodard was the eleventh member of my mother's family (Barnes) and my father's family (Woodard) to serve in the Australian Army. However, I enlisted in 1956, so being the only member to join in peacetime.

Of the eleven members, two lost their lives in World War One (WWI), one being a Barnes and the other a Woodard, and two in World War Two (WWII), once again a Barnes and a Woodard.

Following is a brief history, which covers three generations of all eleven members, their service, units and their fates.

Three Generations of Australian Soldiers
L-R: George William Woodard (Snr) and (Jnr) WWI
William Henry and Norman Francis Woodard WWII Clifford
Walter Woodard, Malaysia and Viet Nam.

These medals represent the four family members Barnes/Woodard who served in WWI.

WORLD WAR ONE

The Barnes family name was perhaps the most popular on King Island, Tasmania where large dairy farmer families existed. In the two world wars, a total of six Barnes family members served from a total population of about five hundred who lived on the island.

Following are the service details of the uncles of my mother, Enid Elvie (nee Barnes) who served in WWI.

William Albert Barnes - Regimental Number 1052

Enlistment Date – 14 April 1915
Age at Embarkation - 25 years
Unit – 26th Battalion, D. Company
Embarkation Details - The unit embarked from Brisbane, Queensland on board HMAT A60 Aeneas on 29 June 1915
Fate - Returned to Australia on 17 May 1917.

Clifford Aubrey Barnes - Regimental Number 3573

Enlistment Date - 13 August 1915
Age at Embarkation – 19 years
Unit – 15th Battalion 11th Reinforcement
Embarkation Details - The unit embarked from Melbourne, Victoria on board HMAT A38 Ulysses on 27 October 1915
Fate - Died on repatriation to Australia
Date of Death - 14 June 1920
Age at Death - 23 years
Place of Burial - Springvale Botanical Cemetery, Melbourne, Victoria.

Circumstances leading to passing - not long after arriving and serving on the Western Front he was involved in a night patrol. Unfortunately, his section ran into a German night patrol where a firefight broke out on contact between these two groups.

C. A. Barnes was wounded in the firefight and as both parties withdrew, he was left wounded in the conflict area. He was taken prisoner by the Germans where he spent the remainder of the war as a German prisoner of war (POW) interred at Limburg, Germany. Clifford was repatriated after the war however never quite made it home to King Island, being disembarked in Melbourne and dying in the Caulfield Hospital on 14 June 1919, aged twenty-three, from influenza (Spanish Flu?).

> *"On Monday last the very sad news received by Mr. and Mrs. Albert Barnes that their son Private Cliff Barnes had succumbed to an attack of influenza in the Caulfield Hospital. The intimation came as a great shock and was especially distressing to relatives and friends from the fact that the popular young soldier was virtually on the threshold of his home. Having been a prisoner of war for a considerable time, the intense joy of his home coming both to himself and relatives can readily be imagined and we feel sure that the sincere sympathy of every islander will go out to the relatives in their hour of sorrow."*

Obituary from the *King Island News* 18 June 1919

Pte. C. A. Barnes.—The following are extracts from a letter sent to Mrs E. H. Percy, King Island, from her brother Pte C. A. Barnes, who is a prisoner of war in Germany:—"At last. Dear Sister, I have the chance of writing you a line or two letting you know how I am getting on. I expect you know by this time that I am a prisoner of war in German hands. Times are very rough here and all I ask you to do is to send me a parcel whenever you can—I mean in the way of foodstuffs. A small parcel of solid food is what we all want here. You dont know how we long for a smoke. If you do this for me I will never be able to repay you. We are having lovely weather now and I am in good health, although times are rough. I hope all at home are well, and I also hope some day, soon, to see you all again and that we will be all sitting around the home table once more complete." The letter was written on June 14, 1917.

Left: BARNES Clifford Aubrey Image from the Australian War Memorial (DA11452)
Right: Extract from the King Island News 19 September 1917.

George William Woodard (Snr) - Regimental Number 3778

Enlistment Date – 2 January 1917
Age at Embarkation – 45 years
Unit – 2nd Pioneer Battalion
Embarkation Details – The unit embarked from Melbourne, Victoria on board HMAT A9 Shropshire on 11 May 1917 Fate - Returned to Australia
Place of Burial – Interred Ivanhoe Cemetery, Burnie, Tasmania.

George William Woodard (Snr) - Regimental Number 3778 Back row second from right.

George William Woodard (Jnr) – Regimental Number 3779

Enlistment Date - 2 January 1917
Age at Embarkation – 19 years
Unit – 2nd Pioneer Battalion
Embarkation Details - The unit embarked from Melbourne, Victoria on board HMAT A9 Shropshire on 11 May 1917
Fate – Killed in action (KIA) in The Battle of Montbrehain on the Hindenburg Line
Date of Death – 5 October 1918
Age at Death - 20 years
Place of Burial – Tincourt New British Cemetery, France.

My grandfather GW (Snr) and GW (Jnr) my grandfather's firstborn, both enlisted in the Army on 2 January 1917 (thereby the consecutive regimental numbers). Both were posted as members of the 2nd Australian Pioneers and arrived on the Western Front in early 1917.

Left: George William Woodard (Snr) - Regimental Number 3778
Right: George William Woodard (Jnr) – Regimental Number 3779.

Two factors prevented my grandfather and his firstborn (my uncle) from enlisting earlier in the war, one is too old and the other was too young. As the war progressed and reinforcements were becoming scarce and frontline units thinning, applications for joining the army were altered as the age for enlistment was raised. My grandfather served as a forty-five-year-old and his son's age now made him eligible for enlistment. I do not believe they enlisted for King and Country but more so for a matter of financial gain. Both the Barnes family on King Island and the Woodard family in Tasmania were farmers and in my grandfather's circumstances with both him and his son joining up, together they had a military income of 12/- (twelve shillings) a day, which was more than farming could produce.

The Battle of Montbrehain on the Hindenburg Line, 5th October 1918 was the last conflict Australians participated in during WWI, where George William (Jnr) was one of the one hundred and thirty-four Australian casualties of the battle. On learning of his son's death, my grandfather was sent home to Australia deemed no longer fit for military service. The following article refers to both my grandfather and his son's circumstances.

'Woodard, George William. 3779

George William Woodard Junior was born in Forestville near Bendigo on the 20th of June 1897. He was the firstborn to George William and Mary Alice Woodard. He was one of eleven children. At some stage, the family moved to Stowport Tasmania as the last six children were born there. As a young man, George became a labourer and spent some time with the local 91st Infantry Battalion (Tasmanian Rangers).

George Jnr enlisted in the A.I.F. in Burnie Tasmania at 19 years of age on the 2nd of June 1917. He must have had his parent's permission to enlist, as his father George Snr enlisted with him.

They were both assigned to be part of the 9th Reinforcements to the 2nd Pioneer Battalion, and they were given consecutive service numbers. It is unclear why George Snr enlisted. He may have done so to do his duty or he may have simply joined to feed his large family. Maybe, he may also have joined to keep his son safe.

They embarked from Melbourne on the HMAT A9 Shropshire on the 11th of May 1917 and when they arrived in England, they both proceeded to the Pioneer Training Battalion on the 17th of July 1917. On the 15th of October George Jnr was sent to Signal School and the next day George Snr proceeded to France and was taken on strength with the 2nd Pioneers. George Jnr finished his signaller course and was taken on strength with the 2nd Pioneers on the 9th of March 1918.

1918 had been a bad year for George Snr, as he had some medical complaints for the first half of the year, which included, diarrhea, myalgia, trench fever and debility. He was however well enough by the 27th of July to return to the front to be with his son.

At Montbrehain on the 5th of October 1918, George Jnr was hit by shrapnel in the left arm and shoulder. He also received a penetrating chest wound. He was taken to the 58th Casualty Clearance Station. He could not be saved and he died there at 5:30 AM on the 6th of October.

Private George William Woodard Jnr lies in the Tincourt New British Cemetery in plot V. H. 35. His mother later chose the epitaph for his headstone, *He Played the Game.*

It is not known whether George Snr was present during any of this.

'He Played the Game' **enlistment poster.**

After Montbrehain the army was wondering what to do with George Woodard Snr. On the 20th of October 1918, the Regimental Medical Officer of the 2nd Pioneer Battalion wrote to the Assistant Director of Medical Services of the 2nd Division.

This man (George Woodard Snr) has been employed on camp duties but is now completely broken up due to the death of his son in the last action. He has applied to be sent back to Australia.

He was sent to England for assessment and was recommended for discharge with 'premature senility, insomnia and rheumatism.' He was sent home to Australia a broken man. He refused any medical help. George Woodard Snr died in 1930 of strychnine poisoning as this troubled man could stand no more.

The youngest son Norman Francis Woodard served with the 2/29th Battalion WWII. He was captured by the Japanese at the fall of Singapore, worked on the Thai - Burma railway and was killed on the 12th of September 1944 when he was being transported back to Japan on the *Rakuyo Maru*. The ship was torpedoed and sunk by an American submarine, which was not aware that the ship was transporting prisoners of war.

Mary Alice would have now lost her husband and a son in both world wars. She died in 1946.'

The above article is my contribution to the book *Just One More Day,* and I wish to acknowledge the author Michael Ganey for its inclusion.

—⦉⦊—

I wish to elaborate more on The Battle of Montbrehain as it was historic for two reasons. As previously mentioned, it was the last battle in which Australian troops participated during WWI and in this action, Lieutenant George Ingram became the last soldier to be awarded a Victoria Cross in WWI.

Following is an abridged version of an extract taken from *Beyond Secrets - A Journey* by Joy Winifred Grange.

'When Major General Charles Rosenthal awoke on October 4, 1918, he must have heaved a great sigh of relief. The men of his Australian 2nd Division had achieved everything asked of them. Their final battle securing the area of Beaurevoir on the Hindenburg Line was achieved with the 7th British Brigade and the 20th Manchester Battalion.

The Manchesters entered Beaurevoir at the same time as the 6th Australian Infantry Brigade secured the frontline between the Torrens Canal and the mountain fortress town of Montbrehain. After almost nonstop fighting since August 8, 1918; Rosenthal's 2nd Division could now be withdrawn and given the long rest promised them and insisted upon by Mr William Billy Hughes, Prime Minister of Australia. They were on their way home. German troops - trapped inside the mountain village of Montbrehain were going nowhere - and no elite German regiment was coming to their rescue. The German forces in France were defeated.

Nevertheless, just before noon, Lieutenant General John Monash ordered Charles Rosenthal to take over the line of the British 138th Brigade (east of Ramincourt), at dusk. Then, using the 2nd Pioneers as infantrymen, he set the 6th Australian Infantry Brigade to take the village of Montbrehain the next morning. So much for the dream of going home.

The 2nd Pioneers, fighting as infantry for the first time, were to sweep diagonally to the east and link with patrols of the 3rd British Brigade. The village of Montbrehain sat square in the centre of the wedge. This undermanned Australian force had a desperate fight on its hands. Each of the four companies attached to the 6th Australian Infantry Brigade had some 300 rifles. Machine gunners of the 5th and the 7th Infantry Companies were shared between all infantry companies. The Pioneers were supported by two guns of the 6th Australian Machine-Gun Company under Lieutenant Wilkinson.

For this undermanned brigade to succeed in capturing the heights of Montbrehain from a firmly established enemy (with his artillery intact) there had to be another factor to even the odds. No doubt this factor was the presence of eight units of field artillery. These field artillery units were all Australian – with years of experience in working closely with the infantry - as close as understanding the importance of every second and every yard.

What was the point of the battle for Montbrehain? Instead of a peaceful conclusion to its years of war; the Australian 6th Brigade had been set to form a dangerous salient. They were to be shot at from three sides. Why couldn't these war-weary Australians have been allowed to wait another twenty-four hours for their promised American relief? Or was this a case of 'the right men for the right task'? Was it that the British General Rawlinson and the Australian Monash were aware that experienced Australians would achieve their objective, while the inexperienced Americans might not? With the village of Montbrehain in Australian hands, the 30th American Division relieved the Australian 2nd Division that evening.'

General Sir John Monash wrote in 'Australian Victories in France in 1918', page 278:

"General Rawlinson wanted to me to retain control of the battlefront for one day longer and to avail myself of the time to advance our line still further to the east. I chose as a suitable objective the village of Montbrehain, which dominated any further advance."

C.E.W. Bean's volume VI of 'The Official War History' page 1043, has reservations about the need for action.

"The taking of Montbrehain was one of the most brilliant actions of Australian infantry during the Great War. Yet, as with many local attacks, it is difficult to feel it was wisely undertaken. It seemed, rather, to make some use of these troops before their withdrawal in accordance with Prime Minister Billy Hughes' demand. The action of October 5, 1918, cost the lives of 30 officers and 400 men. Thirty officers, among them some of the best leaders of the 6th Infantry Brigade and many of the best NCOs and men were killed."

This is an account of the actions of Lt. George Ingram of the 24th Battalion which led to him being awarded the last Victoria Cross of WWI. This abridged extract is from the book Just One More Day by author Michael Ganey.

'B COMPANY'

'Private Ernest Owens was possibly one of the first soldiers in 'B Company' to die. He was with a mate from his hometown, Private Roy McGill, and they were on the jump-off tape just before the advance began, when Owens was hit by shellfire and was killed. McGill was killed later as they neared their objective. Both were in Lieutenant George Ingram's platoon.

At about 100 yards into the advance, Captain George Pollington MM and his men encountered severe machine-gun fire from a post that was very close to them. This post had not been touched by the creeping barrage and the men had to quickly take cover in a shallow trench. Company Sergeant Major George Cumming was also in this trench with his officer, Lieutenant Cecil Boyd. Other members of this platoon included Privates James Parkin, Alfred Hellier and James McCauley. As Cumming turned to Private Hellier to ask him to bring up some Lewis gunners, he was sniped in the head and killed.

Pollington quickly realised that his men must push forward or be slowly picked off by the snipers and machine guns in front of them. Sergeant David Witherden, who was acting as the Company Lewis gun Sergeant, took a Lewis gun forward and rushed within 20 yards of the enemy and laid down effective covering fire. Pollington yelled "Go!" and Lieutenant George Ingram and his platoon attacked from one flank and Captain Pollington from the other. The men leapt forward and yelled as they rushed the enemy positions. This German post was reported to contain nine machine guns and 42 German soldiers. This rush was described as a short sharp hand-to-hand fight, which disposed the Germans to a man.

The Company then resumed its advance for another 100 yards or so when it came under withering fire from several other machine-gun posts. Captain George Pollington was badly wounded in the chest and abdomen. For this action, and at Beaurevoir the day before, he was later awarded the Military Cross.

After Pollington was wounded, Sergeant Witherden continued his one-man assault. He rushed one of the posts alone, killed the crew of four and then turned the captured machine gun around and turned it on the enemy.'

It was about this time that Lieutenant George Mawby Ingram MM won the 24th Battalion's only Victoria Cross. His actions were recorded in his citation.'

Victoria Cross Citation – Lt George Mawby Ingram, M.M., 24th Bn., A.I.F.

"For most conspicuous bravery and initiative during the attack on Montbrehain, east of Peronne, on 5th October 1918. When early in the advance his Platoon was held up by a strong point, Lieutenant INGRAM, without hesitation, dashed out and rushed the post at the head of his men, capturing nine machine guns and killing forty-two enemy after stubborn resistance. Later when the Company had suffered severe casualties from the enemy posts, and many leaders had fallen, he at once took control of the situation, rallied his men under intense fire, and led them forward. He himself rushed the first post, shot six of the enemy and captured a machine gun, thus overcoming serious resistance. On two subsequent occasions, he again displayed great dash and resource in the capture of enemy posts, inflicting many casualties and taking sixty-two prisoners. Throughout the whole day, he showed a most inspiring example of courage and leadership and freely exposed himself regardless of danger."

WORLD WAR TWO

Medals and Commendations of Richard Leonard Barnes, who served in WWII.

Of my six Uncles who served in WWII only one, Richard Leonard Barnes who served continuously from 1939 to 1945 survived without being killed or a POW. Above is a photo of his Service Medals of WWII. No other uncle was awarded any medal not issued to Richard Leonard Barnes. Following is a brief military history of my six uncles involved in WWII.

Richard Leonard Barnes – Regimental Number TX 420 (1918-2003)

> *Place of Birth* - King Island, Tasmania
> *War Service* - 7 November 1939 - 20 November 1945
> *Principal Units* - 2/12 Australian Infantry Battalion and 2/31 Australian Infantry Battalion
> *Decorations* - Medals and Commendations:

1939/1945 Star
Africa Star
Pacific Star
Defence Medal
War Medal 1939/1945
Australian Service Medal 1939/1945
Australian Service Medal 1945/1975 with clasp Southwest Pacific
Foreign Medal
Netherlands War Remembrance Cross 1940/1945

Richard was awarded the Australian Service Medal 1945/1975 with clasp Southwest Pacific after the cessation of WWII.

Being single he volunteered to remain in Borneo and extract Japanese soldiers from Borneo and with many still not believing Japan had surrendered, had remained in a very hostile environment.

Richard Leonard Barnes passed away and was interred in the Currie Cemetery on King Island in 2003. I was proud to have been invited to be a bearer at his funeral. Several members from his war units travelled from Melbourne to King Island for the occasion where I had the pleasure of meeting and sharing their company.

TX 420 Richard Leonard Barnes upon joining 1939 and serving in the Suez Canal 1942.

The Barnes Brothers Military Service World War II

Clifford Keith Barnes
Regimental Number TX 5463

Place of Birth - King Island, Tasmania
Unit - 2/40 Infantry Battalion

This Battalion was garrisoned on Timor as Sparrow Force along with Dutch and Portuguese troops in 1941. The Japanese began air attacks on Timor on 26 January 1942. Two Japanese Battalions plus three hundred paratroopers were inserted into Timor. Following fierce fighting, the Japanese with air support and armour eventually overwhelmed the opposition. The 2/40 Battalion and other troops surrendered to the Japanese on 23 February 1942.

Fate - Killed 12 September 1944 … See article *Death at Sea*.
Place of Burial – Interred at Labuan Memorial Cemetery, Malaysia.

Ronald Charles Barnes
Regimental Number TX 5464

Place of Birth - King Island, Tasmania
Unit - 2/40 Australian Infantry Battalion

Along with his younger brother, Clifford Keith enlisted in the army together (note consecutive Regimental Numbers). His military history coincided with the fate of the 2/40 Infantry Battalion in the fall of Timor to the Japanese in 1942.

Fate - As a POW, Ronald recovered from Singapore at the cessation of war and the Japanese surrender in 1945. He returned to Australia and resettled on King Island.

Eric Anthony Barnes - Regimental Number VX 48348 (Enlisted in Victoria)

Place of Birth - King Island, Tasmania
Unit - A LAA Regiment a Unit of the 6th Division

Enlisted in Victoria, E.A. Barnes served in North Africa then moved to Crete. Crete was overrun by German forces where Australia lost eight hundred killed and three thousand captured in May 1941.

Fate - Eric Anthony Barnes was recovered from a German POW camp in Poland at the cessation of the war and was repatriated to Australia in 1945.

William Henry Woodard
Regimental Number TX 5551

Place of Birth - Victoria
Unit - 4th Anti-tank Regiment
War Theatre - Malaya and Singapore

The 4th Anti-tank Regiment was stationed in Malaya. The Regiment took part in the most successful ambush on Japanese troops during their progressive occupation of the Malay Peninsular at Gemas (South of Kuala Lumpur) where Australian troops killed six hundred Japanese troops. As with all Commonwealth troops they were pushed south into Singapore where they capitulated and became POWs to Japanese forces. He was taken from Changi prison to work on the Burma railway.

Fate - Recovered at war's end from a POW camp in Siam on 20 August 1945 was repatriated to Australia and passed away in Tasmania in 1974.

Norman Francis Woodard
Regimental Number TX 5703

Place of Birth - Tasmania
Unit - 2/29 Australian Infantry Unit
War Theatre - Malaya and Singapore

Like William Henry Woodard, operations in the Malaya Peninsula were forced back into Singapore where Commonwealth troops capitulated to the Japanese forces. Norman was removed from the Burma railway construction to be transported to Japan as part of a POW workforce.

Fate - Killed 12 September 1944 ... See article *Death at Sea*.
Place of Burial – Interred at Labuan Memorial Cemetery, Malaysia.

—ᴍ—

Death at Sea – Extracted from the book *Heroes at Sea* by Don Wall.

"In 1944 the Japanese started transferring the more able-bodied POWs from Singapore by ship to Japan for work parties.

The POWs were transferred by cargo ships, packed in below decks and the ships were never identified as having POW cargos.

In September 1944, one thousand three hundred and nineteen British and Australian POWs were loaded onto the Rakuyo Maru (seven hundred and seventeen being Australian POWs) and set off for Japan.

During this period of the war, American submarines were active in the South China Sea sinking the Japanese cargo shipping.

In the early hours of the morning of 12 September 1944, American submarines attacked a Japanese convoy sinking many ships including the Rakuyo Maru at a location in the South China Sea, south of Hong Kong and west of the Philippines (Luzon)."

Of the seven hundred and seventeen Australian POWs on board, five hundred and forty-three perished including the loss of TX 5703 Pte N.F. Woodard (2/29 Bn) from Tasmania and TX 5463 Pte C.K. Barnes (2/40 Bn) from King Island, Tasmania.

By coincidence, Norman Woodard's brother, Harold had met Clifford Keith Barnes' sister Enid Elvie on King island in 1935. They married and were to become my parents. It is not known if these two soldiers knew each other as they served in different units. These two soldiers were related by the marriage of siblings.

Other Japanese cargo ships lost carrying large numbers of Australian POWs under similar circumstances were Tamahoko Maru, Montevideo Maru and the Kachidoki Maru."

In Memory of
TX5703 Private NORMAN FRANCIS WOODARD
A.I.F. 2nd/29th Australian Infantry Battalion
who died age 36 on 12 September 1944
Son of George William and Mary Alice Woodard, of Natone, Tasmania
Remembered with honour LABUAN MEMORIAL

and

TX5463 Private CLIFFORD KEITH BARNES
A.I.F. 2nd/40th Australian Infantry Battalion
who died age 22 on 12 September 1944
Son of Richard and Grace Maude Barnes, of King Island, Tasmania

Both Clifford Keith Barnes and Norman Francis Woodard have headstones at the Labuan Memorial Cemetery. Labuan Island is situated off the coast of Sabah, North Borneo. Malaysia.

MALAYSIA and VIET NAM CAMPAIGNS

Medals and Commendations of Clifford Walter (Tasi) Woodard - Malaysia – Viet Nam.

Clifford Walter (Tasi) Woodard - Regimental Number 61106

Place of Birth - King Island, Tasmania
Australian Army Career - 17 July 1956 – 25 February 1982
Corps - Artillery
Principal Units - 'Numerous'
Overseas Service - Malaysia 1964 – 1967 and Viet Nam 1969 - 1970
Service Medals:

Australian Active Service Medal 1945-1975 with clasp Malaysia & Viet Nam
General Service Medal 1962 with clasp Malay Peninsular
Viet Nam Medal
Australian Service Medal 1945-1975 with clasp Southeast Asia
Australian Sports Medal
Defence Force Service Medal with 1st and 2nd clasps
National Medal with 1st clasp
Australian Defence Medal
Foreign Medals
Pingat Jasa Malaysia
Vietnamese Campaign Medal

L-R: C.W. Woodard – Pre-Embarkation Photo Malaysia 1964 – Age 24
C.W. Woodard – Pre-Embarkation Photo Malaysia 1965 – Age 26
C.W. Woodard – Pre-Embarkation Photo Viet Nam 1969 – Age 29.

FIVE

MILITARY HISTORY OF 61106 WOODARD C W

I was always going to be a Soldier

Disclaimer: "During my almost twenty-six years of military service I have never kept a diary so some dates mentioned during this time may not be accurate, however, the contents are factual." - Tasi Woodard.

Enlistment: My service was initiated on the 17th of July 1956 in Tasmania.

Discharge: My voluntary discharge was taken on 25th February 1982 in Brisbane, Queensland.

Dedication: Having passed eighty years of age and now as I put pen to paper, it brings back memories of close mates, with some mentioned in this book, who have since passed on. Their comradeship is not lost on the special occasions when their past service is acknowledged.

At the early age of eleven or twelve (1950/1951) I first wore a uniform. Arriving to live in Latrobe, northwest Tasmania I joined the school cadets. Even at that age, I knew that when I was old enough, I would join the Australian Army. My most unforgettable memory of the Latrobe school cadets was when the Prime Minister of Australia Mr Robert Menzies visited Latrobe and our school cadets lined the road to give him a military guard of honour. As he along with the headmaster was inspecting the rank of cadets lining the road, he stopped in front of me and asked me my name. Upon answering he then questioned me, *"When you are old enough will you be joining the Australian Army?"* I replied in the affirmative and then looked behind him as travelling on the opposite side of the road drawn by a horse was a smelly open wagon. I remember the PM remarking, *"Well that's the first time I've ever been followed by a night cart."* There was no sewerage in Latrobe in the early fifties.

Our family then moved to Ulverstone where I again joined the school cadets and eventually was promoted to Lance Corporal. The Tasmanian school cadets had an annual military indoctrination to warfare at Brighton (north of Hobart). Now I believe the year was 1953 when we camped in tents and slept on a palliasse (straw mattress) with two blankets. It was my first introduction to military life, Reveille, roll call, ablutions, mess (breakfast), parade, followed by parade ground drills (a little more complex than school parades), then finally introductions to military weapons.

I had an upbringing on King Island with introductions and usage of a .22 Calibre Browning Repeater rifle and an old Single Barrel 12 Gauge shotgun, so weapons were nothing new to me. Although it was my first introduction to a military weapon; being a .303 Lee Enfield rifle.

My greatest memory of the cadet camp was an exhibition of firepower with a mortar and belt-fed Vickers machine gun, which were impressive to a thirteen-year-old. We followed this exhibition with an assault on the hill which had just been mortared and machine-gunned, by sections at platoon strength. This is known as fire and movement where a platoon, which consists of three sections with nine soldiers per section, has two of its sections lay down fire while the third section moves forward and takes up a firing position. After this, the rear section moves forward and takes up a frontal position. This movement is continued until all three sections have secured their objective. This cadet camp had left a deep impression on me. I left school in my fourteenth year and my next military excursion was when I turned seventeen in 1956.

—⁂—

I was working in Launceston in 1955/1956 on a wage of £6 (six pounds) a week though painfully it was costing me £5 a week for full board. On reaching seventeen years of age and after getting my mother's written approval to join the army they sent me a rail pass to travel by train from Launceston to Hobart where I was met and transferred to Anglesea Barracks. On arriving at Anglesea Barracks, I was put in the hands of a sergeant who in turn showed me my quarters and then took me to the Other Ranks (ORs) mess to show me where I would have my meals.

The Orderly Room was my next stop where I received my regimental number. The sergeant asked me how much money I had on me, I emptied my pockets and I had eight shillings and ninepence (depicted as 8/9). He took me to a pay clerk and told him to make me up a paybook now giving him my regimental number and name and to give me a fortnight's pay. I could not believe it when handed £15, as I have never had £15 in my life. How good is army life, free bed, meals and a heap of money?

At my earliest opportunity, I went down the street and purchased a watch and a wallet for £2/7/9 (two pounds seven shillings and ninepence) … my first watch.

Following medical, dental and other procedures over the next few days, it was on a plane and my first trip to the mainland (Melbourne) where we were taken to a military base Victoria Barracks and grouped with recruits from Western Australia, South Australia, Victoria, New South Wales and Queensland. I was the only enlistment from Tasmania and during a lecture from a sergeant he stated, *"That bloke from Tassie"* and so it became a lifetime nickname. Although written by Asians in a variety of ways 'Tazi, Ta-Si and Tasi' I just settled for the latter as my old father would say, *"A good dog will answer to any name."*

Our intake was all on a train with the next stop Wagga Wagga, New South Wales, then taken by military transport to Kapooka to march into 1 Recruit Training Battalion, where serious soldiering commenced. This was initiated by the basics of parade ground drills, how and who to salute, barrack routines and layouts (very disciplined), meal parades and a huge amount of physical training (PT). Of course, our first parade was to form up at the Q Store for the issue of uniforms, bedding, etcetera. We were even instructed on how to make the bed correctly (military version) thus with a few exceptions started twenty-six years of polishing boots and brass. Following several weeks of parade ground drills and physical training (PT) we were issued with weapons, a .303 rifle, so now it was drilling with weapons and being taught bayonet drills.

Early in our entry to Kapooka, we had a needle parade. I have no idea what we were being immunised against however, it did cause havoc within our intake (no doubt all intakes) with sickness and terrible muscular soreness in the shoulders and upper arms. Our non-commissioned officers (NCOs) had great delight in making us do push-ups under much sufferance. Those not capable of carrying out their orders were subject to much verbal abuse. Further rifle arms training continued, and range practice followed with us becoming competent rifle shots.

We were confined to barracks for several weeks before our first leave pass was issued, which was a visit to the large country town of Wagga Wagga, New South Wales.

Medical problems arose during our time at Kapooka Most if not all of our intake suffered from one if not both outbreaks of measles and crabs. While those who came down with measles were interned in the Kapooka Base Hospital, those who caught a dose of crabs had their bedding taken and had to suffer the humiliation of being stripped and shaven in the groin area with an application of whatever to be administered.

C W Woodard (right) at Kapooka 1956 aged seventeen.

Our recruit training went for some three months. Eventually, we were interviewed by officers on our choices of corps, and I wished to become an Infanteer so I could follow in the footsteps of my earlier two generations of footsloggers. At this point Australia did have troops serving in Malaya during the Emergency however, troops had to be of eighteen years and nine months before overseas active service was permitted.

—⁓—

I was allocated to artillery … so off to North Head, School of Artillery in Sydney. So, it was onto a train with other seventeen-year-olds to Sydney Central with kit bags in our possession. We were met at Sydney Central railway station and like thousands before us crossed the enormous Sydney Harbour bridge awestruck looking out the back of a military vehicle and taking in the beautiful Sydney Harbour en route to the Australian Army School of Gunnery, North Head located at Manly.

In 1957 the Australian Army possessed two types of artillery. Field artillery at the time consisted of 4.2-inch mortars, 25-pounders and 5.5-inch medium artillery. The second was anti-aircraft artillery: heavy anti-aircraft (HAA) a 3.7-inch weapon that could also be used as a field artillery piece and a light anti-aircraft (LAA) weapon; a 40mm Bofors firing a two-pound high explosive (HE) round. These anti-aircraft weapons were a product manufactured and used against propeller-driven aircraft, so after the introduction of jet aircraft, it made these weapons obsolete.

The Australian army did have field artillery in Malaysia however, the same non-posting overseas in an area of conflict until one was eighteen years and nine months of age, restrictions applied. So we young seventeen-year-olds were put on a gunnery course of the 3.7 heavy anti-aircraft (HAA) gun. The 103 HAA Battery was based at Middle Head in Sydney. I despised North Head; the scenery was beautiful when looking south down the Sydney Harbour, and as I was to later learn by experience, the most beautiful harbour city on the planet, however, under the staff of senior NCOs it was pure bastardry.

Following the completion of our gunnery course, we were transferred to 103 HAA Battery. In retrospect, I was later to become aware I had been posted to a unit with the most beautiful surroundings of any unit in the Australian army. HAA in its current form became obsolete thus 103 HAA Battery was retired and replaced in name as 111 Light Anti-Aircraft (LAA) Battery. I was a foundation member of this new unit. We were trained on our new weapons World War Two 40mm Bofors and in time this old equipment was replaced by an electric (battery operated) weapon. I was never impressed with the ability of these Bofors as an anti-aircraft weapon however, I believed they were the best heavy machine gun the Australian army possessed. This belief was justified as approximately ten years later the American army mounted twin 40mm Bofors on track vehicles and used them in Viet Nam as mounted heavy machine guns. These weapons 40mm Bofors fire a two-pound high explosive projectile and were named Dusters by the Americans.

While the unit was based at Middle Head, we had a British army exchange officer posted to us. There were married quarters within the inner grounds and sadly the officer's wife was raped and murdered within the married quarter. The unit was locked down with no member permitted to leave while the law moved in, and the interviewing of all soldiers was carried out. Eventually, the culprit was apprehended and charged under civilian law thus concluding an incredibly sad incident within the unit.

Descending from Mosman one passed Georges Heights, at the time occupied by a field artillery battery, then HMAS Penguin a submarine base before entering the grounds of 111 LAA Battery. Living in members of the battery would proceed to HMAS Penguin, within walking distance where movies would be shown on a nightly basis. One night halfway through a movie, the viewing was interrupted with orders for all 111 LAA Battery members to return to their unit immediately. This may have been in 1958 as huge bushfires were rampaging through the Blue Mountains and burning out the towns in the Blue Mountains area. We were paraded with webbing, all water bottles full and to procure all the firefighting equipment our unit could muster. Once loaded onto unit vehicles we proceeded to the Blue Mountains to relieve army units that had been out there for several days from Holsworthy.

As a child of King Island, I had witnessed scrub burn off on our property, which at the time as a five or six-year-old was quite formidable however, the fires in the Blue Mountains in the Springwood, Lawson and Leura regions were devastating. I have never since been in an environment with fires of this magnitude wiping out towns and the devastation witnessed has always remained with me. We in turn were relieved after several days of firefighting and with red bloodshot eyes, runny noses, wearing smoke-impregnated clothing, hungry and thirsty we returned to Middle Head.

—◊◊◊—

In late 1958 the battery in its entirety moved from Middle Head to North Head. The battery was a part of the 1st Infantry Brigade and in early 1959 partook in the largest exercise that had occurred up to that time since the end of the Second World War. Grand Slam as the exercise was called entailed the whole brigade moving to an area west of Mackay in Queensland for a three-month deployment.

This was my first visit to Queensland and the further north we moved from Brisbane the more I fell in love with Queensland. It was my first exposure to pineapple farms and mile after mile of sugar cane plantations. At Beerwah, a unit refuelling stop, I asked a local what was growing in quantity in paddocks aligning the highway? I saw my first tobacco plantation. Further north the beautiful red soil plains around Nambour added to my admiration of Queensland beside the subtropical climate in which I was now living. My mind was made up somehow, I must get posted to Queensland not knowing that opportunity was to be granted to me next year in 1960.

Later that year in 1959 the whole unit was put through the infantry training course back in Queensland at the Jungle Training Centre (JTC) Canungra in southern Queensland. The jungle is your friend, and it was the type of environment I loved to operate in. However, it was from the JTC experience that I ended up in the military hospital at Yeronga, Brisbane. Living and exercising in the vast JTC area we soon found out we were living in a tick-infested area. One morning after the first light I was found to have five to six ticks in my head, these, in turn, manifested into boil-like symptoms and I was extracted from JTC to Yeronga for several days of care and rehabilitation. It became a necessity that body inspections occurred at first light when on exercise, as I remember on one occasion, we removed fifteen ticks from one soldier's body. On another occasion upon waking one morning, I could not open my left eyelid and when examined, I was found to have one large blood-filled leech attached to my eyelid. A little salt from a twenty-four-hour ration pack removes leeches very quickly. I laid the leech on a log and with my razor-sharp machete ran it down its body and I could not believe the amount of my blood it contained.

In late 1959 the Australian Army raised its second field artillery regiment to be based in Wacol on the Ipswich highway in southern Brisbane. Wacol had been used for years as a National Service Battalion, and with National Service for that era now over a large army camp existed with barracks consisting of World War Two igloo huts covering two ridge lines separated by Bullock Head Creek.

To make up this new artillery regiment named 4 Field Regiment Royal Australian Artillery (RAA). The 105 Field Battery was to be relocated from Holsworthy, Sydney in its entirety by road to Wacol, while a new gun battery was to be formed, named 103 Field Battery by any soldier wishing to be posted to Queensland. With quite a few Queenslanders I volunteered from 111 Light Anti-Aircraft Battery to be posted to Queensland to form up this new field artillery battery. Not only did I get my wish to be in Queensland, but field artillery certainly appealed to me more than anti-aircraft gunnery.

—⁂—

In early 1960 I was assigned to this new unit, so within a few short years I had been a foundation member of two new Australian army units. The 103 Field Battery was to be sent to Malaysia relieving 101 Field Battery following their two-year posting. The Battery Captain (BK) was Peter Badcoe, who was to become a Victoria Cross (VC) recipient in Viet Nam in 1967, the second of four VC recipients during this conflict.

In early 1961 I was cross-transferred from 103 Field Battery to 105 Field Battery. The 105 Field Battery had served in Malaya in the late 1950s during the Malayan Emergency and the unit still retained many of those veterans along with several World War Two, Japanese occupation and Korean veterans. The unit carried a variety of artillery weaponry with each gun crew possessing 25-pounders (phasing out), Italian 105mm Pack Howitzers (phasing in), and a 4.2-inch mortar. This artillery unit may have been the last in Australia to possess mortars.

With new mortars introduced into the Australian Army, they became an infantry support weapon with battalions possessing mortar platoons. It was in 105 Field Battery that I received my first promotion to Lance Bombardier.

Left: Italian 105mm Pack Howitzer in full recoil. On exercise at Tin Can Bay range (Queensland) 1962. The Italian Howitzers phased out World War Two 25-Pounders. Right: On exercise Holdsworthy range (NSW) 1963. I (L) and fellow soldier Donald McDonald with Owen guns.

With the building up of tension in Southeast Asia, the Australian Army raised *Ambrose Force* which consisted of an infantry battalion from Holsworthy and an artillery support unit from Wacol, being 105 Field Battery with other small support units included, for overseas operations. Our battery was streamlined with every two soldiers sharing a tin trunk between them and all webbing, uniforms and weapons on hand. The confinement to barracks was occasionally interrupted when between 1:00 AM – 2:00 AM, the unit mobilised and moved from Wacol to the RAAF Base, Amberley just outside Ipswich, Queensland. This is when loading onto Hercules aircraft and other related activities were practised. The *Ambrose Force* destination was never revealed however, the furphies* were continuous and the strongest was a destination to Laos where the Royal Australian Air Force had access to a base at Ubon, Laos. This destination was never confirmed before *Ambrose Force* was dissolved.

Furphies – rumour(s), false story.

During World War One, an Australian company was contracted to build large containers on wheels to be shipped to the Western Front, Europe, for water supply to the troops. The company's name was Furphy located in the Victorian city of Geelong. A large gathering of troops would concentrate around these water wagons where all sorts of rumours would occur of movements to battle areas, of enemy movements and where future conflicts were likely to occur however, nothing was factual. These rumours were called furphies, which was introduced into the Australian slang and are still used today.

In 1963 I was posted to A Field Battery in Holsworthy, New South Wales (A Field Battery RAA is Australia's oldest army unit) however this posting was to be temporary as by now 111 LAA Battery had been relocated to Holsworthy from North Head.

As the Indonesian Confrontation (Bahasa term – Konfrontasi) was growing in intensity under the then President Sukarno, the army posted any soldier with previous light anti-aircraft experience to 111 LAA Battery, so from field artillery back to an anti-aircraft unit. The Unit was to be moved to Malaya in its entirety by the former Royal Australian Navy (RAN), ex-aircraft carrier HMAS Sydney, now a troop carrier and this was to be its maiden voyage in this capacity.

To better understand the military movements at these times I have included a brief history of Malaya/Malaysia from World War Two, the Malayan Emergency & the Indonesian Confrontation 1945-1966.

Malaysia consists of the Malay Peninsular and the two neighbouring states of Sarawak and Sabah situated on the large island of Borneo. Between Sarawak and Sabah is the oil-rich country of Brunei, which elected not to be a part of Malaysia. The remaining large portion of Borneo is an Indonesian territory named Kalimantan.

Background:

Chin Peng was the leader of the Malayan Communist Party (MCP) in World War Two during the invasion of the Japanese into the Malay Peninsula. He raised a Chinese-Malay guerrilla force to successfully harass the Japanese military during their operation. On the 5th of September 1945 following the defeat of the Japanese the British once again took control of their former colonies of Malaya and Singapore. However, for several reasons, this was to become the start of an uneasy interlude in which the British were not to enjoy their former respect and dominance.

In 1947 Chin Peng became secretary-general of the MCP, which by then committed to seizing power from the British. There were already developing strong political moves by the Malay and Chinese communities to gain independence.

In 1948 the MCP began an offensive for power. Following a series of murders against British plantation owners on the 16th of June 1948, a state of emergency was declared throughout Malaya. From the start, the terrorists conducted stepped-up attacks including murders and ambushes throughout Malaya with some main targets being the valuable rubber estates and tin mines.

By 1950 the terrorist's activities had extracted a terrible cost on the country with approximately fourteen hundred citizens, police and soldiers killed along with considerable economic damage. The terrorism continued unabated and resulted in the assassination of British High Commissioner Sir Henry Gurney in 1951.

The British developed a terrorist strategy called *The Briggs Plan* after their director of operations, British General Sir Harold Briggs, put it into effect. This involved the shifting of thousands of squatters who were mainly Chinese into new defensible villages along with the strict control of people and their food supply. This plan although contentious at the time was instrumental in the defeat of the guerrilla movement. To give support to these plans and the necessary military initiative, an increase in troops and resources was actioned by Britain. A series of special forces were created to operate in the jungle environment and Australia committed a RAAF squadron of supply and transport aircraft and a squadron of heavy bombers.

It was estimated that two-thirds of the MCP was eradicated in 1954. From 1955 and up to the end of the emergency, Australia further committed and maintained additional forces to Malaya including Royal Australian Navy warships, an infantry battalion, an artillery battery and other supporting troops.

During 1957 the emergency was declining with troops finding terrorists increasingly difficult to locate even with air support soldiers probing further into the jungle. On the 31st of August 1957, Malaya was successful in achieving independence from Britain, and Tunku Abdul Rahman was elected as the country's first Prime Minister.

In 1959 the communists were virtually defeated by the Federation of Malaya, as in 1960 only a few hundred hardcore terrorists still led by Chin Peng remained, and they were forced into hiding in the deep jungle on the Thai border area of northern Malaya.

The Malayan government declared the emergency over on the 31st of July 1960 and annually Malaya has a national holiday called Merdeka (Freedom) Day on the 31st of August. There was a high cost of human life, with over eleven thousand people killed during this period, reported as 1,865 security forces, 2,473 civilians and 6,710 terrorists. Some seven thousand regular Australian Navy, Army and Air Force personnel served in the emergency, in addition to military forces from Malaya, Britain, Rhodesia, Fiji and New Zealand. Little was it realised at the time but in less than three years another conflict would envelop Malaya this time with her regional neighbour, Indonesia.

The Formation of Malaysia:

The idea for the formation of Malaysia was proposed by the Prime Minister of Malaya in a speech in Singapore on the 27th of May 1961. Malaysia was to consist of the then Federation of Malaya, Singapore, the Sultanate of Brunei and the British territories of Sarawak and North Borneo (Sabah).

North Borneo (East Malaysia) is part of the third-largest island in the world and excluding Brunei consists of the states of Sabah and Sarawak, which share a common border with Indonesia, which occupies the larger southern section of Borneo (Kalimantan). Both Singapore under Lee Kuan Yew and the Sultan of Brunei Sir Omar Ali Saifuddien elected to remain independent states and not to merge and become a part of Malaysia. The British Government who had been contemplating the future of their north Borneo territories welcomed the concept. President Sukarno of Indonesia thought that this extended grouping of Malaysia was a challenge to his country's power and influence in the region and cited this as an example of neo-colonialism. Currently influencing events in Indonesia were some political problems and a faltering economy. It may be noted, that following World War Two, Indonesia (previously Dutch East Indies) gained its independence from the Dutch, and Sukarno, a military general became Indonesia's first president.

By early 1963 Indonesia had begun a military confrontation (Bahasa term 'Konfrontasi') campaign against Malaysia which was to continue for three years. Confrontation against Malaysia began as a direct economic and social offensive between the two countries, however by April 1963 there were increasing regular attacks across the borders of Sarawak and Sabah by Indonesian guerrilla forces opposing the formation of Malaysia. This resulted in a progressive build-up of British and Malaysian forces in the area.

Following further political and constitutional discussions including the United Nations the new Federation of Malaysia came into being on the 16th of September 1963. In the meantime, the number of raids From Indonesia Borneo (Kalimantan) into Sabah and Sarawak continued and increased after this.

Confrontation – The Malay Peninsula:

During 1964, armed sea raids in the straits of Malacca and Singapore had intensified including acts of sabotage in both Malaya and Singapore. Coinciding with this were large-scale military landings on mainland Malaya. The first of these landings occurred on the 17th of August 1964 when vessels landed one hundred and eight Indonesian troops at Pontian on the southwest coast of Johore. They were quickly captured by security forces.

On the 2nd of September, ninety-six Indonesian paratroopers were inserted by Hercules aircraft near the jungle town of Labis in central Johore. They too were rounded up by Commonwealth Forces.

The 29th of October 1964, saw a force of fifty-two heavily armed Indonesians come ashore in six vessels at the entrance of the Kesang River in the state of Malacca. A counterforce was immediately deployed consisting of D Company 3 Royal Australian Regiment (RAR) and 102 Field Battery. Within forty hours of the operation against the infiltrators, fifty of them were captured or had surrendered without any Australian casualties.

Thai – Malay Border Operations:

For periods during 1964 Australian forces had been engaged in anti-terrorist operations along the Thai border of Northern Malaya. 3 RAR deployed several of their companies on rotation for up to three months in this area, where they were supported by 102 Field Battery and 111 LAA Battery members as extra infantry.

These operations were to ensure that no Indonesian forces landed in northwest Malaya preventing them from contacting the remnants of Chin Peng's political group which suggested that a few hundred terrorists still existed in the Thai- Malay border region.

Throughout the remainder of 1964 and until early 1965 there were continuing Indonesian attacks and sabotage around the Malay Peninsular, particularly in the south and west of Johore State, Malacca and Singapore. Other fewer incidents also occurred in Selangor, Perak and Penang. In one of the larger enemy landings in February 1965, a group of forty-four Indonesians landed on the coast of east Johore and in the ensuing counteroperation, the security forces suffered casualty losses, with several wounded, and resulted in twenty-two enemy killed.

There were more than thirty-five reported incursions into Malaya and Singapore from August 1964 to March 1965. It soon became evident that Indonesian infiltration campaigns into these areas had not been successful, as on each occasion the soldiers had been quickly contained by the Malaysian and Commonwealth Forces. President Sukarno then changed the main thrust of his offensive to North Borneo.

Confrontation Borneo 1965:

By the end of 1964, there had been an escalation in the number of armed attacks into various parts of North Borneo from Indonesia, which was now strengthened by the utilisation of their regular forces.

In response to a direct request from the Malaysian Government, Australia sent 1 Special Air Service Squadron (SAS) and 3 Battalion Royal Australian Regiment to North Borneo in early 1965. 102 Field Battery and 2 Field Troop Engineers were also deployed to support operations.

These units joined more than thirteen battalions made up of British, Gurkha, New Zealand and Malaysian troops stationed throughout North Borneo. Their primary responsibility was patrolling and defending approximately 1,500 kilometres of the mostly rugged border area with Indonesia. 3 Battalion was located at Bau, approximately thirty kilometres southwest of the capital Kuching. 3 RAR carried out platoon-size reconnaissance (recon) and ambush patrols in the border area.

In late April 1965, Indonesian forces launched a battalion-sized attack (approximately six hundred soldiers) against a company base of the 2nd Battalion British Parachute Regiment in the border area southeast of Kuching. The platoon-sized force (thirty-six soldiers) repelled their attacks inflicting casualties on the Indonesians. Following this incident, there was an increase in various military offensives which included well-planned and executed cross-border operations by Commonwealth troops.

In the first seven weeks of these operations, three members of the battalion were killed along with an Iban teacher from an anti-personnel mine incident. On the 27th of May B Company successfully ambushed three enemy motorboats on the Koemba River killing fifteen Indonesians and in mid-June, a C Company patrol was involved in an ambush in the same area, and the subsequent counter-attack resulted in eight of the enemy killed.

At this same time, an A Company Platoon ambushed part of a large enemy force in the border area and with the assistance of artillery, killed seventeen of the enemy with two Australians wounded. In mid-July, C Company had another effective contact against an enemy platoon killing twelve Indonesians and wounding five. By the end of July 3 RAR had completed a successful four months of operational duty and returned to Terendak in Malaysia.

The Special Air Service Squadron:

Since their arrival in North Borneo, 1 Squadron of the Perth-based SASR had been concentrating their operations in the central Brigade area, which covered Sabah and parts of Sarawak, with their headquarters in Brunei. Their primary role remained one of recon, operating in four-man patrols in the mountainous and jungle terrain along their border area and often within enemy territory. In the latter half of their tour, they were tasked with more offensive cross-border operations. This included close recon and surveillance of the enemy movements and camps sometimes up to 10,000 yards (9,140 metres) within Indonesian territory. Some of these patrols also included an ambush role which resulted in killing and wounding a number of the enemy without casualties of their own. In early August 1965, the unit returned to Australia.

Coup in Indonesia:

The Communist Party of Indonesia (Partai Komunis Indonesia - PKI) was the largest non-ruling communist party in the world and had an increasing political influence within Indonesia. On the night of the 30th of September 1965, there was an aborted coup attempt against President Sukarno, with the PKI implicated which resulted in the killing of six senior generals. Consequently, there was widespread upheaval with brutal and violent eradication of life and arrests throughout the country and after several months, the military eventually restored control and the PKI was outlawed. In March 1966 President Sukarno, who was later dismissed from power, delegated his authority to General Suharto who was proclaimed President of Indonesia in 1968.

Confrontation Borneo 1966:

The Australian commitment to the defence of North Borneo and the Malay Peninsula continued during 1966. In January, 2 Squadron SAS arrived to relieve a squadron of British SAS in the West Brigade area of Sarawak, their role was like that of 1 Squadron in 1965. Since the attempted coup in Indonesia, their regular force activity in Borneo had started to lessen. In the following months, the squadron extended its operations throughout the brigade area and was able to obtain a range of valuable information for the security forces, particularly on enemy locations and movements. Active across-border operations were halted at the end of May, due to renewed talks between the Malayan and Indonesian military officials, discussing the ending of the hostilities. Further routine surveillance patrolling by 2 Squadron along the border area did not detect any sign of enemy activity, which reflected the general wind down in the confrontation. In 1966 the squadron returned to its regimental base in Western Australia.

4 RAR was the second Australian battalion to serve in North Borneo arriving in late April. They operated from similar positions in Sarawak as that of 3 RAR in 1965, however, because of the coup the situation in Borneo regarding military activity along the border area slowly decreased. In June 1966, a platoon from C Company successfully engaged a number of the enemy near the border area of Sarawak. In the following ambush encounter, these platoons engaged another part of this force which resulted in numerous enemy killed and wounded. The battalion continued its operations in this area in conjunction with a Gurkha company and patrols from 2 Squadron SAS, which resulted in the withdrawal of the targeted enemy groups.

On the 11th of August 1966, a peace treaty was signed between Indonesia and Malaysia thus bringing an end to the confrontation conflict. Soon after this 4 RAR completed their tour and returned to Malaya. Their departure marked the end of Australia's active involvement in the Borneo campaign.

It was reported that a total of 114 members of the Commonwealth Military Forces were killed during the conflict, which included 18 Australians and there was a total of 181 soldiers who had been wounded. Indonesian casualties were reported as 590 killed, 222 wounded and 771 captured.

—m—

Leading up to the 24th of May 1964 the unit of 111 LAA Battery RAA, 7th Field Engineer Squadron and a detachment of Iroquois helicopters from No5 Squadron Royal Australian Air Force (RAAF) were loaded onto HMAS *Sydney* at Garden Island in Sydney Harbour. These units together with ammunition, guns and equipment embarked on the HMAS *Sydney* for Malaysia and left port on the night of the 24th of May 1964 in reaction to the ever-increasing Indonesian confrontation over the formation of Malaysia. The forming of Malaysia included the eleven states of Malaya, Sarawak and Sabah, the latter two situated in the northern part of Borneo. On departure from Australia, the HMAS *Sydney* was escorted by the Australian destroyers HMAS *Parramatta* and HMAS *Yarra* as the president of Indonesia (President Sukarno) vowed the HMAS *Sydney* would not reach Malaysia.

The convoy sailed north entering the Bismarck Archipelago passing between New Britain and New Ireland then proceeded northwest crossing the equator north of Papua New Guinea at 143° east on the 31st of May. This is particularly memorable as the ship had a crossing-the-line ceremony occurring on my twenty-fifth birthday. The convoy then proceeded to the Philippines passing Zamboanga on the West coast of Mindanao before sailing due west to Jesselton (now Kota Kinabalu) in North Borneo. The HMAS *Sydney* dropped anchor in Gaya Bay offshore from Jesselton.

Two hundred soldiers and attached personnel of the 7th Field Engineering Squadron disembarked with a wide range of stores and heavy equipment along with eight million rounds of small arms ammunition and two hundred tons of mortar ammunition to begin defence project work in Sabah. The unloading was supported by two Landing Ships, Medium (LSM) the *Vernon Sturdee* and the *Harry Chauvel* and several smaller amphibious craft.

While anchored, Navy divers were employed underwater for the duration of the anchorage period while the destroyers continued sweeps across the anchorage area.

During the voyage, the *Sydney* refuelled the *Yarra* (an education of refuelling on the move) while the troops were kept active in PT, gun drills, maintenance of weapons and equipment and live firing off the stern of the ship with small arms at released targets. I may add here that each soldier was allocated a large 26 oz can of *Fosters* beer each evening and needless to say, the most popular troops on board were the non-drinkers.

On departing Sabah, the HMAS *Sydney* remained under escort and sailed west southwest to arrive at Singapore on the 9th of June 1964, after spending sixteen days at sea. In Singapore, the artillery troops disembarked and proceeded by rail to Royal Australian Air Force (RAAF) Base Butterworth, North Malaya. A small detachment of military personnel remained on board, me included. After several days in Singapore, HMAS *Sydney* departed and preceded north up the Straits of Malacca (separating the Malay Peninsular from Sumatra) to Penang Island.

Two events occurred on this part of the voyage. On the first night after departing Singapore the HMAS *Sydney's* emergency alarm sounded all through the ship, shuddering with reversing engines and repeated calls of *"close all Z hatches"* thus preventing a collision with an oil tanker in the congested and narrow Straits of Malacca. The other event occurred on the second day when the HMAS *Sydney* was approached by a small Indonesian armed patrol boat and was greeted by onboard personnel with continuous hand gestures (not of a friendly nature). At anchor in the Malacca Strait north of Penang Island off the northwest coast of Malaya, the unit preceded to unload its military equipment, guns, trucks and associated stores onto the beach. So, in June 1964, we proceeded from the beach to RAAF Base Butterworth, thus ending the maiden voyage of the HMAS *Sydney* as a troop carrier.

HMAS *Sydney* at sea in May/June 1964 after departing Sydney on the 24th of May.
On the flight deck are secured vehicles and guns of the
111 LAA Battery RAA en route to Malaysia.

In May 2014, a reunion was held at Garden Island, Sydney Harbour, to mark the 50th anniversary of the departure of the HMAS *Sydney* on its maiden voyage as a troop carrier. Ex-Navy, Army and Air Force personnel with family members in attendance, were accompanied by a naval band and speeches then followed by a huge luncheon to mark the occasion.

On arrival at the RAAF base, it was jaw-dropping to witness the weaponry at this facility. The first and most notable observation was seeing the V Bomber force employed there, which consisted of the Victor, Valiant and Vulcan aircrafts. The Vulcans were a nuclear delivery vehicle and with an undisclosed operating ceiling and top secret, were believed to be capable of a nuclear delivery several hundred miles from its target. It was never officially disclosed to us that the Royal Air Force (RAF) did have nuclear weapons in Malaya however, with the presence of the Vulcans along with accompanying Victors and Valiants, it left little to the imagination. The base also possessed several exceptionally large ground-to-air missiles.

The RAF also had a squadron of Javelins all-weather interceptors deployed there, which were continually in the air at night-time with the Indonesians often buzzing a line through the Malacca Straits that depicted Malayan/Indonesian airspace. The RAAF had two squadrons of Sabres deployed which later were replaced by the French Dassault Mirages and Canberra Bombers. The Royal New Zealand Air Force (RNZAF) also had Canberra Bombers present with all Air Forces having support aircraft availability including Hercules, Caribou (from 65/66), RAF Beverleys and Argosys along with the RNZAF Bristol Freighters. The RAF contribution also included the Sea King and Belvedere helicopters and Australia provided the UH-1B Iroquois helicopters to support operations on the Thai-Malay border.

Left: A Victor Bomber landing at Butterworth 1964.
Right: A Valiant Bomber airborne at Butterworth 1964.

Two photographs of a Vulcan Bomber lifting off and airborne at Butterworth 1964.

Our army unit was the only Australian army unit posted in North Malaya and did participate in border operations (as infantry) on the Thai border. From the Emergency operations Chin Peng and the remainder of his force retreated into southern Thailand, however, did periodically venture into northern Malaya harassing kampongs in that regional area. Along with the 3rd Battalion troops from Terendak, we functioned as a reaction force to Chin Peng's raids. We were not the only military force in North Malaya as the British had a Green Jacket battalion stationed at Minden Barracks on Penang Island.

Our unit was deployed around the Butterworth base. Besides operations, we conducted many infantry types of exercises in the jungles of the states of Kedah, Perak, Selangor and Penang Island. In the State of Perak, I discovered the most amazing rainforests. I love the jungles as they become one's best friend however, the jungles of the Cameron Highlands are the most beautiful I have ever had the fortune to operate in. The rainforests of the Cameron Highlands are five to six thousand feet above sea level, quite cold at night-time and very dark where one cannot see your hand in front of your face. Unfortunately, it is also tiger country. On my first visit to the area I was informed, *"You will not see any dogs in the kampongs up here ... tigers love dogs."*

When harbouring* of an evening, the harbour would be quite compact with vines or toggle ropes tied to each occupant's hoochies for all-night relief on the machine gun post.

*A harbour is where a unit before the last light will secure an area and position personnel in a manner, which gives the unit all-round fire defence with overlapping arcs of fire.

Such were the heights of the Cameron Highlands that at times one could look down on clouds covering lesser heights and valleys. From the shores on the west coast of Malaya, one travels only twenty-five miles (forty kilometres) inland from an equatorial climate to this region, which can be quite cold during the night. Such was the height of the huge trees and the majestic coverage of their canopy that no daylight or sunshine reaches the forest floor, thus there was no undergrowth.

I received my second promotion to bombardier whilst serving in Malaya.

We visited the ambush area where Chin Peng's guerrillas ambushed and killed Sir Henry Gurney, the British High Commissioner in Malaya, in October 1951.

The reason for our visit was to assess the perfect ambush location as ambushing was prime teaching within the Australian army of jungle warfare. Chin Ping's comrade Siew Ma with thirty-six guerrillas chose this site along the winding gap road leading uphill to the popular expatriate highland retreat of Frasers Hill sixty miles north of Kuala Lumpur. One three-hundred-yard segment of steeply inclining roadway running to a sharp bend was so severe that drivers of all forms of transport needed to slow to a crawl. The ambush party placed itself in the lush undergrowth on the hillside of the road, the perfect ambush location, which included an escape route. Following two days of laying in the ambush area, his patience was rewarded, with firstly a Land Rover appearing, dropping through gears as it negotiated twists and turns back down the road. The Land Rover when coming into view carried half a dozen armed police. One hundred yards following was a black limousine, a Rolls Royce and once into the killing zone the Land Rover and Rolls Royce were ambushed with the Rolls Royce eventually stopping forty yards from the Land Rover. The High Commissioner exited the Rolls Royce and had taken no more than three or four steps before he fell face down in a clatter of rifle fire. A scout car with a Bren machine gun blazing arrived and the ambush party retreated along its escape route without one casualty. Siew Ma claimed the life of the most senior foreign diplomat in Malaya.

The lesson for us … we were observing a perfect ambush location, which you must take into consideration the many factors in selecting such sites. In a further chapter, I will write of the comparisons in lying in ambush situations in Malaya compared to Viet Nam.

On another jungle venture in the state of Perak I was to come to grief with an unseen predator when we were operating and sleeping in swamp areas for many days, which landed me in the RAAF hospital for more than a week at Butterworth, another story (see Chapter Military Oddities – A Silent Killer).

From living in the jungle for weeks at a time surviving on twenty-four-hour ration packs and at times on resupply we would get a ten-man ration pack which would give us more variety of food. On insertion, we would be carrying a minimum of three days' rations complete with webbing, three water bottles, and a large pack consisting of a spare set of greens and sleeping gear. Then adding in weapons and minor commodities, you could be laden with up to thirty kilos of gear and operating on the lowlands in equatorial conditions so after a week of movement we lost many kilos of body weight.

Each man needed to carry three water bottles to replace fluids from constant sweating. Water bottles were refilled from natural resources however, all personnel carried water purification tablets to be added to refilled bottles that could not be consumed for twenty-four hours. Fluid intake was continually required, however it needed to be controlled.

Following periods living in the boondocks (jungles) a lot of our troops would develop a fungus growing on parts of the body, primarily the inner thighs and crotch, and upon return to Butterworth would dispatch the uniform and for several days wear nothing but a Malay sari, sitting in the sun and letting sunlight eventually kill the fungus which was the best cure.

On one occasion while moving through the jungle we came across a burnt-out kampong (Malay village). During the Malayan Emergency if a kampong was found to be supplying Chin Peng's guerrillas with food the population was removed and the kampongs burnt down. Arriving at this burnt-out kampong we found a small clump of banana trees bearing fruit, however very green fruit and after living from ration packs for the best part of the week, two of our sections thought fresh fruit would certainly be a little luxury. Within an hour or two, our fresh fruit eaters could shit through the eye of the needle at ten paces. Following a further two days of continuous runs, their condition deteriorated to such an extent, that they had to be extracted back to Butterworth. They had become so weak they became a liability … so a lesson was learned, do not eat green bananas.

**Left: Children from a kampong photographed while patrolling along the rice paddies.
Right: Water Buffalo feeding by a kampong were used for tilling the rice paddies.**

What were the advantages of living on RAAF base Butterworth? Surviving on ration packs on jungle operations and returning to the RAAF base was like moving into a five-star luxury complex as far as the food was concerned with a huge smorgasbord of food available to us. We considered the RAAF personnel to be pampered however, we never complained of being exposed to their offerings.

While operating on jungle operations more than once we were unfortunate enough to upset the locals. When moving through jungle tracks in operational mode, silence is imperative. Suddenly, the jungle would explode from above us because we had intruded into the territorial boundaries of the local gibbon tribe. They would wait until we were under them then all hell would break loose, twigs, branches and even their shit would be rained down on us. If we thought we were in an area undetected we had been exposed as the racket in the jungle could be heard miles away, a warning that something foreign was intruding in their territory. If any enemy forces were in the vicinity, it was a convenient early warning system.

Our biggest loss during these jungle excursions was the unfortunate death of a platoon sergeant through an anti-personnel mine incident. He became a casevac and his body was extracted from the incident area.

I must make it clear that our unit's deployment to Butterworth was chiefly as an airfield defence unit manned with electric-driven 40mm Bofors which were inadequate in the age of jet aircraft. We occasionally had practice airstrikes on the base by our own Canberra Bombers and as the Canberras operated against ground forces from a few hundred feet, we were quite ineffective in our defence.

———〰———

Leaving the base for jungle operations and exercises was a break from the airfield defence where one could enjoy jungle operations and reacquaint ourselves with infantry skills and tactics. My time in Malaya was in 1964, followed by five months back in Australia then returning to Malaya for a further two and a half years (July 1965 to December 1967).

Not all our time was spent sitting around an airfield or moving around in jungles. With more than one hundred thousand Commonwealth troops in Malaya/Singapore and being a sports person, it was like a continuous Commonwealth Games. Of all the forces in Malaya/Singapore, by far the biggest component was the British with a huge naval fleet in Singapore, which was accompanied by Royal Australian Navy (RAN) and Royal New Zealand Navy (RNZN) support. There were also Royal Airforce Bases in Singapore at Tengah, Seletar and Changi along with a V Bomber force and an all-weather interceptor squadron of Javelins at Butterworth.

Commonwealth army units were based at Terendak (Malacca), further up the peninsular from Singapore, and consisted of troops from the UK, Australia, New Zealand, the Gurkhas from Nepal and naturally the Malay Rangers. Along with part of a Gurkha Brigade, our small artillery unit and a UK Green Jacket battalion were the only army components north of Malacca.

Although seeing action on the Malay Peninsula, later most of the confrontation was carried out in Kalimantan (Borneo) with troops being fed into that area through Kuching, the capital of Sarawak. Australian artillery was sited along the Sarawak/Kalimantan border to support the infantry and Special Air Services (SAS) operating in Borneo proper.

Some action took place on the Malay Peninsula with Indonesia completely getting the tides confused and making a landing craft invasion across the Straits of Malacca, four hundred metres out from the land on the mudflats at low tide. They were easily taken by direct artillery fire and what was not killed, conceded when realising their hopeless situation.

Indonesia had C130 Hercules aircraft and landed two aircraft loaded with paratroopers in Malaya however, they were rounded up without conflict after being reported by local villagers. Indonesia believed they would be welcomed with open arms by the locals.

———〰———

As the Indonesian threat began to wane our families were allowed to join us in Malaya. The RAAF had families stationed on Penang and when we arrived in 1964, we moved into very nice housing in Georgetown on Penang Island. My eldest son was a pupil at the RAAF school in Penang until our departure in December 1967.

The family had an education about living and learning the way of life in a southeast Asian country, especially with the overly sensitive area of religion. Malaysia is a Muslim country, however, does have a rather large Hindu and Buddhist population, which is always a delicate subject when relating to politics.

Army life never altered that much for the serving soldiers however, off-duty time was now spent with family. Being on Penang Island, transferring to Butterworth was by military vehicle and ferry to the mainland and return.

When the external situation created by the Indonesian President Sukarno failed it was back to him having internal problems within his country. President Sukarno was Indonesia's first President, himself an ex-army general with the country being administered and run by him and his Generals. He now had internal problems and it quickly became *reds under the beds.*

As with many Asian countries over the centuries, the Chinese had migrated and although not running countries politically, did run countries through commerce and trade. As with Chin Peng, a Malayan of Chinese extraction, Indonesia with its huge population had many Indonesians of Chinese extraction, who did hold much of the wealth within the former Dutch East Indies. It was now declared that a Chinese Communist element within Indonesia was attempting to overthrow the new country of Indonesia formed following World War Two. We believe that within Indonesia from 1966 to 1967 some two hundred thousand Indonesian Chinese were slaughtered by the Sukarno regime.

This also spilled over into Malaysia and with many of the population consisting of Malayan/Chinese, an internal problem exploded within its boundaries. It got so extreme (I can only talk of Penang Island) that a twenty-four-hour curfew was placed on the island owing to riots and murder within the city. I can recall outside one married quarter, a local jumped off his bicycle and hid under the vehicle overpass of the stormwater drain into the driveway. It did not deter the local armed force as he was shot dead under the vehicle overpass in Green Lane Georgetown, Penang Island.

Earlier, school buses were ambushed, school children decapitated, and their heads stuck on bamboo poles lining the main roads. It was the death penalty being outdoors on the streets of Penang. Our wives were taken by military vehicle under armed escort to do their shopping at the Navy Army Airforce Institute (NAAFI). This was a British shopping complex at Minden Barracks which was occupied by the British Green Jacket battalion on Penang Island and then returned to their housing again under armed escort.

Commonwealth troops were not allowed to interfere with any local incidents as these troops occupied Malaysia for external threats only. The internal problems in Penang finally petered out and normality returned at the expense of many deaths of all ages, which was an education for Australian families.

The threat to Malaysia by Sukarno's Indonesia lessened to such an extent that Commonwealth troops slowly but cautiously began to withdraw from southeast Asia. Sukarno wisely saw that he was on a hiding to nothing by threatening the existence of Malaysia and the British Commonwealth Forces.

One of their higher-ranking officers from the airborne Indonesian troops who dropped into Malaya stated, *"We believed we would be welcomed with open arms by the Malayan kampongs as we were there to rescue our Muslim brothers from British tyranny."*

From a pilot officer of the Javelin squadron in Butterworth to me, *"If the 'balloon' goes up here, Indonesia will not have a plane that can fly nor a ship that can float within twenty-four hours."*

Confrontation in Kalimantan (Borneo) slowly subsided. Our ground troops returned to Singapore and Malacca then eventually were phased out of southeast Asia, and I am sure, much to the delight of the Indon Forces. Our unit remained at Butterworth and me seeing out a two and half years (July 1965 – December 1967) second stint was returned to Australia by Christmas 1967 following my family, which left Malaya in November 1967.

Malayan Veterans attended a reunion at Twin Towns, Coolangatta Queensland in 1999. L-R: Reg Miller, Henry Walters, myself and Junior Suthers (sadly all deceased).

GLOSSARY OF TERMS AND ACRONYMS

To better understand the terms and acronyms within this chapter of my memoirs, following I have inserted a glossary of weapons, aircraft and general dialogue used by the military, which relates to the Malaysian and Viet Nam campaigns.

Glossary of terms and acronyms of weapons used by Australian troops in both the Malaysian and Viet Nam conflicts:

*weapons used only in Malaysia

7.62	heavy barrel light machine gun
12-gauge*	automatic shotgun
Bren gun*	initially a .303 then converted to a 7.62mm magazine-fed
Claymore mine	anti-personnel directional above-ground mine
F1	9 mm sub-machine gun
GPMG*	7.62mm general-purpose magazine-fed machine gun (British)
Hand Grenade*	white phosphorus
Hand Grenade	shrapnel and percussion (British and US)
M 14 mine	anti-personnel mine with a danger radius of approximately one metre
M 16 mine	anti-personnel mine which was the deadliest AP mine in Viet Nam with a lethal danger radius of several metres - often called the 'jumping jack' mine
M-16 rifle	5.56mm Armalite assault rifle (US)
M26	high explosive grenade
M-60	7.62mm general-purpose belt-fed machine gun (US)
M-72	66mm light anti-tank weapon also called an IAW
M-79	40mm grenade launcher or more affectionately, the *'Wombat gun'*
OMC	Owen Machine Carbine, a 9mm submachine gun
SLR	7.62mm self-loading rifle

Glossary of terms and acronyms of aircraft used by Commonwealth Forces in the Malaysian campaign:

Australian and New Zealand (RAAF and RNZAF)

Bristol Type 170 Freighter	short-distance aircraft freighter
C-130	four-engine cargo transport aircraft (Hercules)
CC-08 Caribou	Canadian-designed STOL (short take-off, landing) transport aircraft
Dassault Mirage III	French fighter aircraft purchased by the RAAF
DC-3	propellor driven aircraft
MK-20 Canberra	jet bomber
Sabre	fighter aircraft
UH-1B Iroquois	troop carrier helicopter referred to as a *Huey*

British (RAF)

Argosy	fast turbo troop jet carrier
Belvedere Helicopter	rotor fore and aft troop carrier
Beverley	large propeller-driven troop and cargo carrier
Javelin	all-weather interceptor fighter aircraft
Lightning	jet fighter
Sea King Helicopter	troop and supply carrier
V Bombers	strategic nuclear strike force aircraft known as Vulcans, Victors and Valiants

—m—

Glossary of terms and acronyms of aircraft used during the Viet Nam war:

B-52	strategic jet bomber (US)
C-123	twin-engine transport aircraft sometimes called a *baby Herc*
C-130	four-engine cargo transport aircraft (Hercules)
CC-08 Caribou	Canadian-designed STOL (Short take-off, landing) transport aircraft
Canberra	jet bomber (RAAF)
Cessna	fixed-wing light aircraft
CH-47 Chinook	twin-rotor heavy-lift helicopter
CH-54 Sikorsky	heavy-lift helicopter, also known as a *sky crane*

Cobra	assault helicopter
DC-3	propellor driven aircraft
F-4 Phantom	jet bomber
F-86 Super Sabre	jet bomber
UH-1B Iroquois	troop carrier helicopter referred to as a *Huey*

—m—

Glossary of terms and acronyms used during the Viet Nam war:

1 ALSG	1st Australian Logistic Support Group (Vung Tau)
1 ATF	1st Australian Task Force (Nui Dat)
2IC	Second in Command
2LT	Second Lieutenant
AATTV	Australian Army Training Team Viet Nam
ANZAC	Australian and New Zealand Army Corps; a combined Australian/New Zealand unit
AO	area of operation
APC	armoured personnel carrier
ARVN	Army of the Republic of Viet Nam – the South Viet Nam regular army
BC	Artillery Battery Commander
BDR	Bombardier
BG	Battery Guide
BK	Captain - artillery
BSM	Battery Sergeant Major
bund	an earthwork formed to protect equipment from direct fire or blast, the raised pathways between paddy fields
casevac	casualty evacuation
Charlie	Viet Cong, from the phonetic spelling of VC, 'Victor Charlie'
chopper	helicopter
CO	Commanding Officer
contact	to engage in a battle with the enemy
CSM	Company Sergeant Major, a warrant officer

DF	defensive fire, a registered artillery target
Digger	nickname for the Australian soldier, a legacy of trench warfare
Dustoff	acronym 'Dedicated untiring service to our fighting forces' a helicopter for casualty evacuation
FO	forward observer for artillery and mortar fire
FSB	Fire Support Base – a base that included artillery and/or mortars to support patrolling forces
GNR	Gunner
grunt	an infantryman, sometimes called grunters, the noise they make pulling on their packs or climbing into APCs
gunship	a helicopter, normally an Iroquois mounted with rockets and machine guns
H and I	Harassment and Interdiction – artillery fired onto a suspected enemy area of movement
harbour	a night defensive position, usually circular with MG sentry posts
HE	high explosive ordnance
HMG	heavy machine gun, usually around .50 calibre or 12.7 mm and above
Ho Chi Minh Trail	a series of trails from North Viet Nam through Laos and Cambodia into South Viet Nam
hootch/hoochie	nickname for personal shelter or lodgings
HQ	Headquarters
Huey	Iroquois helicopter
JTC	Jungle Training Centre, Canungra, Queensland
J, the	jungle
kampong	a Malaysian enclosure or village
KBA	killed by aircraft
KIA	killed in action
kiwi	nickname for New Zealanders
LBDR	Lance Bombardier
LOH	light observation helicopter – a Sioux or Bell
LT	Lieutenant
LTCOL	Lieutenant Colonel
LZ	landing zone – an area in which a helicopter could land

mama-san	a woman in a position of authority, especially one in charge of a geisha house or bar
MAJ	Major
MC	Military Cross - a decoration for gallantry for officers, unable to be awarded posthumously
medevac	medical evacuation, the Hercules aircraft flight returning to Australia
MIA	missing in action
MID	Mentioned In Dispatches - an oak leaf attached to the campaign medal ribbon as an award for outstanding service
Military Region	there were four Military Regions (known as 1-4) from the DMZ to the Delta, in South Viet Nam
Mini-team	A three- or four-man team of engineers from which splinter teams can be formed to provide engineer support usually for mine warfare, mine detection and mine clearing
mm	millimetre (calibre)
MM	Military Medal - an Imperial bravery award for soldiers
MMG	medium machine gun, usually around .30 calibre
Montagnards	Vietnamese tribal hill people who formed their own units during the war
mortars	artillery weapon which fires explosive shells
napalm	firebomb of petroleum jelly
nasho	a National Serviceman conscripted into the Army for two years' service
NCO	non-commissioned officer
NVA	North Vietnamese Army
OC	officer commanding, a sub-unit commander
pad	a helicopter landing point or area
paddy	a field for growing rice that can be flooded when planting the crop
pit	entrenched fighting position for ground troops
province	a political region – there are 44 provinces in South Viet Nam
RAP	Regimental Aid Post
R & C	rest and convalescence - leave earned after injury or illness or arduous duty, and taken locally
R & R	rest and recreation - leave earned after six months on operations in South Viet Nam and usually taken outside the country

RAA	Royal Australian Artillery
RAAF	Royal Australian Air Force
RAE	Royal Australian Engineers
RAEME	Royal Australian Electrical and Mechanical Engineers
RAR	Royal Australian Regiment, infantry
recce/recon	reconnaissance
ROK	Republic of Korea
RSM	Regimental Sergeant Major, a Warrant Officer Class One
RVN	Republic of (South) Viet Nam
SAS	Special Air Services (Regiment) – operated in small groups as long-range reconnaissance patrols
SOP(s)	standard operating procedures
Spooky	nickname for the C-47 fixed-wing close air support gunship (also known as *Puff the Magic Dragon)*
TAOR	tactical area of operations
TET	Chinese New Year – a moveable date based on a lunar calendar
TOC	tactical operations centre – command post
tracks	nickname for tracked vehicles
Uc Dai Loi	Vietnamese term for Australians meaning *people from the great southern land*
US	United States of America
VC	Viet Cong – a renaming of the Viet Minh
VCI	Viet Cong Infrastructure
Viet Minh	the term applied to Vietnamese resistance fighters from the first Indochina (French) war
WIA	wounded in action
WO1	Warrant Officer Class One – usually a Regimental Sergeant Major who is the senior NCO in a unit
WO2	Warrant Officer Class Two – a rank below WOI, usually a Company/Battery Sergeant Major
WP	white phosphorus
XO	Executive Officer – 2IC of a military unit

—∿—

Goodbye Malaya - Hello Viet Nam

"Get this soldier out of here, he's going native. Get him home and into a unit going to Viet Nam." - **So was decided the next stage of my military career.**

Similar to Malaya, I have included maps to better understand the military movements at these times and some further background, which relates to the campaign. The uniqueness of the Viet Nam War was that it was a conflict with no fronts. Unlike previous wars, many small and large battles were continuous throughout South Viet Nam.

Brief on South Viet Nam:

The Americans divided South Viet Nam in Corps I – IV from the demilitarised zone (DMZ) south to the Ca Mau Peninsular incorporating its forty-four provinces. The Australian Task Force (ATF) was deployed in Corp III in the province of Phuoc Tuy. By the mid-sixties, the ATF was established at Nui Dat with Vung Tau being the Task Force's logistics support base, situated on the ocean. Vung Tau was also the repatriation hospital for wounded soldiers with the more serious returned to Australia. Although Phuoc Tuy Province was the tactical area of responsibility (TAOR), Australians were deployed in surrounding provinces on operations in Corp III.

Left: My six years of operations were performed in this region of southeast Asia.

The Australian Army Training Team Viet Nam (AATTV) operated within American
units throughout Corps I – IV of South Viet Nam and the forty-four provinces.

III Corp Tactical Zone (CTZ) where Australian Forces were based and
operated out of Nui Dat, Phuoc Tuy Province, South Viet Nam. War Zones
C, D and the Iron Triangle were Viet Cong strongholds near Saigon.

Deforestation – US Defoliation Process:

The Americans carried out several ways of deforestation to deny enemy troops movement in daylight thus cutting in half their movement tonight hours only. The enemy had no airpower so the Americans could cover these areas by gunships during daylight hours. There were two methods of deforestation with the first involving sky cranes inserting D8 bulldozers into areas and while operating abreast, and under the cover of gunships, they proceeded to gouge out huge fire trails chequerboarding the landscape. The second method was to aerial spray chemicals by two-engine Baby Hercs (C-123s). Often these fire trails were utilised and occupied by setting up Fire Support Bases (FSBs).

Fire Support Base:

FSBs included artillery or mortars to support patrolling forces so when a battalion is given an area of operation (AO) an FSB is established. The occupation of an FSB consists of a Battalion Head Quarters and the Command Post, an artillery gun battery, six 105mm howitzers, the battalion mortar platoon, and other support units as required. If on location, centurion tanks and armoured personnel carriers (APCs) are stationed within the FSB, and a helicopter landing zone (LZ) is centralised within this area. In establishing the base it has 360-degree all-round protection by those in its occupation. Viet Nam is the first war in which field artillery was routinely inserted and extracted by helicopter.

On most occasions, our artillery was inserted by Chinook helicopter. Vietnam was the first war in history where artillery was inserted by air.

Establishing a Fire Support Base:

From the time our gun battery is inserted the first forty-eight hours are virtually nonstop in the development of local defence whilst giving support to the infantry as required. Inserted with the guns is a small unit-operated bulldozer, case model 310G which immediately begins bulldozing up mounds (bunds) completely around the gun. The development of these bunds by the gun crews includes the construction and sandbagging of an ammunition bay, an M60 machine gun bunker and sleeping bays all with overhead cover. Our Command Post, which also includes an overhead cover, is dug in underground by the case dozer. The Command Post is run by our Gun Positional Officer (GPO) with his survey sergeant as 2IC. The GPO carries the rank of Lieutenant (LT). The battery captain (BK) is the senior officer within our unit on the site and his responsibilities included the setting up of local defence in our perimeter of the FSB. The local defence includes laying of a barb-wired barrier secured by star pickets, inside the wire trip flares are overlapped then inside the flares are claymore mines which are activated from within the M60 machine gun bunker. Both flares and mines were deactivated during daylight hours. The M60s are sited with arcs of fire overlapping within the perimeter wire. As we only carried a limited supply of gun ammunition upon insertion, the battery guide (BG) a warrant officer (WO), was instrumental in the further distribution of ammo when it was flown in by Chinooks.

The insertion of a 6 RAR (ANZAC Battalion) company by eight *Hueys* into an AO. In the foreground is the early development of an FSB - Viet Nam 1969.

Gun Ammunition:

On insertion, our gun ammunition included XM 546 anti-personnel artillery rounds (6 rounds carried by the crew) along with a small supply of high explosives (HE) and white phosphorus (WP). Resupply is immediate by Chinook of all the other types of ammunition. This included M1 HE, which can be fitted with a variety of fuses, such as point detonating (PD) and variable time (VT) fuses. M134 illuminating contains a magnesium compound flare and when ejected from the projectile it burns brightly for several minutes suspended by a parachute. M60 WP or base eject M84 smoke were also supplied. This occurs as the establishment of the FSB continued. Last light and first light patrolling outside of our perimeter are carried out daily, and following the last light patrols, the flares and claymore mines are activated.

The Gun Crew:

Our M2A2 howitzers could provide flexible fire at normal angles, high angles and with open sights (barrel parallel to the ground). They are a crew serviced weapon and a full gun crew consists of seven personnel although on occasions we would be down to even five due to other factors. The gun crew personnel comprise a gun sergeant, who is in total control and command of all aspects of their gun crew's responsibilities. Bombardier (BDR), second-in-charge (2IC) of the crew whose main responsibility is the tender and preparation of all gun ammunition as requested and required. A lance bombardier (L/BDR) assistant to the BDR and gun ammunition numbers. Two gun layers gunners (GNR) one for line, one for elevation, remaining gunners ammunition numbers.

Gun Crew Weaponry:

An artillery gun crew was perhaps the most heavily armed group in Australian forces on operations in the Viet Nam war. The reason a gun crew carries such a variety of weapons is that they have the luxury of being inserted and moved by helicopter though when acting in the capacity of infantry they are required to scale down.

Small arms weapons carried by an individual gun crew with all members being able to operate each weapon, include:

One each of an M60 machine gun, an M72 light anti-tank weapon and an M79 grenade launcher, three each of M16 Armalite rifles and SLR rifles, and six each of claymore mines and hand grenades.

Charlie Gun 101 FLD, BTY, 1 FLD Regiment RAA supporting 6 RAR (Anzac Battalion) Viet Nam 69/70. Moving from FSB Discovery to FSB Lion (Operation Marsden) October 1969.

L-R: L/BDR Paddy Winters, (Rear) 2LT. Merv Fennel (Section Safety Officer), GNR D. H. Doring, GNR Les White, GUN SGT Tasi Woodard, GNR Gary Franks (Dec), BDR Neville Jolliffe (Dec), (Absent) GNR Les Giles, awaiting a Chinook for aerial movement.

Arriving back home at Christmas in 1967 from Malaysia and following extended leave I reported to 1 Field Regiment RAA at Enoggera Barracks, Brisbane in February 1968. The unit had already completed one tour in Viet Nam and was preparing for its second. I was promoted to sergeant and became one of the six gun sergeants in 101 Field Battery.

As the strength of the unit was building up with national servicemen and regulars the training became more intense with long exercises in the Tin Can Bay and Wide Bay areas including a unit completing a very intense two weeks through the JTC at Canungra, South Queensland. This was compulsory for all units and individuals before the movement to Viet Nam. This training was without artillery weapons and was purely infantry training.

Before departure, my Battery Sergeant Major (BSM) and I attended a demolition course at Wallangarra in southern Queensland as all operational units had to carry members conversant with and the carrying of demolition materials, which were used periodically on operations during the tour.

Tours of duty for individuals and units were usually for twelve months, under the circumstances which prevailed my tour lasted for almost fourteen months (April 1969 - May 1970) having spent two Anzac Days and almost two birthdays during my tour.

— m —

I was placed on the advance party for our unit along with four other soldiers. We arrived in Nui Dat via Tan Son Nhut (Saigon) in time to accompany the 104 Field Battery we were to relieve, on their last operation in the country. Being involved in this operation certainly gave me a head start for when our unit arrived and was to accompany our battalion, 6 RAR Anzac Battalion on operations in May 1969. On departing Viet Nam in May 1970 our other gun battery 105 Field Regiment was the first unit to return to Australia followed by HQ Battery then 101 Field Battery thereby completing the regimental exchange. I must add here that the only Corps that were relieved and exchanged on a unit basis were infantry battalions and artillery field regiments. All other units remained in the country and individuals were replaced within the units in a trickle reinforcement system.

Between operations we spent some time at the Horseshoe, which was a smaller, fully occupied military FSB some six kilometres from Nui Dat, then thirty-six hours on R & R in Vung Tau and a week back in Australia (February 1970) to be with the family, before returning to Viet Nam.

Finally, our unit departed Viet Nam in May via Qantas from Saigon and arrived in Sydney. My experiences overseas featuring many serious soldiering and the lighter side of military life are featured in the chapter Military Oddities.

— m —

Following an extended leave, our regiment was split with 105 Field Battery and HQ Battery being posted to Wacol, Brisbane while our 101 Field Battery was posted to Enoggera, Brisbane. I believe on reforming the battery we had only some thirty-five to forty personnel left (a battery is usually one hundred and thirty personnel strong), with our national servicemen being discharged, officers reposted and I being the only gun sergeant retained in the unit as others were posted throughout the country.

My senior officer was English, an ex-British major, who on enlisting in the Australian Army dropped a rank to captain, with myself being the most senior NCO in the unit. Following in-depth meetings with my ex-British officer, he explained he did not have a full comprehension of Viet Nam operations, nor did he have full knowledge of Australian weapons and equipment. So I was requested by him to run our battery, which was small in numbers, while it began to build up in strength. With the remainder of the regiment being undermanned, we could not at this stage train as a regiment, therefore small unit training was implemented. Besides individual gun drills, I included map reading skills followed by extensive practical map reading exercises on Bribie Island, which was a flat, heavily timbered island off the Sunshine Coast in Queensland.

A big emphasis was put on small arms weapons training as we carried quite a range of weapons and other military hardware. Gradually our subunits were being built up with the incoming national servicemen and regular soldiers. The unit was on notice that we would be deployed to Viet Nam in February 1972, 1 Field Regiment's third tour.

The regiment was at its full complement of strength by mid to late 1971 when in November the unit was to stand down as no further battalions or regiments were to be deployed to Viet Nam. However, individuals to units still in Viet Nam would be redeployed (trickle system) to keep those units up to strength until the individual units could be withdrawn from the conflict in a coordinated though complex exit from the country.

Except for specialised small groups, the Viet Nam War was over for Australia in 1972. However, the USA never completed the withdrawal from Viet Nam until 1975, continually putting more burden on the Army of the Republic of Viet Nam (known as the South Viet Nam Army or ARVN) for their defence, which became a complete debacle and in turn, was overrun by the North Vietnamese and Viet Cong. History shows that the military equipment left in South Viet Nam, including Air Force by the USA, enabled North Viet Nam to become the fourth largest equipped army on the planet.

In a rough estimation, it is believed some three million Vietnamese were killed in the conflict while the USA lost some 56,000 troops and Australian losses were 522.

What now for the Australian Army? National Service was eventually phased out, which left our Army with a surplus of senior NCOs within the Regular Army.

From 1972 on, my postings included the Field Regiment, a brief period to 6 Brigade Task Force Enoggera, then back to the field regiment at Wacol and then my longest posting during this period, which was a three-year posting to the Land Warfare Centre (LWC) in Canungra. I had been through the Jungle Training Centre/Land Warfare Centre on three occasions as it was a compulsory course before overseas deployments to areas of conflict. Now being on staff I must say I have never in my military career have been in a unit, which placed such a high priority on staff care, although I may add one was expected to carry out his appointment within his posting of the highest degree of excellence or be marched out.

From 1979 to my discharge in 1982 I was into civilian rugby, coaching with Southern Districts Rugby Union at Annerley in the Brisbane competition. I can thank the Army that following my three years at Canungra, I was posted to my first introduction to a reserve army unit, which was 5/11 Field Regiment RAA on cadre staff, located in Annerley and walking distance to the Souths Rugby Union Club. I firmly believe it was a two-way posting as it gave the Army a little public relations (PR) having a military member as a Director of Coaching of a club within the Brisbane and Queensland primary rugby competitions.

While serving in my posting at Annerley, the Army offered me a promotion to Captain from WO2 however, I was to take up a posting of my choice to either Perth (Western Australia) or Launceston (Tasmania). My priority was not to leave Queensland, so I elected to finish my army career at forty-two years of age, following almost twenty-six years of service. Thus, taking my discharge on the 25th of February 1982 at Northern Command Personnel Depot.

A farewell by my unit members.

Extract from *The Army Newspaper* 1982

"Footballer Retires"

"Following a long and distinguished Services Rugby career, Tasi Woodard is retiring from the Army. He Captained/Coached numerous Army Unit teams as well as the Queensland Army, Queensland Combined Services and Coached ASRU (Australian Services Rugby Union). He had the distinction of Captain/Coaching two undefeated premiership teams in consecutive years 1967/1968 in two different countries (Malaya/Australia). Tasi was the Director of Coaching' of the 'Southern Districts Rugby Union club in Brisbane in 1980/1981."

SIX

MILITARY ODDITIES

"The willingness of future generations to serve in our military will be directly dependent upon how we have treated those who have served in the past"
George Washington.

George Washington undeniably comprehended the national importance of fairly treating those who have served in uniform - wisdom that has evaded Australia's political elite for decades.

I believe any long-serving military member would have many memories and amusing stories relating to what occurred during their service at home and abroad. I have mixed tales to tell, many amusing some devastating and sad as such is the life of servicemen and women. Following are a few short stories of events that I wish to share.

1: Just a Common Soldier

I thought it applicable that this touching article is included in this book. Having lived now in Caloundra on the Sunshine Coast, Queensland for more than twenty-five years, I have travelled south to Brisbane and north to various other places to attend funerals of past ex-military servicemen whom I have served with, both at home and overseas on no less than sixteen occasions. I remain in touch with the families of these men that I was close to within the Army.

JUST A COMMON SOLDIER
(A Soldier Died Today)

He was getting old and paunchy and his hair was falling fast,
And he sat around the Legion, telling stories of the past.
Of a war that he had fought in and the deeds that he had done,
In his exploits with his buddies; they were heroes, everyone.

And tho' sometimes, to his neighbours, his tales became a joke,
All his Legion buddies listened, for they knew whereof he spoke.
But we'll hear his tales no longer for old Bill has passed away,
And the world's a little poorer, for a soldier died today.

He will not be mourned by many, just his children and his wife,
For he lived an ordinary and quite uneventful life.
Held a job and raised a family, quietly going his own way,
And the world won't note his passing, though a soldier died today.

When politicians leave this earth, their bodies lie in state,
While thousands note their passing and proclaim that they were great.
Papers tell their whole life stories, from the time that they were young,
But the passing of a soldier goes unnoticed and unsung.

Is the greatest contribution to the welfare of our land
A guy who breaks his promises and cons his fellow man?
Or the ordinary fellow who, in times of war and strife,
Goes off to serve his Country and offers up his life?

A politician's stipend and the style in which he lives
Are sometimes disproportionate to the service that he gives.
While the ordinary soldier, who offered up his all,
Is paid off with a medal and perhaps, a pension small.

It's so easy to forget them for it was so long ago,
That the old Bills of our Country went to battle, but we know
It was not the politicians, with their compromise and ploys,
Who won for us the freedom that our Country now enjoys.

Should you find yourself in danger, with your enemies at hand,
Would you want a politician with his ever-shifting stand?
Or would you prefer a soldier, who has sworn to defend
His home, his kin and Country and would fight until the end?

He was just a common soldier and his ranks are growing thin,

But his presence should remind us we may need his like again.
For when countries are in conflict, then we find the soldier's part
Is to clean up all the troubles that the politicians start.

If we cannot do him honour while he's here to hear the praise,
Then at least let's give him homage at the ending of his days.
Perhaps just a simple headline in a paper that would say,
Our Country is in mourning, for a soldier died today.

© 1987 A. Lawrence Vaincourt
Reprinted with permission

2: Two Near Misses

#1 Sydney Pre-1964:

Our unit was deployed to the Holsworthy (New South Wales) artillery range participating in exercises as near to active service operations as could be simulated. We had an enemy air force, which I believe was the University of New South Wales Squadron flying Meteor Jets (The Royal Australian Air Force had used these aircraft in combat during the Korean War).

The impressive Gloster Meteor fighter jet.

On this occasion, the squadron was making strikes on our position in the late morning while our land troops were well dug in and camouflaged. It was fascinating watching these jets screaming down on us, levelling out after making their projected strike, soar back into the blue, loop around after gaining altitude and diving on us for repetitive simulated strikes. On one occasion we observed a diving Meteor however, his diving strike just came on and on, and in a nanosecond, my recollection was, *"Shit! He's leaving his pulling out late."* This proved to be correct as when the Meteor was attempting to level out it hit the ground on the perimeter of our defensive position at a speed and force that was beyond my estimation.

A great ball of flame erupted and we could see fragments of the aircraft cartwheeling forward of the Meteor's impact zone. The exercise came to an abrupt halt. The Holsworthy range was completely closed off to all unwelcome observers such as the press, as sentries were posted to all entries and exits to the training area. We scrambled and began retrieving bits and pieces strewn over the large area forward of the crash scene. At the impact site, the earth was smouldering and smoke was filtering out of the rubble. We were ordered to look for any remains of the pilot. Such was the crash impact; the most gruesome find was the pilot's helmet containing the skull devoid of any features and a boot was also found containing a lower part of the leg.

A crash investigation team descended on the area and began their task. We were never informed of the outcome and finalisation of the investigation however we did become experienced in the possibilities of mishaps in airstrikes against ground troops. The loss of a pilot was devastating, however, but for a very minimal distance, the total loss of life could have been worse.

#2 Viet Nam 1969:

Our battery was flown in by CH-47 Chinook helicopters and as usual, the priority is to survey in the six battery guns while at the same time maintaining great urgency in the early development and construction of the FSB because it is at this time, we are most vulnerable to enemy ground attack. The reason for firstly surveying in the artillery pieces is so our infantry companies will have instant artillery support, while they are being inserted into their AOs.

At this FSB establishment, the battalion mortar platoon was next to us erecting mortar and weapon pits. Supplies were being shuttled in mainly by Chinook, ferrying in ammunition and supplies necessary for the full defensive establishment of the FSB.

Chinooks approach the FSB at a height of about 1500 feet (out of range of effective small arms ground fire) then sharply turn and descend steeply into the Landing Zone (LZ) releasing their under-slung external load. The under-slung load hangs some three to four metres below the aircraft and with the helicopter moving on a curved descending path, centrifugal force keeps this load under control and so when at a safe level, the cargo hanging directly underneath is lowered to the ground and once released, the Chinook flies out. If they were carrying troops, they virtually hovered just off the ground and discharged their internal load from the rear ramp and on extraction immediately fly out.

On one occasion we were watching a Chinook approach the FSB and as usual, it turned steeply to descend into the LZ. The Chinook's underslung load contained two hundred rounds of mortar ammunition and many claymore mines representing several tons of external play load. On this attempted delivery we watched as the sling between the Chinook and the external load completely lose its tension and the external cargo began to freefall and pass the carrier.

Incoming Chinook with an underslung load.

This in turn dragged the CH-47 straight down on itself causing a shattering explosion and the eruption of a large fire upon impact. This took place just off the LZ and was approximately sixty to eighty metres from a section of guns and crews (three guns and fifteen to eighteen soldiers). One soldier from each gun immediately ran to the crash site to be of any assistance if possible.

There are five personnel on a Chinook crew; a pilot and co-pilot, two side machine gunners on M-60s and a loadmaster. I located myself at the rear end of the crashed chopper with its body completely broken in half. It had its rear ramp down so I could see through the length of the aircraft.

Sadly, I saw either the pilot or co-pilot, who one would assume had a broken back as he was still strapped into his harness with his head between his feet. The other was an Afro-American gunner half hanging out of his side window laying over his machine gun however, he was completely on fire. From my position, I could not detect any other crew. The intensity of the fire grew and it was impossible to get any closer to the burning aircraft. Then the explosions started, firstly from the machine gun ammunition and then the cargo so we immediately sought a safer distance from the wreck.

This incident occurred late morning and so throughout the afternoon and night, the explosions continued never ceasing until the next morning, which left smouldering wreckage. A US crash investigation team was flown in following first light and even then, it was not until late afternoon that the wreckage was approachable. The investigation continued over the next few days while we continued with our side of the war.

A Sky Crane helicopter lifts out a major portion of the Chinook that crashed into our FSB in 1969. Unfortunately, all the American crew was killed.

I am not sure if the report was true but the feedback on the cause of the gruesome incident was that a coffee mug was on the floor and became jammed beneath one of the pilot's controls pedals. To us it did not seem feasible that this could be the cause, however as nearly all our movement around South Viet Nam was by Chinook, we always checked to ensure the pilots were not drinking coffee. I believe this practice was outlawed following this crash incident. Years later around 2015, I was talking to an ex-army helicopter pilot about the incident and he confirmed that the investigation outcome was blamed on the coffee mug.

One mug of coffee = five lives and millions of dollars in loss.

3: Dance of the 'Flaming Arseholes'

I have seen this dance performed on three occasions, the first in the Other Ranks (OR's) canteen at Holsworthy, south of Sydney in New South Wales and twice more on different occasions at bars in Georgetown Penang, Malaya.

To perform this dance firstly the performer must have consumed a considerable amount of alcohol. Secondly, this dance will only be performed if there is a reasonable audience. Thirdly an empty table must be produced as this dance is performed on the table so all the audience can view the act.

Several pages of a newspaper are rolled up tightly forming the shape of a length of pipe. The performer then climbs on top of the table with much applause. The applause increases as he removes his trousers and throws them from the table. The performer then places the cylinder of rolled-up newspaper between the cheeks of his buttocks as the applause increases. The performer then lights the bottom end of the newspaper, as the paper commences to burn upwards the performer commences to *Soft Shoe Shuffle* while gyrating on the table. The shorter the paper burns the louder the applause. At last, the performance ends when the paper has almost burnt out and the performer is under some pain and duress. I have noted that the more alcohol that has been consumed before the event the higher the paper has been allowed to burn. At last, the left-over remnants have been removed and discarded, the performer then does several pirouettes to now much applause, then descends from the stage and resumes his seat. After replacing his clothing, the performer does not buy any more alcohol that evening and on two of these occasions carried out of the venue following the consumption of his freebies.

I have never attempted to perform the *Dance of the Flaming Arseholes* for two reasons; I cannot dance, and I have more respect for my scrotum.

4: Breech Blocks and Fingers

The training was very intense before our unit's move to Viet Nam and a lot of time was spent at both Tin Can Bay and Shoalwater Bay artillery ranges firing all our different types of ammunition; HE, WP, Illumination, Time Fuse, etc.

We would as single guns stop, bring the gun into action and direct fire at a designated target with competition amongst the individual gun crews quite intense. Night firing was constant, as we were later to learn in Viet Nam, not only on operations but even back in Nui Dat you would be involved in nightly fire missions. On this occasion, at Shoalwater Bay, a night fire mission was called with my gun ranging. This is when all the six battery guns are surveyed and one gun is used for adjusting fire into a target area. When the target is achieved then a salvo from all six guns may be utilised.

Following several shots and adjustments to the ranging, we reloaded and when ordered to fire we could not close the breech block following the placing of another projectile into the breech. My loading number was pushing the projectile and the layer was attempting to close the breech without success. I pulled my ammunition number to one side and tried to punch the projectile home; however, it would not completely enter the chamber and it would ease back slightly as if some spongy matter was preventing the final inch or so of full insertion.

The conversation from the command post to me and back went somewhat like this:

GPO *"Charlie Gun … fire!"*

Gun Sergeant (me), *"We are experiencing some kind of fouling in the breech … will clear as soon as possible."*

We do carry a small night torch for such emergencies. I ordered the breech to be fully opened and then slightly pulled back the cartridge case. Jammed in between the rim of the cartridge case and preventing the cartridge case from being fully driven home was the end of a finger. My ammunition number, Dennis was standing in the background saying nothing.

GPO: *"Charlie gun. Have you cleared the obstruction yet?"*

"Yes," I replied," *We have had a finger sheared off and was jammed behind the rim of the cartridge case."*

GPO: *"Get your finger out on Charlie gun."*

The ranging in continued followed by a battery salvo. Now Dennis served on my gun for thirteen months, the duration of our Viet Nam tour and I'm pleased to say Dennis returned home to Australia with all his remaining fingers intact. Dennis is still alive and well and residing in Mackay, Central Queensland.

5: Snake Tales

Ram Chandra:

During a large military exercise held west of Mackay in Queensland in 1959, we were fortunate to be introduced to one Ram Chandra. At the time, Ram was perhaps the greatest authority on Australian snakes within the country, the first survivor of a deadly Taipan strike in Australia and I believe the first handler in the country to milk specimens for anti-venene treatment.

The Army lent Ram Chandra an Army Land Rover and trailer to visit every unit deployed and hold talks on snake identification as he had live specimens of many species of Australia's deadliest snakes also skeletons of heads, which became an interesting subject. During his lectures, he would fetch a box from the trailer, manipulate the content then dive his hand into the box and withdraw a snake, which included Death Adders, Tigers, Red Belly Blacks, Taipans and the deadliest of all, the Eastern Brown, which is also known as the Fearsome Snake.

When it came to the skeletons of snakeheads it becomes obvious why the Taipan is so deadly. Compared to other snakes, the Taipan's fangs are up to 20 millimetres long and when it strikes its prey the fangs penetrate very deep, and secondly, it pumps huge volumes (more than any other) of its potentially fatal venom into its victim. It can grow very large (more than two metres) and whereas most snakes on feeling footsteps approaching will attempt to evade the presence, they are extremely aggressive and will attack. I believe it is the only snake that can strike the length of its body backward.

Ram Chandra was the most informative person we had ever been in the presence of on snake matters. He did show us his leg which had been attacked by a Taipan and one can only describe it as a victim of polio, thin and wasted.

Kiwis and Snakes:

I believe a Kiwi would prefer to face almost anything in preference to a snake. In early 1960 whilst stationed in Wacol with 4 Field Regiment, the Australian and New Zealand Armies initiated troop exchanges; being small components within a regiment or battalion for cross-training in the ANZAC tradition. We were the first unit to receive a New Zealand (NZ) component called Trans-Tasman 1.

It was amusing to see NZ troops out in the bush standing around in a group and poking huge ant nests with long sticks. Of course, NZ does not have ants, snakes, and any other Australian bush critters.

While back in Wacol Barracks one of our troops had killed a snake in the area and placed it into a Kiwi soldier's bed, all coiled up with its head facing the victim. On pulling back his blankets the poor man let out a horrific scream and almost had a heart attack. He grabbed a blanket and pillow and refused to sleep in his bed, preferring to stay under a tree where he spent the remainder of his time in Australia.

Now if you want to scare a Kiwi …

Kampong Commotion:

It was in the Cameron Highlands (Malaya) where a British patrol entered a kampong amid a huge disturbance among the villagers. The British troops arranged for the men, twelve in all to hold this huge python now quite dead, so they could take a photo of the event. It took twelve men to support this gigantic python and one could quite easily see the outline of a kampong goat it had swallowed. I only saw the photo and wished to this day I had got one.

It brings home that while operating in this environment one is sharing, moving around and sleeping in their space. We had encountered snakes on a few occasions in the wilds but nothing like the python that feasted on a kampong goat.

An Owen Gun and a King Cobra:

While patrolling through a rubber plantation in the north Malaya state of Kedah, the forward scout armed with an Owen submachine gun, came to a sudden halt when confronted by a huge King Cobra which had reared up perhaps half a metre from the ground with his hood fully flared out. An impressive snake specimen, however deadly.

The forward scout immediately slid off the safety slide and gave his aggressor a half magazine of 9mm rounds. There was only one winner however, we wished the confrontation had not occurred as we left behind a magnificent creature.

6: Long Houses and Skulls

Borneo is an equatorial region. With the equator passing through this area it has little seasonal change and experiences constant rainfall resulting in huge jungles. British North Borneo (now Sabah) like Sarawak was a Malaysian state that bordered Borneo (Indonesia Kalimantan) proper. This small country became a protectorate of Commonwealth troops although most of the Australian personnel consisted of field engineers (construction) during the Confrontation period.

Sabah is more aligned with Australian history due to the horrific Death Marches of Sandakan, the infamous Japanese prisoner of war camp during World War Two.

Venturing into the interior from Jesselton (now Kota Kinabalu) the state capital of British North Borneo, we entered a native village being met and made welcome by the village headman, who in turn became our guide. It was difficult to assess the village population as the women, who with children were very shy though wanted to observe these strange visitors. Perhaps the village population was probably fifty to sixty strong. This village was a communion where no one owned anything, including the pigs, fowls and goats as everything belonged to the village.

The construction of the village was interesting as the main building is called the Long House which had a very useful purpose. It is high set with entry by stairs only. All the villagers were accommodated and slept in the Long House. We were invited into the Long House and although having a lived-in odour about it, the place was very clean. The most interesting feature within the Long House was that well up the walls were shelves and along these shelves were many human skulls.

Over their long history, tribal attacks on other villages were the norm with themselves also on occasions being invaded. Throughout their history it was always payback attacks however, no one ever explain how it all was initiated from long past generations. I am not aware if cannibalism still existed.

The reason for the Long Houses being, is if the village was attacked by a neighbouring tribe, all the males were already assembled in the one area with weapons on hand. Add to this that with the Long Houses being elevated the enemy had to scale stairs while assaulting the defender, while the defender always had the upper hand fighting a foe on a lower level. I am not aware of the skulls within the Long House are of invaders or trophies from successful attacks on other villages.

7: Aboriginal Origin

When living in Queensland in my early service career I played many sports with Aboriginals in both the military and civilian scenes. This included Australian Rules, rugby and rugby league, cricket and athletics. Besides being good soldiers I admired them for their sporting prowess and became close friends with some, with whom I had a long association.

On arriving in Malaya in 1964 and experiencing my first direct meeting with an indigenous Malayan I almost fell over as I swear, I was looking into the face of an Australian Aborigine. For some time, I pondered the likeness and after spending four years in Malaysia and learning their history I came to this conclusion.

In history, Malayans claim they initially came out of India through Bangladesh into Burma (Myanmar), through Siam (Thailand) then down into the Malay Peninsula. Undisputed history tells us that tens of thousands of years ago sea levels were estimated to be some two hundred metres lower than what it is today. Migrating overseas was a less challenging exercise than what currently exists. It is believable that Tasmania was connected to the Australian mainland in those times as I'm led to believe that the deepest part of Bass Strait was only one hundred and twenty metres. Having visited and stayed at Seven Spirits Bay in northern Arnhem Land there is undeniable proof that trading between Indonesians and Australian Aborigines existed long before the white settlement of Australia was initiated. Seven Spirits Bay is the closest point of the Australian mainland to Indonesia. Could it have been possible that Malaysians immigrated south through Borneo, the Indonesian archipelago and the first point of arriving on our continent could have been Seven Spirits Bay?

Over the centuries the seas rose to current proportions, and migration over the millennium ceased thus isolating our continent (and Tasmania). My belief in this concept will never waiver, that Australian Aboriginal ancestry was initiated in India, through Malaya and into Australia. Before that it is accepted, we all originally came out of the African continent.

8: The 'Wanky Wank' Bar

I am sure the mere mention of the *Wanky Wank Bar* brings a smile to many an old salt. Departing Australia in May 1964 on the HMAS *Sydney* on its maiden voyage as a troop carrier and arriving in Singapore on the 9th of June our unit disembarked and was transferred to North Malaya by train. However, a small army detachment of our unit remained on board to maintain our unit's equipment before delivery to North Malaya via the Malacca Straits. Being aboard for sixteen days since the HMAS *Sydney* departure friendships were forged with some mariners.

On my first night in Singapore Harbour shore leave was permitted and I was invited to join some sailors on shore and have an introduction to some Singapore highlights. Our first 'port of call' (naval language) was to an establishment very close to the naval dockyards and named the 'Wanky Wank' bar by naval personnel. The name alone does not require any further description, the beers flowed and the very lovely young ladies were shouted Singapore Teas at a ridiculous price (Saigon Tea in Viet Nam) while the sailors imbibed in beverages of a more alcoholic nature.

As the night wore on the more serious nature of the visit was initiated taking place under the tables of the venue. Following the relief of the exercise, serious consumption of alcohol continued. At least with sex drive annulled without fear of gonorrhea or a much worse disease contracted, alcohol intake was the main objective with the enjoyment of the female company, a relief (no pun intended) from several weeks at sea.

I was a party to assisting a few legless matelots back to the ship. Thus, concluded my first night out in an Asian city, certainly an education in the company of some very fine and abled-bodied mariners.

9: Rope Burns and Embarrassment

Soon after we arrived in Malaya in 1964, we practised being deployed into the jungle by helicopter. This deployment consists of the helicopter hovering above the height of the jungle foliage and the troops lowering themselves by an external rope being cast out of the chopper. This procedure was to be carried out to insert troops quickly into any area where a clearing was not available.

Lining up on a temporary helipad we were soon accompanied by a Royal Air Force Belvedere a double rotor system forward and aft (a smaller version of the American Chinook) and could carry nineteen fully equipped troops. Also accompanying us was one of our senior officers who gave us a verbal introduction to the Belvedere and then declared he was going up in the helicopter as he was to give our troops a demonstration on not only how to extract ourselves from the chopper but also the speed in which we should leave, descend and clear the area. Our officer climbed into the Belvedere and it immediately ascended to a height of some twenty to twenty-five metres where it hovered.

A rope was thrown out and the officer reached out, grasped the rope and with an incredible speed descended to the ground. He regained his feet, stood in front of and facing us, standing at ease (hands behind the back with the back of one hand in the palm of the other and legs astride fifteen to eighteen inches). The officer then explained to us that was how we were to extract ourselves from the helicopter. We stood in amazement and watched the blood dripping from his hands between his legs.

Now for those who have never suffered rope burns, it is one of the most painful burns one can endure. I have been exposed to minor rope burns so can relate to this painful exercise. Our officer quickly left while we in turn climbed aboard and departed in a hovering helicopter repeatedly until the procedure became second nature. Our demonstrating officer, much to his embarrassment, was next seen with bandaged hands. Rope burns do take a long time to heal. Perhaps he was the only officer in Malaya to wear gloves for a prolonged period.

10: Kiwis and Jungle Animals

I was never a witness to either of these incidents however, it does not take long for these unusual events to be passed around by bush telegraph. Both incidents occurred during the Indonesian Confrontation in the years 1964 and 1965. These gruesome encounters occurred firstly with a Malayan tiger and the other with an elephant in Kalimantan (Borneo).

The Tiger Incident:

While operating in the Cameron Highlands area of Malaya, a Kiwi soldier was sleeping under his tent's half shelter. In the early hours of one morning, a tiger by stealth approached the sleeping soldier and closed his jaws around the top of the soldier's head then commenced to drag him out from under his shelter. Of course, the soldier yelled and screamed immediately waking his comrades in the harbour area, who ran towards him and started firing shots.

Thankfully, the tiger released his prey and fled from the area leaving the victim thrashing around in extreme shock. The man was evacuated out of the area and immediately into hospital, where still emotionally scarred by the incident was returned home to New Zealand.

I never heard of the outcome of the poor unfortunate; however, one would assume he would have trouble sleeping at night.

The Elephant Incident:

While patrolling in Kalimantan (Indonesia Borneo) a New Zealand patrol walked into a small herd of elephants which unfortunately had one very upset and intolerant bull elephant, that immediately charged the patrol. Before appropriate action could be taken, he stampeded amongst the soldiers crushing one to death during the rampage.

The bull elephant was dealt with and along with the poor victim a hasty retreat was made from the remainder of the herd. Of course, the body was evacuated from the area. Not a good day for hunting Indons.

11: A Silent Killer

Earlier in Chapter 4 *A Military History* I mentioned coming to grief with an unseen predator while operating in swamp areas in the State of Perak, Malaya.

For two days before returning to the RAAF base I was starting to show symptoms of the flu, with a running nose, dry eyes and getting an ever-increasing headache. I was pleased to get back to Butterworth where I was told to report to the RAAF hospital and after taking my temperature I was immediately interned. Over the next two days I deteriorated and after the many blood samples extracted looking for a cause of my symptoms, an ex-British major (medical specialist) visited me and after ten minutes said, *"This man has leptospirosis. Cardiograph him to see if he's fit enough for immediate treatment."*

In the early sixties while stationed at Wacol I listened to a Sergeant, who served on active services during the Malayan Emergency in 1958. He came down with leptospirosis while on active field operations and was admitted to the hospital in a very bad state. One of the systems of the disease is that it builds up fluids in the spinal column thus pushing the brain upwards into the skull, which creates ever-increasing headaches. In my case, it resembled lying in a train tunnel with an approaching locomotive.

The sergeant explained (obviously in a worse state than I suffered) that he had to undergo spinal taps, withdrawing the fluid from his spinal column. He stated that it was the most painful thing he had ever experienced. He also said that while in his delirium, when he heard the trolley coming for another spinal tap, he would proceed to lock himself in the toilet. He would be forcibly removed from the cubical and then carried back to his bed where another extraction would be performed. The medical personnel eventually got on top of his disease and following recovery and rehabilitation, he was eventually returned to his unit fully fit for service.

Having this knowledge behind me when the doctor stated I had leptospirosis my first question to him was, *"Do I have to have spinal taps."* He looked at me with a raised eyebrow realising I must have some knowledge of the disease.

With great relief, I was overjoyed to hear him state, *"No. You are not that far gone."*

My medical documents stated:

"Admitted 3.7.67 episode of fever on admission, general malaise, muscular aches and pains, painful eyes on moving them, some neck stiffness and tender over liver and headache. Begin on penicillin 600,000 units four-hourly then after twenty-four hours, six-hourly.

Blood pressure down to 70/45 then slowly recovered."

I can recall that following my first injection I believed my body was seemingly more above the slab than on it with the penicillin at war with the symptom. I had a nurse in attendance 24/7 during the first two days, then I slowly began recovery needing to spend ten days in the hospital.

The doctor saw me before discharge and explained to me that they believe the disease entered my body through a cut on my thumb. I could recall cutting it on a lid of a small can of food from a twenty-four-hour ration pack. He also explained the chances of contracting the disease are very remote as it is usually realised from a rat's body through urine and the disease will only keep alive from ten to twelve seconds on discharge. I returned to my unit fully fit for all duties. Over the twelve to thirteen years during the Malayan Emergency and the Indonesian Confrontation, six Commonwealth troops died from leptospirosis.

12: The Identity Discs and Brothel Saga

On proceeding overseas every soldier gets issued with identity discs (ID) also known as tags, that must be always worn when in or out of uniform and is a chargeable offence if found without wearing them. These discs are issued in pairs, worn around the neck in a necklace style and are engraved with the following information: *Australia, Regimental Number, Surname, Initials, Religion and Blood Group.*

When our unit was posted to the RAAF base Butterworth in North Malaya, we had attached other groups from different Corps. i.e. Corps of Signals and the Corps of the Royal Australian Electrical and Mechanical Engineers (RAEME) who were technical people that could make damaged equipment operational. They are called the Light Aid Detachment (LAD). When our LAD was moved into the RAAF workshops, they had at their availability the latest engineering equipment that could repair anything from aircraft to weapons.

We arrived in Malaya in 1964 and by 1965 were aware of the better places to visit in Georgetown, Penang Island for a very enjoyable night out for the right price. It was in 1965 that a Momma San, who is an owner of a house of pleasure from one of the more popular houses in Georgetown arrived at the base and demanded to see the Commanding Officer which in our case is Battery Commander (BC) of the army unit that resided at the RAAF base. Following a much-heated discussion she was escorted into the BC's office, he in turn sat her down and calmed her down, then asked to know why she wanted to see him. Momma San demanded the BC get his appropriate soldiers to not only collect their IDs but pay up for services provided at her house of pleasure. She stated that these soldiers would turn up at her premises and explained that they had no money but would leave their IDs in her care and come payday would honour their outstanding payments and reclaim their IDs. With that Momma San reached into her bag, pulled out another bag and unloaded many sets of ID tags onto his table. The BC commenced searching who were the offending soldiers using their tags for such immoral purposes.

The BC was surprised to find all discs had fictitious regimental numbers on them, finding he had former Australian Prime Ministers in his unit along with names such as Michael Mouse, Donald Duck, Clark Kent, Donald Bradman, Edward Kelly and even the then President of the USA Lyndon Johnson's ID.

How embarrassing!!! The BC had to explain how she had been conned. Amid much yelling and screaming, she insisted that this matter was going to be taken higher than his authority and he and his unit were to be exposed for their behaviour and she would shame him, his soldiers and the Australian Army. Following to promise her he would get to the bottom of this activity and have the culprits pay their dues was the only way he could remove her from his office.

An immediate muster parade was called for. The law was laid down and all sorts of punishment were promised if the culprits of this devious practice could be found. One did not have to be a Rhodes Scholar to work out where this was initiated however, the practice was ceased. I do not know if the Momma San carried out her threats of taking this matter to a higher authority, though if by chance an old Malayan veteran should read this, in some cases, I am sure a satisfactory smile will come to his face for past free pleasures.

13: The Long Way Home

As the year wore on married personnel were allowed to fly home for Christmas. I along with quite a few other married personnel, elected to be home and enjoy Christmas with family. So in the latter part of December, we boarded the train in the afternoon at Butterworth for the overnighter to Singapore, which was a trip of about 450 miles. On arrival in Singapore, we were transferred to Changi Airport and the next morning boarded a Qantas jet. About an hour after the Singapore departure we were flying back over Butterworth and Penang and onto Thailand. Upon leaving Thailand, the aircraft flew west out into the Indian Ocean. The reason for this diversion is that we were not permitted to fly over Indonesian air space.

Well over the Indian Ocean we then headed south and finally landed at Cocos Islands (Keeling Island) where we were confronted by a huge board stating: *'Welcome to the Cocos Islands, five metres above sea level. Do not swim in this area as the sea contains'* ... followed by a list almost a metre long of nasty marine creatures. It appears that if it can kill you it abounds in the ocean surrounding the Cocos Islands.

We decided that there was no time for swimming, so following a meal and the aircraft refuelling we departed the Cocos Islands heading south, south-east to our next port of call, Perth. Following a short stopover, it was off again across the continent to our destination of Sydney to be reunited with our families for a Merry Christmas and New Year.

14: Uc Da Loi

This was the Vietnamese term meaning, *People from the Great Southern Land* (Australia) or in short, *Men from South*. So, this is how they referred to us in Viet Nam, not that we minded, as we much preferred that than how they referred to the Americans.

Reference to use:

'Uc Da Loi Number One' - when paying ridiculous prices for a Saigon Tea (a watered-down non-alcoholic drink) followed by personal service.

'Uc Da Loi Number Ten' - when refusing to do any of the above.

15: Ambushing

Malaya:

Ambushing in any environment involves many factors to give the ambush party total superiority in any engagement including holding the high ground, a good visual zone, an efficient killing zone and an effective escape route. So, reconnaissance is necessary to consider these and many more factors, so it is in your favour. Once the ambush area is selected the party moves in well before the last light to familiarise themselves with the area, organising individual fire zones including where the ambush party can observe without being seen. Of course, camouflage and concealment are high priorities. We layout trip flares (for night ambushes) and the placing and sighting of claymore mines for ambush initiation. Once laid total silence is required and movement is forbidden with communication by toggle ropes or jungle vines. Overnight ambush parties differ greatly from longer duration ambushes where a lot more logistics are necessary.

I can remember several night ambush parties in Malaya and I write of these and compare them with a likewise experience in Viet Nam.

During my first experience in Malaya, we were deployed in a very dense fringe of the jungle, elevated and looking over some open ground with a well-used pedestrian trail in front of us. While following the dusk and moving into total darkness we observed what appeared to be someone approaching smoking a cigarette, then another, then many followed by hundreds; our introduction to a swarm of fireflies.

Our next experience although with sleeves rolled down, shirts buttoned up and bush hats on, was the invasion of insects - after all, we were in their territory. Small insects found their way inside one's clothing while bigger insects would crawl over us and of course being pitch black, no identification was possible. We had known the jungles in Malaya were rife with centipedes, snakes and a plethora of unidentified insects so one could only lie in silence and let them run over you. The urge to ignore those that got inside your clothing was difficult and there was no way any of the ambush party dozing off as *creepy crawlies* kept one alert. First light was always welcomed where one could *debug* himself and find what had spent the night with you, obviously enjoying and sharing your body warmth. Malayan jungles also have tigers, so we were always listening to the sound of larger fauna within the environment.

Viet Nam:

If the battalion regimental sergeant major (RSM) wanted an all-day reconnaissance party to check out a geographical feature or a night ambush party from the FSB, on a rotation basis from our six gun sergeants one would become a section commander with soldiers from each gun crew making up a section. I have done both of these tasks firstly reporting to battalion HQ and with the RSM to go over a map of where he would want us deployed, whether an all-day reconnaissance or a night ambush.

One night ambush was actioned in an area that sometime earlier had been defoliated by Agent Orange. I write on this subject to draw to the attention of readers how two countries, not that far apart with one in an equatorial region and the other in a monsoonal region, can be utterly devastated by who was running the military forces within those countries. The British in Malaya and the USA in Viet Nam.

I was ordered to set up a night ambush in a particular area, not that far from the FSB as an enemy movement was suspected on a nightly basis. Following reconnaissance, an area was selected and the ambush party moved out mid to late afternoon. With the ambush set, we settled in for the night and as the night settled the changes in the environments became obvious. Not an insect was detected, not a bird in the area and not even a living animal to be heard, it was just total and complete silence. This was the eerie experience of an area completely devoid of any living thing except for us.

The upside of this was that any movement at all could be detected from a fair distance. No engagement was made during this night ambush; however, a lasting comparison was noted that, unlike Malaya, nothing lived or made a sound in the defoliated forests.

So, night ambushing in the Malayan jungles differed immensely from some experiences in Viet Nam, being the reason for writing on this subject.

16: Puff the Magic Dragon

To appreciate the military might of the USA one would have to have served with them operationally though, for me, I witnessed it in Viet Nam.

Once we arrived in Phuoc Tuy Province a tour of the airfield in Nui Dat took place to show us what military capabilities were available to us as support weapons. A most impressive initial presentation to us was a Huey Cobra, which at the time claimed to be the fastest helicopter ever produced. It was a flying platform carrying rockets, grenade launchers and a brutal undercarriage machine gun. The chopper was extremely narrow with the pilot in his compartment sitting on top and rear of the weapons operator. The weapons operator had sights on his helmet visor and what he looked at the machine gun could engage. The chopper took off, rose to some height then flew directly down on us. From a ground point of view, it was a very narrow target flying at tremendous speed with a payload that we would not see coming. Remarkable!

The USAF had numerous types of strike weapons. With aircraft it was the F-4 Phantoms and Super Sabres, being carriers of napalm, rockets and machine guns, that supported us on occasions. Often, we saw the huge B-52 bomber on a course somewhere and on occasions witnessed them delivering their payloads from great heights.

The American heavy artillery was something to behold with nothing similarly held by the Australian army. Their long-range artillery could fire a large projectile well more than twenty miles (thirty kilometres) requiring air clearance before engaging targets. The heavy artillery varied from self-propelled (on tracks and looked like tanks, however, were thin-skinned vehicles) to large pieces that could be delivered into the field by Sky Cranes.

Of all the inspiring firepower the US possessed, the one deadly weapon of destruction I was amazed by, was watching in action *Puff the Magic Dragon*. On a night, you could sit on the bund of our artillery position and watch the conflicts taking place all around us, which could be a machine gun in action in one direction, aerial flares being dropped/fired in another or an artillery bombardment falling elsewhere.

However, for me watching Puff at night-time was the ultimate. The old DC-3 was invented before World War Two and was an aircraft that could carry a load more than its weight. On these occasions, they carried nothing but Gatling guns and the ammunition to feed them. These machine guns fired at a rate of six thousand rounds a minute with every fifth round being a tracer bullet. The beauty of this craft is that it could fly very slowly in ever-decreasing circles and virtually shoot up a grid square of one thousand square metres in one operation. Watching them operate at night-time was like watching a flamethrower which is a vision I will never forget.

17: An Experience with Napalm

Perhaps the most horrific and devastating weapon used in Viet Nam was napalm. Napalm was a most successful weapon used against enemy bunkers and their tunnel systems as upon exploding it would suck all the oxygen out of the air, consume it and therefore tunnels would become airless voids. If an enemy was not instantly incinerated, they were likely if especially well underground in tunnels to be devoid of oxygen and choke to death.

My first experience with napalm was a strike some four to five hundred metres from my location where an active bunker system was discovered. A closer strike on the perimeter of our position occurred when at last light a Bell helicopter (call sign Possum) came into our position and immediately reported an enemy force of some forty to fifty and was moving towards our location. The pilot was ordered to again become airborne and track their movement. He reported that they had moved directly in front of our gun positions some 150 – 200 metres from our perimeter.

My 105mm howitzer gun was a perimeter gun and was ordered to fire HE projectiles at ground level into the heavily timbered front with a traverse left and right following each round. In the meantime, perimeter lights (lights that flick on and off and can only be observed from the air) were laid along our perimeter and the USAF was called in for a napalm strike. Two F-4 Phantom aircraft approached and following each other dropped their pair of napalm containers, looped around and on their second approach fired rockets into the area while on their third circuit machine-gunned the target. It was interesting to watch the machine guns, one would suggest a type of Gatling gun, as the aircraft would appear to temporarily pause in flight during this part of the operation. As the F-4 Phantoms departed the scene, they were replaced by pair of Super Sabres that identically repeated the operation. Overkill … Perhaps?

18: Formidable Centurions

Brief background:

By 1955 Australia had purchased from the United Kingdom (UK) one hundred and seventeen Centurion tanks. Claimed by the Australian press, *"Australia buys the Super Tank"* and ran the headline, *"Centurion is 52 tons of death."*

During the 1950s the centurions were upgraded with modifications to the MK3 to the MK5 standard by replacing their coaxial Besa 7.92 mm machine guns with the Browning .30-inch machine guns. Armour plating and other significant modifications included the fitting of a .50-inch L6A1 ranging machine gun (RMG) with associated alterations to sights and other equipment including an armoured fuel tank (one hundred gallons) to the rear of the hull.

Thus modified, the tanks were unofficially designated Centurion MK5/1 (Aust) and except for only one, the tanks were deployed to South Viet Nam in 1968. Further modifications were carried out in Viet Nam because of operational experience in this country. Those who doubted the Centurion's ability to operate effectively in the country's dense jungle and soft paddy fields were soon silenced. Irrespective of terrain or season (monsoonal) the tanks and their crews acquitted themselves extremely well and undoubtedly saved the lives of many, especially infantry soldiers.

The Centurion's 84mm gun could fire several different natures of ammunition; HE, armour piercing as well as smoke and canister. Canister was a highly effective anti-personnel round that worked equally well in clearing jungle growth from enemy bunkers and once exposed, the bunkers could be engaged more effectively by tanks and infantry. On many occasions the Centurions, remembering weighing fifty-two tons would drive over enemy bunkers, track turn crushing them and all who occupied therein. The Centurions featured in the battle of Binh Ba and no doubt saved the lives of many infanteers from the 5th Battalion who were instrumental in the battle in 1969.

Centurion ARN 169013 in 1968 with crew commander Sergeant Jock McConnell (Left). This tank had a chequered career in Viet Nam being damaged by a mine in September 1968. In mid-November it detonated an offset mine along Route 2, damaging the right track and wounding Jock McConnell, the operator Trooper (TPR) Terry Cosgrove and driver TPR Mick Hannaford. (Hannaford was to die of wounds inflicted by a mine while driving ARN 169017 less than a month later).

Jock McConnell's tank and others were used for ambushing along the riverways of a night-time. A lot of enemy movement was carried out at night on the rivers moving troops and resupplying units operating in specific areas. The Centurion would be located overlooking the waterways, camouflaged and loaded with canister shots, which in turn took a very heavy toll on watercraft. Canister shot is like a huge shotgun with pellets very much like a reinforcing rod cut up into small pieces.

Sergeant Jock McConnell (left) of C Squadron 1st Armoured Regiment waiting for darkness to envelop their tank ambush on the Song Rai River in 1968. The tanks were highly effective in sinking VC cargo and troop-carrying sampans as they moved along the two-kilometre-wide river.

The Centurions were withdrawn from Viet Nam in August 1971. Fifty-eight Centurion tanks served in Viet Nam from 1968 to 1971.

19: Jock McConnell and Me

When I was posted to the Land Warfare Centre in 1977, Jock was already on staff. We were both WO2 Class Warrant Officers and immediately became good friends. I was the Captain/Coach of the Canungra Rugby team and Jock became the team manager. Jock was an outstanding manager and would never fail to acquire any item I required for team enhancement and at times would procure items not requested by me, however, it was always best not to ask where the items came from.

I was transferred back to Brisbane in 1980 and did lose track of Jock's movements. An old friend who I served with in Malaya, Alan Jago called me in 2004. Alan had met and served with Jock in Viet Nam with both being involved in the battles of Coral and Balmoral; Jock as a tank commander and Alan from the Corps of Royal Australian Electrical and Mechanical Engineers (RAEME) where he worked in the field repairing tanks. Alan informed me that Jock was now separated from family and residing at Bribie Island on the Sunshine Coast, Queensland and was not in good health; could I get in touch with him?

In doing so I spent three consecutive Anzac Days with him on Bribie Island staying for three to four days surrounding the event, bending the elbow and reliving our service careers. On these occasions I stayed with Jock in his unit and from my bedroom I could hear him rasping in breath and coughing throughout the night, which would not have been a pleasant experience for him. I spoke with Jock about his health impediment and he explained that his state of health had come about due to his Centurion service before and during the Viet Nam Conflict. The Centurion tanks were asbestos-lined for fire prevention and when the tanks fired, the inside of the Centurions was filled with asbestos dust. Following the prolonged firing, the dust hung in the confines and settled inside the tank. They were living and travelling in a constant asbestos environment and he stated that many *tankies* suffered from lung problems however, the Army would never accept responsibility for the health aspect of past serving members.

Jock was a very popular member of the Woorim suburb of Bribie Island and he did a lot of voluntary work for the surf club, we of course ate there during my stayovers. I got to know the surf club members with whom I gave my contacts if they ever needed to get in touch with me regarding Jock's welfare.

On my second Anzac Day visit to Bribie Island, I gave Jock a copy of Gary McKay's book Jungle Tracks which was a history of the Armoured Corps service in Viet Nam. Jock featured in the book on several occasions and it was my pleasure to give to him Gary McKay's outstanding history of the 1st Armoured Regiment and its involvement in Viet Nam. I wrote inside the book, *"To Jock McConnell from Tasi Woodard. Anzac Day 2005"* and signed it. I again spent Anzac Day 2006 with Jock and I noticed his health was deteriorating. Sadly, later that year I received a phone call from the Woorim Surf Club informing me that Jock had passed away the previous night. I requested the club members when cleaning out his unit to secure the book Jungle Tracks and I would collect it from them at Jock's funeral, on 13 July 2006.

The funeral was held at Mt Gravatt Cemetery with a massive gathering of surf club members and many retired armoured corps personnel, such was his standing within the Corps. With book in hand and in attendance with my and Jock's close friend Allan Jago, we farewelled our comrade.

Sadly, Alan passed away in 2008 with multiple health problems and I was requested to and proudly became a bearer at his funeral. His funeral was also large with attendance from his RAEME Corps, Armoured Corps and RSL members.

Left: Mid 1960s Malaya. Three very close friends. L-R: Ross McCann, Reg Miller and Allan Jago (all deceased).
Right: Allan was a veteran of the Battles of Coral and Balmoral in Viet Nam 1968.

20: Low-Level Extraction

While on operations the resupply of artillery ammunition was usually by Chinook helicopters by the means of external slung loads. Delivery of another means was experimented with and that was simply by an Australian Caribou flying low over the FSB, pushing the payload out the rear end and employing parachutes, the payload would gently fall to the ground.

We were warned of the coming delivery and had to get behind our well-bunded gun pits. The Caribou was approaching and sure enough, just outside our immediate perimeter, the first payload was extracted out of the rear of the aircraft. This means of resupply looked favourable and probably a much cheaper delivery service than the Chinooks. Earlier an American crew member had told me that the use of Chinooks by the Australian Army cost $12,000 per hour. As we were the only support nation in the conflict paying our way, cheaper alternatives to accomplish an objective were worth exploring.

On this occasion, the parachutes failed to open and this payload upon hitting the ground exploded in one huge cloud of dust, dirt and shrapnel. Oh well … back to the Chinooks. I do not believe that low-level extraction of military artillery ammunition was attempted by the Australian Army again for the duration of our participation in the conflict … LLX (Low-Level Extraction) was taboo.

Ammunition for 101 Battery - During Operation *Ross* an airdrop of 105-millimetre ammunition failed to open over FSB *Discovery*.

21: The Losing of an Officer

Being involved in an environment of warfare one can expect casualties and Australia lost some five hundred and twenty-two troops during the Viet Nam conflict. Officers are not exempt. Our small subunit sadly lost one of our finest and most popular officers when he initiated an M16 anti-personal mine (aka Jumping Jack).

Our artillery unit supplies an officer, usually a lieutenant or captain, who is accompanied by a sig/ arty to each of the five infantry companies. He is known as a Forward Observation Officer (FOO) or simply as a FO party. The FO is directly in communication with the command post of the gun battery and is responsible for directing artillery fire onto a target designated by the infantry officer in command (OC). In this case, our FOO was attached to A Company 6 RAR Anzac Battalion.

Lieutenant Bernard A. Garland was married just before our unit departed from Australia in May 1969. During a twelve-month tour, each soldier gets a five-day break (not including travel time) with the most common destinations being Hong Kong, Singapore or home to Australia to family. Lieutenant Garland chose Singapore with his wife flying up from Australia for a belated honeymoon. On Bernie's departure from Singapore back to Viet Nam, little did he or his wife know it was to be their last rendezvous.

In April 1970 on the Battalion's last operation in Viet Nam (Operation *Townsville*), the battalion was extracted and returned to Nui Dat to prepare for their return to Australia on the 23rd of April. On the 22nd of April, Lieutenant Garland was killed by an M16 anti-personal mine explosion. When his death was filtered back to us, I can remember one of his fellow officers sitting on a log unashamedly sobbing, such was Lieutenant Garland's popularity. His death was felt by all ranks in our unit.

22: The Naked Gun

The Naked Gun – *Charlie* Gun is caught with their pants down.

There are two seasons in Viet Nam being the Dry and Wet monsoonal seasons. The latter is where one lives and operates in mud and rain virtually up to your armpits and you are never dry. At times you abandoned your gun, weapon, and sleeping pits (your sleeping pit was usually dug into the bund of your gun pit) as keeping your ammo dry was a challenge and had a higher priority than keeping individuals dry.

During one Dry season, we had been inserted overland by APCs with them towing our guns while under Centurion tank support. We had been on continuous operations for some time, constantly moving with little time for personal hygiene. On arriving at a location that was to become a temporary FSB the guns were put into position and as always, the foremost priority regarded local defence.

While establishing this FSB, a very dark and ominous cloud cover began to form over us and it began to rain. Not to lose the opportunity to refresh and get some personal hygiene I told our crew, *"Get your gear off and we will shower."* A cake of soap was produced and there we were standing in the rain naked, soaping ourselves up and cleansing when a fire order came through our tannoy system ordering, *"Single gun mission 'Charlie' gun."* Our six-gun battery in alphabetical order was 'Alpha, Bravo, Charlie, Delta, Echo and Foxtrot'. My gun was *Charlie* gun and if only a single gun mission was required our GPO was to have his little game.

The rain had passed over and there was an Australian artillery gun crew in the middle of South Viet Nam starkers, carrying out a fire mission clothed only in boots and in some cases earmuffs with me holding a tannoy lead acknowledging the fire orders. Oh, for a camera (an afterthought).

My thoughts went back to the School of Artillery at North Head, Sydney where the gun drill was carried out in full dress in a very strict precise manner. My thoughts were, *"How I would love to have a photo of this mounted in the gun park at North head."*

With the fire mission completed and now dressed we continued with the development of the FSB. I'm sure our GPO enjoyed his little game however, we thought it was quite amusing also as it may have been a first during the war.

Years later in 2017, I was attending an artillery unit reunion in Perth (one I had served in Australia with) but not the one within Viet Nam. As the night proceeded and memories of the war were recalled I was with a group with an ex-RSM who served in Viet Nam as a gun sergeant and he brought up the incident, *"Did you hear about a gun crew in Viet Nam that was caught and carried out a fire mission completely naked?"* There was much banter and laughter, including myself though I never divulged my participation in the incident.

23: The Haircut

The Tet Offensive commenced on the Chinese Lunar New Year recorded at midnight on 29 February 1968. The National Liberation Front (NLF) being the Viet Cong armed communist political revolutionary organisation, mobilised almost its entire military force in South Viet Nam from the DMZ to the Delta, which involved all four Corps. The Tet Offensive casualties included the ARVN 3,557 with US 1825, Free World Forces 92 and enemy losses of 45,005 killed in action (KIA). There were 23,009 allied forces wounded in action (WIA). Civilian casualties recorded were 14,300 killed with 24,000 wounded. Refugees caused by the offensive are registered as 599,858.

Since the Tet Offensive, the Australian forces in Viet Nam were built up to their greatest wartime numbers, being some eight thousand troops. During this time Australia had three infantry battalions with supporting units mainly artillery, armoured, field engineers and supporting arms on call.

A Field Artillery Regiment (two gun batteries) along with a New Zealand Gun Battery were allocated to each battalion and accompanied them on operations. Our 101 Field Battery, parent unit First Field Regiment RAA was attached to the 6th Battalion's second tour in 1969/1970, which was an Anzac Battalion consisting of three Australian Rifle Companies and two New Zealand Rifle Companies. The usual rotation of battalions on operations consisted of one month on operations and a fortnight back in the Australian task force base at Nui Dat, Phuoc Tuy Province. As one battalion completed a month of operations it would be replaced by the battalion, which had completed a two-week stay in Nui Dat while the third battalion was halfway (two weeks) through its month of operations. This was the system the rotation was based on, however during wartime systems can be thrown out of sync for several reasons. We departed Nui Dat in mid-October and were not to return until the end of the year, the 28th of December 1969, some two and a half months of continuous follow-up operations.

In late November following six weeks of continuous operations, our unit's soldiers were beginning to look like women regarding the length of their hair. We were occupying FSB *Discovery* at the time our Battery Captain (BK) organised a barber to be flown out of Nui Dat on the first available chopper to stay the day and then fly out on the last chopper of that day back to Nui Dat. The barber's mission was to give approximately fifty-five to sixty troops a haircut during his daylight visit.

My Gun Positioning Officer – Lieutenant (GPO) spoke to me, *"Sergeant Woodard ensure your Lance Bombardier gets a haircut during the barber's stay. He is among the most needy of shearing".*

I fronted my Lance Bombardier, *"Paddy, the GPO has told me to tell you, you above all must have a haircut. He considers the length of your hair is disgusting, ensure you line up for the barber's visit".*

Come last light the last chopper exited out of the FSB with the barber onboard. I have no idea if he did execute sixty haircuts that day or not, however, Paddy had not been shorn.

The next morning, I was approached by the GPO stating, *"Sergeant Woodard did you tell your Lance Bombardier to get his haircut yesterday?"*

"Yes Sir." "Charge him for disobeying a lawful command."

So, during twenty-six years of service with many years as a junior and senior NCO, I charged my first and only member of the Australian army.

During our fortnight stay in Nui Dat, the unit sends in small groups to Vung Tau for a thirty-six-hour Rest and Recreation (R & R) stopover. Paddy was charged and found guilty of disobeying a lawful command and forfeited his thirty-six hour R & R to Vung Tau as his penalty.

24: A Depressing Mini Operation

We left Nui Dat with the 6 ANZAC Battalion in mid-October which was the initiation of our longest continuous operation on tour, which eventually ended on the 28th of December 1969, lasting some two and a half months.

Flying out by Chinook we established FSB *Discovery* just to the east of Tan Ru for Operation *Ross*. This continuous operation ended at FSB *Picton* near the Nui May Taos and become Operation *Marsden*. In between FSB *Discovery* and FSB *Picton* we occupied FSB *Tasman*, FSB *Banks* and FSB *Lion*. Some of the FSBs were occupied by a section of guns (three guns and their crew) as they became mini operations upon awareness of enemy movement and unit locations. This depressing mini operation I'm referring to is the occupation of FSB *Tasman*.

In November only a section of guns (mine included) was flown in to support A & B Companies from 6 Battalion. We were flown in by Chinook and my gun emplacement was about twenty metres from a part of an underground Vietnamese village, something that was completely foreign to me. A large construction of timber was raised approximately half a metre above the ground seemingly for underground ventilation. This system was roughly twenty metres by ten metres and I had no idea how many of these constructions were in the area or how big the village was. It was raining quite heavily on our insertion and very uncomfortable when occupying and establishing an FSB.

The extraordinary feature of this occupation emanating from the underground quarters was the children crying and the adults attempting to hush them up. I was not surprised that having a Chinook helicopter landing virtually on top of their residence would terrify any child. I believed the adults would have the situation in hand temporarily until we were called on to give artillery support to our infantry.

The children kept crying.

Within fifty metres of our position, a very low barbed wire compound was erected, probably no higher than fifty centimetres, the same in width and about one and a half metres in length. This cage was a series of star pickets driven into the ground and then enclosed with barbed wire. The sad aspect of this cage was that it was occupied by a Vietnamese man lying in the rain unable to turn over or stretch out. The only clothing, he was wearing was a pair of underpants.

This underground Vietnamese village was occupied by American Marines whose numbers were unknown. A Marine Sergeant approached and introduced himself and advised me he would be taking out a night ambush party through my position late afternoon and would be returning after first light the next morning again through my position. As it was an ARVN (South Vietnamese Army) party not to get *trigger finger happy* being approached by Vietnamese early in the morning.

I asked him to accompany me to the caged personnel not fifty metres from my position. I pointed and asked, *"Viet Cong?"* The reply, *"No. ARVN deserter"*. I could do nothing except shake my head at such a practice.

The rain continued; the children kept crying.

Late in the afternoon when evening was starting to close in, I was anxiously waiting for the night ambush party to pass through my position. Eventually, I got in touch with the marine Sergeant, *"It's getting late. When is your night ambush party going out?"* As we all know when a night ambush party is sited the completion is all in place before the last light.

The reply, *"We have cancelled the ambush party because it's too wet."*

My reaction was, *"What the fuck are we doing here in Viet Nam?"*

The rain continued; the children kept crying.

When occupying an FSB a lot of work is required preparing different types of ammunition, temporary weapon pits, organising fire arcs, all-night vigilance on an M-60 machine gun, setting out a local defence with trip flares and Claymore mines, etc.

We were not required for any fire support throughout the night and I believe thankfully for the local underground residents, although all through the night the children kept crying. I have no idea how many Vietnamese were confined in their underground residence however, I'm sure there were a lot of children. Slowly the dawn approached and after standing to I sauntered down to the ARVN deserter to check on his welfare. He had been removed at some time during the night.

The rain continued; the children kept crying.

We were told to *"prepare to move"* the next morning and after about twenty-four hours of occupation and not firing a shot, a Chinook lifted us out and we returned to FSB *Discovery*.

The last sound I heard before the arrival of our Chinook was children crying ... poor miserable human beings!

The consequence of this little operation still plays on my mind as I very rarely visit shopping centres. On occasions that I have and a child starts throwing a tantrum whether crying or screaming, I must leave the premises.

Many years ago (last century) I was visiting Tasmania to meet a niece who I have not seen since she was a child. Here she was now a married woman with two small children.

She casually said, *"Uncle Cliff. We will have to come to Queensland to visit you."*

I replied, *"You and your husband are welcome however, do not bring your children."*

I have not seen nor heard from her since.

Inside a Chinook while being transported to another operation. I am reflecting on the left and the soldier on the right with the M-60 is another Tasmanian … Kelvin Howe.

25: American Heavy Artillery

As I have previously mentioned the American firepower was intimidating and effective. Following are examples of the USA's heavy self-propelled (SP) artillery used in Viet Nam. These pieces were based in Nui Dat.

These pieces had a twenty-two feet (seven metre) long barrel and could propel a huge missile well more than twenty miles (thirty kilometres), covering three provinces in Viet Nam. To achieve such a range air clearance was necessary owing to the missile's high trajectory in flight.

C W (TASI) WOODARD

Left: Another SP 155-millimetre heavy artillery piece.
Right: This SP piece is not a tank. It is a soft skin vehicle with the functions of a tank.

26: B-52s

Only on one occasion during my tour in Viet Nam did I witness a B-52 strike close. We were on operations about one mile (sixteen hundred metres) from their strike zone, which was a large mountainous complex. The enemy held this position and was well dug in, occupying the caves in the mountains that had never previously been attacked.

Even though the bombers operated at about 30,000 feet they were quite visible as we watched three B-52s approach nose to tail in alignment. Even at that height, their accuracy was impeccable. Still being approximately one mile from the target area you could feel the impact of the explosions through the very ground we were standing. Witnessing their massive payloads falling and experiencing the tremors of the strike was something to behold.

Left: A typical run by a B-52 Stratofortress dropping 340-kilogram bombs.
Right: The aftermath of a B-52 strike. Often when moving by helicopter over the country to operational areas one would notice parts of the landscape pockmarked by huge craters where B-52s had previously made strikes.

106

27: A Long Op – Operation *Marsden*

The Nui May Tao is a steep two thousand feet high rocky mountain rising abruptly from the flat countryside. It sits on the junction of three provincial boundaries and thus lies in the far corners of Phuoc Tuy, Binh Tuy and Long Khanh Provinces.

The Nui May Tao had served for many years as a secure haven for a complex Viet Cong system of logistics and supply areas. From 1965 to 1969, 84 Rear Services Group had control of the systems and was responsible for procurement, storage, transit coordination and disbursement of munitions, weapons and supplies. This area maintained local and main force units in Viet Cong *Area E,* which serviced the Provinces of Long Khanh, Bien Hoa, Phuoc Tuy and western Binh Tuy. The remote Nui May Tao had escaped regular operations and therefore had been free to develop this way.

Phuoc Tuy Province, South Viet Nam.

On leaving Nui Dat in mid-October we were to proceed on our longest continuous operations and did not return until the end of that year in 1969. The initial operation was Operation *Ross* followed by Operation *Marsden.*

In the meantime, our battery or sections occupied the FSBs of *Discovery* east of tan Ru, *Tasman* and *Banks* near Ap Binh Chau, *Lion* in Xa Thua Tich then finally onto FSB *Picton*. All along the infantry were continually engaging with and having huge successes against enemy forces, capturing large amounts of weapons, ammunition and food with very few casualties.

On occupying FSB *Picton* our battery was fully inserted by the 1st of December. By the 3rd of December, eight rifle companies were committed to the area around the Nui May Tao. On the same day, a platoon of three 155-millimetre howitzers from the US artillery arrived in *Picton* to support the operation.

A 155-millimetre American Howitzer. This artillery piece was often flown into operational areas by Skycrane. In this case here to accompany our field battery in supporting 6 RAR ANZAC Battalion in 1969 during Operation *Marsden* in the Nui May Tao. Note the background, as this area had some time previously been defoliated.

The rifle companies were moved into their AOs and so the clearing out of the Nui May Tao began. A Company was designated to gain the heights of the western side of the May Tao to clear through Nui Gop to the highest point. The company worked its way gradually to the top and there established its FSB named *Castle*. It was defended by company headquarters and contained one section of mortars, which provided fire support and harassed the Viet Cong in the re-entrants on the mountains.

Down at the main operational FSB *Picton* on the lowlands our battery 101 Field Battery, was not currently involved with fire support as the much larger American 155-millimetre howitzers were more devastating than our smaller 105-millimetre howitzers, firing high angle over FSB *Castle* into the Viet Cong held re-entrants. I approached my boss (the BK) and requested to be allowed to be flown into FSB *Castle* and spend some time with A Company in their occupation. With the request approved, I armed myself and along with some rations and my field sleeping kit I was inserted into FSB *Castle* to be met by the Company Sergeant Major (CSM) WO2 Myles.

WO2 Myles was later wounded in a mine incident, which killed our Unit Officer Lieutenant Bernie Garland on the 22nd of April 1970, during Operation *Townsville*. The CSM allocated me a position on the defensive perimeter of the FSB.

Left: FSB *Castle* with the Australian flag raised on a dead tree. Nui Gop was the highest point of the Nui May Tao and was occupied by the Company's HQs of the 6 ANZAC Battalion RAR accompanied by a section of mortars (December 1969). Right: A sentry post at FSB *Castle* with an M60 machine gun and heavy barrel 7.62 SLR. Note the continuation of the Nui May Tao in the background.

Left: The mortar section fired twenty-three contact missions. The barrels need to be cooled following long periods of firing. Right: My host at FSB *Castle* CSM WO2 Myles with a Vietnamese interpreter.

The 6 RAR ANZAC Battalion operation in the Nui May Tao in December 1969 was an outstanding success. During the month it contacted, ambushed, killed and captured enemy forces. The battalion also uncovered huge bunker systems, workshops, weapons caches, and a large hospital complex, which contained a dental surgery, and a massive administration area. Weapons captured included mortars, heavy and other machine guns, massive amounts of various calibre rifles including shotguns and submachine guns plus tonnes of munitions and ammunition. As well as weaponry, great amounts of food, equipment and medical supplies were seized.

It may be mentioned that for four days voice aircraft were used calling on the Viet Cong to surrender where they would receive medical attention, food and protection.

By the end of December 28, Operation *Marsden* was complete.

My lasting memory of my visit to A Company on top of Nui Gop (FSB *Castle*) was of the 155-millimetre projectiles from the US artillery just clearing Nui Gop and descending into the Viet Cong occupied re-entrants throughout the nights. It sounded like freight trains continually passing overhead. One can thankfully be grateful to be on the other end of an artillery breechblock.

Operation *Marsden*

Enemy Casualties Included: KIA – 22. WIA POWs – 21, detainees – 5, graves - 12 (13 bodies)

6 RAR Losses: KIA – 3, died of wounds – 1.

From intelligence summary:

"Operation *Marsden* was a highly successful attack resulting in severe disruption of the VC medical and resupply systems. His supply chain which began at rear services base located in the Nui May Tao has been destroyed."

28: Santa Claus Stories

#1:

The usual rotation of battalion operations was one month of operations and then two weeks in Nui Dat. While occupying the Nui May Tao on Christmas Day 1969 a Huey flew in, and out jumped Santa Claus with a big red suit on including a red hat with the traditional white pom pom. Externally he was wearing his basic webbing, carrying an Armalite rifle and with a holstered pistol hanging from his belt, a sure giveaway that Santa was an officer.

He strolled amongst the troops with the usual greeting, *"Ho, Ho, Ho. Merry Christmas."* Some response was directed at him from concealed weapon pits and camouflaged areas. *"Fuck Off Stupid"* was the most common reply with us all knowing that when Santa returned in the Huey it would be to Nui Dat to an Officers Mess quenching his thirst on tinnies and more than likely sitting down to a nice Christmas dinner.

#2:

This story took place well after my discharge from the Army. In December 1991, my wife Ailsa and I were in a quandary at what to do and where to go for Christmas and New Year. At a drop of a hat, I decided that never visiting Vanuatu we would go for nine days and take in both Christmas and New Year.

We booked our flights and accommodation at a resort called La Lagoon which was situated a few kilometres out of Port Vila. Unfortunately, our departure and arrival times took place during darkness denying us an opportunity to view the lovely islands from the air. Departing Brisbane at 2300 hrs Christmas Eve and with a three-hour flight saw us arriving at Vanuatu at 0200 hrs Christmas Day. We were graciously shown to our accommodation and even though right on the ocean, we could not help but go immediately to bed.

At 0600 hrs a loud knocking on our door awoke us and we were curious as to who could be visiting us at this time. I went and opened the door and standing before me in a full Santa suit with a huge tray of mixed fruit was the blackest Santa I had ever seen. I immediately burst into laughter much to the surprise of Ailsa so I invited Santa inside, thanked him and gave him some merry Christmas wishes.

To this day when Christmas rolls around and I see a Santa Claus my memories immediately flashback to two Santas in very different circumstances and countries.

29: Miscellaneous

Burning Them Out:

In the dry season, bunkers found occupied by the enemy were often burnt out by artillery firing white phosphorus into the area to start fires.

My gun *Charlie* Gun firing WP (White Phosphorus) ammunition into a target area.

XM546 Anti-personnel 'Splintex':

While back in Nui Dat my gun was towed by APC to the *Horseshoe* to give an ARVN company a demonstration on the effect of Splintex, the anti-personnel round we carried. This round carries some five thousand darts (50 mm long) and when fired explode into two bursts of two thousand five hundred darts each which can be adjusted to explode from a few metres from the muzzle up to approximately four kilometres.

The photograph illustrates our demonstration to the ARVN troops, firing Splintex at figure targets placed at various distances from our howitzer. The ARVN troops were allowed to inspect the figure targets following the demonstration and were amazed by the subsequent carnage.

The company commander was WO2 Alan Cleasby Australian Army Training Team Viet Nam (AATTV) with whom I served in Malaya (a photo of Alan is in the inaugural Wallabies Rugby team Malaya in 1965).

When moving by Chinook helicopter with the gun underslung for operations, each gun crew member carried a Splintex round with him in case we are inserted into a hotspot.

Home of the SAS in Viet Nam:

SAS Hill

Any soldier who served at Nui Dat would immediately recognise the Australian Task Force's (ATF) most prominent feature, SAS Hill. The Australian Special Air Service Regiment (SAS) had to occupy the highest point in Nui Dat to ensure effective communications with their long-range patrols.

**Left: Baria, the capital of Phuc Tuy Province and not far from Nui Dat. Here is a photo of a section of Baria's town hall - obviously well fought over.
Right: Salvage - A Chinook helicopter airlifts the remains of an Iroquois helicopter shot down by the ground fire and never quite made it to our FSB in its attempt to do so. The crew was retrieved.**

30: Honey Bears and Rabies

An artillery regiment in 1969 consisted of three batteries, two gun batteries (each battery having six artillery pieces) and an HQ battery heavily involved with operational and unit administration. The unit strength was approximately three hundred personnel. During the Viet Nam War, while the gun batteries were deployed with their battalions on operations, the HQ Battery was mostly employed at the Australian Task Force base in Nui Dat.

This allowed HQ Battery to have a mascot and in their case it was a Vietnamese honey bear whose name escapes me. On the evening before Viet Nam's departure, already replaced by the newly arrived HQ Battery, our HQ Battery held one last boozy farewell, unlimited alcohol, and a ration allocation of perhaps the best in twelve months. As the night wore on and the troops became incapable of sound reasoning so became the mascot, being fed copious amounts of alcohol. Now we all know if you get a large group together on the grog you will end up with a nasty among the party, so became the mascot at some late point in the evening. The Honey Bear, quite drunk went berserk, clawing, biting and attacking anyone within proximity. A weapon was quickly produced and a final goodnight and goodbye were administered to their mascot.

George Mason with unit mascot *The Honey Bear*. George is the one wearing a hat.

Now five members of their subunit believing they are off to Oz the next day woke up to a terrible medical issue. Those that had been savaged by the mascot had to remain in Viet Nam to endure an anti-rabies program. Now I am not aware of this procedure, but I believe it is a little painful owing to having a series of injections inserted into the intestine through the stomach area. I am not aware of how long this procedure's time factor endured.

The moral of this story is, *'If you visit Viet Nam and adopt a honey bear as a mascot … don't get it on the piss'.*

31: Home

Going Home - May 1970:

Following almost fourteen months in the country, from April 1969 to May 1970 we were transported by Caribou from Nui Dat to Saigon to board a Qantas flight direct to Sydney.

Going Home – Luscombe air strip Nui Dat.

Arriving Home - May 1970:

When our unit arrived home to Australia from Viet Nam, protests against the war were rife and violent in the USA and to a lesser degree were picking up in Australia. Troops arriving home before we were being abused, spat upon, red paint was thrown on them and taunted as baby killers, etc.

The protests were escalating and were becoming a worrying concern to both the law and the government. The Federal government downplayed that Qantas was flying troops home from Viet Nam, even though our arrival at Kingsford Smith Airport (Sydney) was scheduled to arrive in the early hours of the morning.

Before landing in Sydney we had a stop in Singapore and so as not to be identified as soldiers upon arrival at home, we were to wear our non-military shirts similarly to when we entered Viet Nam. We were issued with leave passes and told, "As soon as you get off the plane disappear!!!" We disembarked from the plane at 0230 hours without any problems and were either met by family or friends or merged into the civilian population. In my case, a friend delivered a car for me and I commenced my drive home from Sydney Airport to Brisbane, at that time approximately one thousand kilometres.

32: Big Red - World Champion

An old comrade of mine, Len McMullen with whom I had served within different units over a long period, himself a Malaysian and Viet Nam veteran, found us both serving in the same unit in Brisbane. We were both warrant officers and it was to be our final postings before taking our discharge in the early eighties.

Len purchased a property, *Mulgowie* west of Ipswich and was running cattle preparing for his military discharge. In 1979 Len arrived at work quite excited and told me that over the weekend he had caught the biggest sand goanna he had ever seen on his property. We discussed this capture and Len said he had him locked up safe and sound.

Now approaching was the annual Bushman's Carnival held at Cecil Plains, a gymkhana featuring all the events applicable to a country carnival. Also, a feature of the Cecil Plains' annual Bushman's Carnival is that they have the distinction of being the holder of the world championship goanna racing with recorded world records which they had held over many years.

So Len and I put our heads together and pondered over the opportunity of placing this captured goanna in one of the most anticipated events of the Cecil Plains carnival. After making inquiries we learned the goanna race was held over fifty metres being a pure sprint and an entry fee like all professional events as applicable. We decided to enter Len's goanna and after much discussion, we finally agreed on naming him Big Red. Now neither of us know much about goannas, let alone racing them. Like how do you train goannas for racing? There was no one we could turn to who had experience in this sporting contest. We decided just to comply with the racing committee's instructions and let him go.

Len McMullen - Primary owner of Big Red.

On the day of the carnival, the goanna race was late in the afternoon and a fair amount of Queensland's favourite drop had been consumed by many, then the goannas were put on display and the betting was initiated. Now Big Red was not the favourite as he was racing against the current world champion, though he did well in the stakes, as in Big Red's favour was his size. Many punters questioned Len and me about his racing ability and we were truthful in relating that he had never raced before, a novice, which kept his odds looking healthy. Len and I did place a reasonable bet on our runner to attempt to recover our entry fee and perhaps to pay for a little celebration, with any luck.

Race time and with a large crowd on either side of the fifty-metre track, tanked up and quite verbal ... *"They're off!"* With much cheering, yelling and screaming from the punters the goannas took off, with Big Red wearing a green sash with the number seven on it, bolting from the start. 'Big Red' hit the front within the first ten metres and the further the race continued the bigger his lead increased. Big Red won by some three metres, not only winning but smashing the current world record by more than two seconds. Now Len and I jumped around and embraced each other realising not only had Big Red won, but we now owned a world record holder and were cashed up.

Now the sad part of this great victory. Following Big Red crossing the finishing line he did not stop and was last seen entering a timberline some two hundred metres away. Without our world champion, Len and I celebrated well into the night with supporters, whom we assumed had put a wager on Big Red. They were not only congratulating us but were also supplying us with the amber fluid. The following morning not feeling that well, we discussed our good and bad fortunes ... we owned a world champion but had no idea where he was.

At this time I was producing my homebrew and after consulting Len, I thought it appropriate a beer label should be produced in honouring a winner and world record holder. Len was fully supportive of this suggestion hence two labels were struck.

All homebrew was labelled as such, one for lager and one for bitter being the two labels, one at the beginning of this story and one at the end. The motto is bastardised Latin *'Tu Sanqini Bute'* simply meaning *'You Bloody Beauty.'*

The homebrew was labelled on two occasions. Left label for lager (being the beginning of this story) and the right label for a bitter ale (being the end of this story).

Later in the eighties, an entrepreneur named Bernie Power built a large brewery named Powers Brewery at Yatala, which is halfway between Brisbane and the Gold Coast. The release of his first line of beer was ironically branded Big Red. Len and I thought it appropriate that in Bernie Power naming a release of Power's new brew it should be bought to his notice that he had run second. So I wrote to the newspaper about the fact and in April 1991 in the daily Sunday newspaper, an article appeared around the story just told.

Sadly, Len passed away some years ago with a multitude of illnesses and following many operations the old body could not handle the constant flow of surgery.

RIP my dear friend.

33: Conclusion

To conclude Military Oddities many more yarns and historical facts could be included. Some sad, which included the loss of two unit members while serving in Malaysia, to the unusual coincidence that our unit departed Australia with the currency being in pounds, shillings & pence then returning home to decimal currency.

I could write about the many differences between serving under the British in Malaysia and serving with the Americans in Viet Nam, where even though we were under Australian control, the overriding authority was the USA. During my time in Viet Nam, I did experience three joint operations (USA, Australian and the South Vietnamese Army – ARVN) which in itself was an eye-opener in the difference between the Australian and American ground operations.

Although the Army only occupied twenty-six years of my life it was the dominating period and I may add the most adventurous, important and memorable. My overseas service of some six years not only gave me a great education on life in Southeast Asia about Malaysia, Singapore and Viet Nam it certainly made me appreciate the fact that I was most fortunate to be born Australian.

Following my military service, I have visited other Asian nations including South Korea, Thailand, Taiwan, Hong Kong and the small North Borneo nation of Brunei. In general, I have high regard for the majority of Asians as they are most courteous and friendly.

After my discharge in 1982 and for the next thirty-four years my wife Ailsa and I have journeyed to many points of the compass however, just like my life in the military it was always most pleasant on returning home to Australia.

—∭—

SEVEN

POST-MILITARY SERVICE EVENTS

Upon completion of my military service, I ensured that I did not divorce myself completely from service events. Because of lifelong friendships, it was wonderful to catch up with those friends at events such as ANZAC Days, Viet Nam Veterans reunions, Unit reunions and occasionally a prearranged get-together of old rugby mates and fellow veterans.

1: Dawn Services

Being a former soldier in the Australian Army and following my service I had two military ceremonies on my *bucket list,* which were strong desires within me. The first was that I wished to attend the Dawn Service at Gallipoli and another was to attend the Dawn Service at Villers-Bretonneux in France.

Gallipoli (Turkey):

My wife Ailsa always wished to see the Greek Islands so the obvious outcome to pursue and to *kill two birds with one stone* was to attend the Gallipoli Dawn Service followed by a tour of Turkey and then the Greek Islands. So in 2001, we ventured off with a tour group to attend the Gallipoli ceremony.

We were fortunate to spend two days (the 23rd and the 24th of April) on the peninsular in the company of a lieutenant colonel from the Australian Army as a tour guide who was fully conversant on the Gallipoli campaign. During this time, our guide moved us by foot over the Anzac area, explaining and showing us the prominent locations that made the history of the failed campaign. Being an ex-soldier it became apparent the immense and difficult task the ANZAC troops were confronted with.

Arriving at where the ceremony was to take place on a hillside overlooking Anzac Beach where the landings occurred only a small platform existed. This platform was for the band, flag poles and military personnel (Turkish, Australian and New Zealand) for ceremonial activities and seating for VIP personnel only. We did have the time to meander amongst the cemeteries and monuments during our time which gave us an invaluable insight into the disaster our ANZACS were confronted with.

We left by bus from Assos at midnight travelling to Canakkale on the coast, then onto a ferry over the Dardanelles to the Gallipoli Peninsula. We arrived at approximately 0230 on ANZAC Day and took our positions on the hillside among many young Australian backpackers and other touring groups. Come to the dawn service when overlooking the beach where the landings took place, a mist rose from the ocean which lent to quite an eerie experience followed by the moving ceremony. We also attended the midday Lone Pine ceremony where so many troops on both sides, slaughtered each other over such a short distance. During the Battle of Lone Pine, seven Victoria Crosses were awarded.

Midday service 25th April 2001 at Lone Pine Gallipoli. A large monument at Lone Pine was erected over the once held Turkish trenches which in turn became a tomb of the dead.

Leaving the Gallipoli Peninsula was the initiation of our next leg, which was a western Turkey tour for over a week and then departing for the Greek Island experience. Our first island visit by sea was Rhodes, then to Athens, to Istanbul, flying to Singapore and then returning home.

Villers Bretonneux (France):

In 2012 the second Dawn Service on my bucket list took place. We individually made our way to France and gathered at our accommodation in Arras by train from Paris, where our battlefield tour with Made Easy Tours commenced.

Following a week of touring the Somme in the footsteps of the ANZACs on the Western Front in both Belgium and France, the 25th of April arrived. Once again, we arrived in the early hours of the morning to sit in front of the huge monument and cemetery at Villers Bretonneux where thousands had gathered for the ceremony. The monument has engraved in it the names of Australian troops that have no known graves. Following the Villers Bretonneux Dawn Service, our next visit was to the special ANZAC services held in Bullecourt. This was at the Slouch Hat memorial in the nearby Australian Memorial Park with its statue of the bronze Bullecourt Digger, where we shared a moving experience of the service with the French villagers.

Australian War Memorial -Villers Bretonneux, France 2012.

A photo was sent to me from Graham and Wilma Boyd (New South Wales) taken in the village of Villers Bretonneux on ANZAC Day 2012 following the Dawn Service. It is amazing to the degree how the locals dress up the gardens for ANZAC Day.

Battlefield areas visited during our tour included Arras (Wellington Tunnels), Le Hamel, Villers Bretonneux, Bullecourt, Peronne, Mont St Quentin, Pozieres, Mouquet Farm, Newfoundland Park, the Thiepval Memorial, Albert, Vimy Ridge, Fromelles (Cobbers Corner and VC Corner), Hill

60, Hooge Crater Cemetery, Polygon Wood, Broodseinde, Passchendaele, Tyne Cot, the massive Langemark German Cemetery and Ypres.

When considering all these locations above which were situated in such a relatively small area, just illustrates how brutal the engagements would have been for all soldiers involved and the wake of carnage that historically prevailed.

2: Menin Gate and the Last Post

On the afternoon of the 29th of April 2012, when departing the Somme in northern France and proceeding to Ypres in Belgium I was approached by our tour guide and driver Colin Gillard and he said, *"I was invited to lay a wreath on behalf of Australia at the Menin Gate ceremony on the evening of the 30th of April 2012. Did I wish to participate?"*

I asked Colin, *"How come I was invited to do this?"*

He stated, *"The Menin Gate committee knows I do Australian tours in the ANZAC Day period and did he have anyone in his tour group who could be invited to participate?"* Colin nominated me.

I of course replied, *"I would be honoured to participate."*

A Brief History of Menin Gate:

The Menin Gate – Ypres, Belgium.

The Menin Gate Memorial to the missing is a War Memorial in Ypres, Belgium dedicated to the commemoration of British and Commonwealth soldiers who were killed in the Ypres Salient of the First World War and whose graves are unknown. The gate marks the starting point for one of the main roads out of town that led Allied soldiers to the front line. Some 55,000 men and women passed this way never to return.

A total of 54,896 names are inscribed within the huge gate which straddles the main road into Ypres. The names inscribed by nation are as follows: the United Kingdom 40,244; Australia 6,198; Canada 6,983; British India 4,217; South Africa 564; British West Indies 6. New Zealand and Newfoundland have their memorials to the missing elsewhere in Flanders. Some 300,000 Commonwealth soldiers were killed in the Ypres Salient.

Five major battles over Ypres occurred during the Great War such as its strategic value. The first battle halted the Germans' advance; the second battle marked a second German attempt to take the city in April 1915; the third battle is commonly referred to as Passchendaele, but this battle was a complex five-month engagement.; the fourth and fifth battles occurred in 1918.

Menin Gate is regarded by many as the most important British War Memorial in the world. It may be noted that Tyne Cot (site of the Battle of Passchendaele) is the biggest Commonwealth War cemetery in the world having twelve thousand graves. At this location, there exists another wall containing the names of a further 34,984 Commonwealth soldiers who have no known grave. So, in a seven-mile area in the Ypres Salient, there are almost 90,000 dead with no known grave.

The Menin Gate provides comfort, a place to visit and remember, because to borrow from Field Marshall Lord Plumer's speech when the gate was unveiled in July 1927, *"He is not missing, He is here."*

The Menin Gate Ceremony:

The Menin Gate Ceremony in Ypres is the longest continual military ceremony, performed nightly and was initiated on the 9th of July 1927. Except for the German occupation during World War Two, between May 1940 to September 1944 the ceremony has been played every evening at 8:00 PM under the Menin Gate.

On accepting the invitation to lay a wreath on behalf of Australia I had to report to a Menin Gate Marshall, thirty minutes before the ceremony to be advised on the ceremonial procedure. Invited to accompany me during the ceremony was Richard Young of Orford, Tasmania and Terrence Kerr of Glenroy, Melbourne who recited the Exhortation during the ceremony. Both members had kin killed/buried on the Somme during the Great War.

> ON INVITATION LAID A WREATH ON BEHALF OF AUSTRALIA ON THE 30TH APRIL 2012 AT THE MENIN GATE CEREMONY, YPRES, BELGIUM IN MEMORY OF THE 60,000 AUSTRALIAN CASUALTIES OF THE GREAT WAR – WWI
>
> C.W. (TASI) WOODARD W.O.II RETD

Ceremony Invitation

L-R: Richard Young (Tasmania), myself and Terrence Kerr (Victoria).

I have never been more in awe of an occasion and felt so humbled to be participating in such an event, a memory I shall dearly carry to my passing. During the ceremony, I could not help but wonder if my Grandfather and his firstborn (buried on the Somme) and two Great Uncles' footsteps had in the past walked or marched into the Great War along Menin Road.

The ceremony is attended by hundreds of spectators when Menin Gate is closed to all traffic and areas are roped off. We were requested to have our photos taken with the famous Menin Gate Buglers from the Ypres Fire Brigade, who present the music for the official program.

L-R: Terrence Kerr (Victoria), Menin Gate Buglers, myself and Richard Young (Tasmania).

Mr Woodard, lest we forget.

A nice little gift was presented to me following the ceremony on the 30th of April 2012 by the Menin Gate committee.

The American War Memorial at Omaha – an area of 175.5 acres

Headstones 9,387 ... Missing In Action 1,557

From Belgium, we visited the D-D Landings, the American Cemetery and Memorials, onto Mont-Saint-Michel to Paris and then returned home.

3: 2018 Centenary of Battles – Western Front

In 2018 Australia celebrated a century of battles on the Somme (France) and Belgium in those countries and on the dates on which the battles occurred. I viewed some of them being broadcast live in Australia.

At the commencement of the 2018 battle reunions, I had no idea that I would be involved in the final reunion held on the 5th of October 2018. This was the last day of Australian involvement in the Great War with a final assault on the German-held Hindenburg Line and the liberation of the town of Montbrehain, which had been under German occupation since early 1914.

The Celebration Banner is displayed outside, on the Town Hall.

The Battle of Montbrehain:

Under the leadership of Australian Lieutenant General John Monash, Montbrehain was liberated by troops of the Second Australian Division. One hundred and thirty-four Australians were killed during the battle with one of them being my uncle George William Woodard (Jnr), enlistment no. 3779.

All living relatives of the fallen soldiers were invited to attend the Montbrehain ceremony. The Victorian group administrating the Australian involvement informed me that through their research for relations of the battle deceased, they found many great-nephews/nieces, though I was the only living nephew that they could locate. I believe the reason being is that my uncle was the firstborn of a large farming family and he was much older than my father. If my uncle had survived the war, he would have been aged forty at the time of my birth.

It should also be noted that Lieutenant George Ingram was awarded a Victoria Cross (VC) during this battle, which was the last VC awarded in World War One.

Lieutenant Ingram served in the Victorian Police Force before his enlistment into the army and it was because of this that the Victorian Police Force were the main contributors to the Montbrehain reunion even sending the Victoria Police Pipe Band to the occasion. The Victorian Police also produced a large metal plaque with the names of the one hundred and thirty-four Australians killed and presented it to the town of Montbrehain, which in turn was mounted in the town square following a presentation.

The presented plaque commemorates *The Fallen*.

Following the plaque mounting a photo was taken of myself and my son Norman (who accompanied me on tour) pointing to my Uncle's name on the plaque.

Being a member of the Caloundra RSL (Queensland) I was requested to present an RSL (The Returned and Services League of Australia) plaque and scroll to the Mayor of Montbrehain, Mr Gabriel Derson. The presentation was carried out following the commemoration ceremony at the Calvary Cemetery, Montbrehain.

Presenting Mr Gabriel Dirson (Mayor of Montbrehain, France) with a plaque on behalf of Caloundra RSL (Queensland, Australia) October 5th, 2018.

COMMEMORATION DU CENTENAIRE DE LA LIBERATION DE MONTBREHAIN

5 OCTOBER 1918 - 5 OCTOBER 2018

Caloundra sub branch member
EX WO Tasi Woodard presenting a
certificate and plaque to
Mr Gabriel Dirson (Mayor of Montbrehain, France)
on behalf of the Caloundra R.S.L sub branch on
the 5th October 2018 at the commemoration
ceremony at the Calvary Cemetery Montbrehain.
The ceremony is in memory of the
liberation of Montbrehain which took place on the
5th October 1918, the battle was the last action in
WWI by Australian troops. Montbrehain, on the
Hindenburg line was liberated by troops of the
Second Australian division. During the battle
Lt George Ingram was awarded
the last V.C. of WWI.
3779 George William Woodard (Jnr) was one of the
134 Australian troops killed during this action.
A large plaque naming the 134 killed was unveiled
and presented to the mayor at city hall.

Commemoration Letter.

Laying a wreath at the Calvary Cemetery, Montbrehain accompanied by Patricia Vance (Victoria) and my son Norman.

My son Norman and I visited my uncle's grave at New British Cemetery, Tincourt outside Peronne.

During our battlefield tour before the Montbrehain ceremony on the 5th of October, I again was invited to accompany an Australian group to lay a wreath at the Menin Gate Last Post ceremony.

Menin Gate Ypres, Belgium revisited in October 2018.
L-R: Peter Smith (Tour Guide – England), Frank Kelly (ACT - Australia),
Stephen Ford (NSW - Australia) and Tasi Woodard (QLD - Australia).

4: An Evening with Athletic Royalty

In 2006 I was invited to attend a military reunion in Adelaide of a South Australian-raised unit to relieve a unit in Malaysia. I remained in Malaya and was taken on strength of the relieving unit upon their arrival in Malaya in 1966. This unit consisted of many soldiers from the 1st and 2nd National Service intakes initiated at the commencement of the Viet Nam War and this reunion was held to celebrate the 50th anniversary of the raising of the South Australian unit.

The reunion was attended by some two hundred and fifty guests as parents, wives and families of the unit's members, with the guest of honour being the South Australian Governor, Marjorie Jackson, known during her athletic career as *The Lithgow Flash.* At the Helsinki Olympics (1952) Marjorie won two Olympic Gold medals in the 100 and 200-metre sprints and became the first Australian female to break a world record as well as the first to win track and field Olympic Golds.

Marjorie featured in the last British Empire Games held in Auckland, New Zealand, winning four Gold medals, and again featured in the first Commonwealth Games held in Vancouver, Canada in 1954 winning a further three Gold medals. She held every Australian State and National Sprint title contested from 1950 to 1954 and was never defeated in thirty-three contests at Australian and International levels.

Besides Olympic medals, Marjorie Jackson received a Member of the British Empire (MBE) and an Order of Australia (OA) while in 2007 she received an Olympic Order, the highest order bestowed by an Olympic committee.

Marjorie became only the second Australian inducted into the International Association of Athletics Federations Hall of Fame. To be eligible for membership in the Hall of Fame, an athlete must have won at least two World or Olympic titles and set a world record. Jackson set thirteen World Records in her career with her 200 metres time of 23.4 seconds at the Helsinki Olympics beating a mark that had stood for seventeen years. Her induction took place in a ceremony held in Monaco on Saturday, November the 16th, 2013. The only other Australian female to achieve the Hall of Fame honour is a fellow sprinting legend, Betty Cuthbert.

So indeed, I was in the company of athletic royalty. During the reunion, I was approached by Sid Penhaligon, a fellow soldier who I had served within Australia and was the RSM of our unit in Viet Nam and who in the past was an athlete of some renown. Sid requested me to meet and have a photo taken with the Governor as she and I of all the guests were the only two to have been awarded the Australian Sports Medal.

Sid Penhaligon (L) and I standing behind the Governor of South Australia, the great Marjorie Jackson.

5: A Freakish Reunion

In early 2016 I was viewing some old slides I had taken in Viet Nam during 1969 and I came across a slide that I had forgotten about. So being curious and a receiver of the quarterly publication of the *Queensland RSL News* I decided to submit the image from the slide and the following article to the publication.

SEEKING INFORMATION ON WOMAN FROM NUI DAT

Can any reader recognise the WRAAC/ nurse in this photo taken at Nui Dat on December 28, 1969?

In 1969, the usual rotation of battalion units on operations was one month operations, two weeks back in Nui Dat. Our unit departed Nui Dat for operations in mid-October 1969 and found ourselves on continuous follow-up operations up until, and including, the Christmas period.

On December 28, 1969, we were extracted from the Nui May Tao and returned to Nui Dat. On landing at Nui Dat heli-pad and exiting from a Chinook helicopter, I was surprised to see this uniformed woman standing by herself on the outskirts of the heli-pad.

I approached her and asked if I could take a photo of her. When asked why, I replied she was the first woman I had seen in two-and-a-half months. She consented to the photo being taken.

Perhaps a reader of the *Queensland RSL News* may recognise this woman. If so, I would be overjoyed to learn of her whereabouts as I have photos taken from the original slide I would be pleased to pass on to her or her family. Please contact CW Woodard on 07 5437 2645.

Article from the quarterly publication of the *Queensland RSL News* 2016

Much to my surprise some weeks later I received a card from Fremantle, Western Australia in which I refer:

> *"Dear Tasi, thank you so much for going to so much trouble in locating 'the girl in the photograph.' My family and everyone I show the newspaper article to are quite amazed (taken some forty-seven years previously). Carolyn Evcott from Surfers Paradise with whom I served in Viet Nam during 1969/1970, sent me the newspaper cutting stating, 'Is this you?' It certainly was. I will locate a recent photo and send it to you."*

Regards, Rosemary Griggs (Ex-Red Cross 1969/1970 Viet Nam).

I was wrong. Neither was Rosemary a WRAAC or nurse but served with the Australian Red Cross. Rosemary stated she was stationed in Vung Tau however when seating was available in a helicopter flying Vung Tau to Nui Dat they could fly in/out to visit the wounded in the field hospital situated in Nui Dat. The more seriously wounded would be hospitalised in Vung Tau or repatriated to Australia if need be.

I produced photos of Rosemary from the slide and sent them to Fremantle for her and her family. I received a Christmas card from Rosemary with a photo of her marriage to Charlie, a retired ex-farmer. Rosemary does voluntary work for Save the Children Australia. Thank you for your past service, Rosemary.

Charlie and Rosemary (nee Griggs) Mitchell. Wedding day 26th of September 2016 at Riverbank Winery in Swanbank Valley, Western Australia.

6: One Last Parade

Reginald Alfred Miller was a very proud West Australian whom I first met when I was posted from Queensland to Holsworthy, New South Wales in 1963. Reg was already a member of the unit that I was attached to and I quickly became good friends with him through rugby.

Reg's military service only lasted twelve years with him taking an early discharge due to an unsatisfactory posting. He returned to Western Australia and took on employment in the mining industry. Reg did serve two tours in Malaysia firstly during the Malayan Emergency and secondly during the Indonesian Confrontation and I served with Reg during his latter overseas posting.

Following his military discharge, we always kept in touch and following my discharge did on his invitation to spend several weeks in Perth with him and his wife Tracy. Eventually, Reg and Tracy left Western Australia and moved to Cairns in Queensland. Although still quite a distance apart our contacts became more frequent through the visits to the Sunshine Coast/Cairns and on the odd military reunion.

In 2009 we were invited to Cairns for Reg's seventieth birthday which we attended. Even then it was obvious his health was deteriorating as he was on medication and losing weight and muscular definition. Within the year he was wheelchair-bound and eventually placed into palliative care.

We also attended Tracy's seventieth in 2010 and Reg arrived at the occasion in a wheelchair. Unfortunately, during the evening's function, an ambulance had to be called and Tracy escorted Reg back to his hospital.

Before that event, while sitting next to Reg he said, *"Tasi. I am coming down to Caloundra to spend next ANZAC Day with you."*

My reply to him was, *"Reg, to shift you would be like shifting a hospital. You stay here and I will come up and spend ANZAC Day in Cairns with you,"* and you could see he was overwhelmed with my response.

On the 24th of April 2011 I arrived at Cairns airport to be met by Tracy, dropped my gear off and she took me to the hospital. I had just walked through the front door when a nurse approached me and asked, *"Are you Tasi?"*

On confirming my identity her response was, *"Thank Christ you're here. He's driving us crazy."*

A sentimental reunion took place over the next few hours. On departing the nurse explained the hospital would supply a wheelchair for the ANZAC Day Parade and a time for pickup was decided upon. On arriving at the hospital, the following morning, the nurse informed Tracy and I that Reg had been up since 0230 spit polishing shoes, ironing his shirt, sprucing up his clothes, drinking coffee and clock watching. Arriving at the Forming Up Point (FUP) it was a parade through the main street of Cairns of approximately 1.6 km to the large park where the ceremony was to take place, however only several hundred metres to the Cairns RSL from the park.

Attending the ANZAC Day Parade Cairns on 25th April 2011.

Following a massive session at the RSL we took Reg home to his and Tracy's unit as he was allowed to spend the night at home (his last).

134

Ailsa and I had organised a tour of several weeks in the Kimberley, Western Australia, in early May so after several more days in Cairns with Reg, it was finally home, packed then off to the Kimberley's. Before departing Cairns, I assured Tracy, that we would contact her on our return home. When I did, I was informed he had passed away during our absence, dying of renal cell carcinoma, which had spread to his lungs.

I received a lovely card from Tracy thanking me for sharing ANZAC Day with him, with her chosen words, *"I shall go to the grave believing Reg just hung in there then let go following ANZAC Day … for one last parade."*

Reginald Alfred Miller
8 July 1939 – 11 May 2011
RIP my friend.

EIGHT

MY RUGBY CAREER

I never rose to a great level of rugby as almost all of my career was service-related, however, I did leave a lasting impression in North Malaya from 1964 through to 1967 and also in Queensland Services Rugby from 1973 to 1978 inclusive.

"Gunner Woodard report to the rugby pitch at 1500 hours with your football gear."

This was the directive I was given to training with a rugby team, a game I had never played nor I believe had ever watched up to this point in time.

As a seventeen-year-old, I walked straight into the North Shore Australian Rules team in the top Sydney competition, not that I believed I was the best Aussie rules player representing North Shore from the School of Artillery at North Head.

So here I turned up to the unit's rugby team under the coach, Sergeant Russell Parker who in his mid-forty years of age I believe would have been a forward in his younger days as he was quite a big man. He would have known I was a novice to the game and preceded to instruct me on the laws of the game and positional play. The hardest aspect of the game for me to comprehend was the offside laws as none exists in Aussie rules. It soon came to note that I possessed a fair turn of speed and I could place kick a ball further and more accurately than any other team member, so for my first game I became a winger and goalkicker. I was just instructed if I was passed the ball all I had to do was sprint to the try line. I cannot recall the other unit team we played against, however, the first time I was passed the ball I just ran. The cover defence finally caught and tackled me and while picking myself up from the ground, teammates ran to me and congratulated me on scoring a try. I converted my try as goal kicking to me was not a pressure skill. As it turned out, in all my service career I was the primary goal kicker in any team I played for.

Following some competition matches it was decided that my ball skills were wasted on the wing so I was drafted into the inside centre, which is the position I retained in all levels of rugby from

1957 to 1968. I can only thank our unit's outside centre, Snow Singleton being an ex-rugby league player hailing from the Hunter Region in New South Wales, for the education and direction he gave me in my new position. And to this day I believe he was more instrumental in my success in this position than any other coach. We became a lethal centre pairing at this level thanks to his tuition and direction. I was informed of Snow's passing some years ago … thank you, Snow.

I continued in Services Rugby in Sydney through the years 1958 and 1959. I was posted to a new field regiment that was raised in Brisbane in 1960 and it didn't take long for our unit to start making an impression on the Services Rugby in Southeast Queensland. Here I received my first captaincy of a rugby team. Now the Services had an A Grade and Reserve Grade side in the Brisbane Rugby Competition and within the Services was known as the General Officer Command (GOC's) team. I was drafted into the A Grade GOC's team and played once again in the position of inside centre through the years 1960 to 1962 until I was posted back to Sydney in 1963.

I may add that playing in the GOCs team was the cause of my CO's disapproval of my absence from unit exercises, however, rugby training at Duncan Oval on Tuesday and Thursday afternoon and playing in the Brisbane competition on weekends were considered as a GOC's parade and therefore not to be missed.

I may add here, that when the Indonesian Confrontation started in 1964 followed by the Viet Nam War, such as the depletion of troops from Australia to overseas deployments the Services team was forced to withdraw from the Brisbane competition.

During my time playing with the GOC's team, I met and became known to Captain Colin Khan (Genghis to all, but not to his face), who was in an administrative capacity in the GOC's team. The reason I mention this is that I will talk about him later in this book. When posted back to Sydney I represented my unit and was selected in Corps matches (Artillery). Then came my unit's move to Malaya.

With one hundred thousand Commonwealth servicemen in Singapore and Malaysia in 1964, Malaysia became the powerhouse of rugby in Asia. Following the defeat of Japan in two tests in Malaya in 1965, the Malayan Rugby Union (MRU) drew the curtain on Commonwealth servicemen representing Malaysia at internationals. This was brought about as they were aware that following the waning of the Indonesian Confrontation, Commonwealth servicemen would be withdrawn from the country. We agreed with the decision as I recall only one Malaysian played in the test against Japan. When the Commonwealth servicemen departed, Malaysia would not have a team at the international level.

Rugby in Malaya consisted of two conferences, the North Malayan states and the South Malayan states along with Singapore. Being in a small Australian army unit based at the RAAF Base at Butterworth, we automatically belonged to the North Malayan conference. So, for the sporting fraternity when not involved in all things military, which was the reason for being there, Malaya became a rugby mecca, participating in three competitions, being; Base, Penang State and the North Malayan conference.

Competition One – Base Competition:

On our unit's arrival at Butterworth in Malaya, our small Army unit (company size of approximately one hundred and thirty troops) went straight into the base competition consisting of three RAAF (Squadron teams), two RAF teams, one Australian army team and the Green Jacket Battalion (UK), which was based on Penang Island at Minden Barracks. I was the captain/coach of our army team.

Competition Two – Penang State Competition:

Penang State had their competition consisting of teams from the Penang Sports Club, Penang Blues, Royal Air Force, Australian Men's Sports Club (AMSC) and the Green Jacket Battalion. The AMSC was by far the strongest team in this State competition and since its inception had not lost a game in the several years it existed. The team was drawn from the whole RAAF Base.

During the base competition in early 1965, a WO2 from base squadron Blacky Blackwood approached me and suggested that a team be raised from the single personnel from the Base and our Army unit. It would be called the Wallabies and if I was interested would I be its inaugural captain/coach? To date, the single personnel from the base played for the ASMC a team based in Penang and drawn from the RAAF married personnel based in Georgetown. He explained it would even up the State competition, being more competitive with the second team drawn from RAAF and Army members.

The concept appealed to Blacky and me, and with the approval from the RAAF heavies along with our army BC's agreeance, the Wallabies Rugby Club in Malaya was born, to become the sixth club in the State competition.

The original Wallabies Rugby team 1965.
Back Row (L-R): Bill Bailey, Larry Hayne, Wayne Hall (Vice-captain) [All RAAF] Dingers
Bell, David Levy, Tilley Devine, Tasi Woodard (Captain/Coach), Adrian Lohman [All Army]
Front Row (L-R): Blue Leslie, Doc Luxford, Alan Cleasby [All Army] R.
Wright, M. Jeffrey, Peter Ashworth, Ray Gillies [All RAAF]

In 1965 we became runners-up to the AMSC in the Penang State grand final. In 1966 we won the grand final and in 1967 went through winning the grand final undefeated. In 1966 the Wallabies had become so popular that a Wallabies second side was raised, which added the seventh team to the Penang State competition.

At this time, our founder WO2 Blackwood was a member of the Sydney, Australian-based Western District Rugby League Club at Ashfield which wore a black jersey with a white 'V' (In 1999 the Western Suburbs Magpies later amalgamated with the Balmain Tigers and became West Tigers). At this time the AMSC was sponsored by the Sydney-based St George Rugby League Club and wore their colours (a white jersey with a red 'V') with the donation to them in jerseys and socks.

Blacky with a short holiday during a return trip to Sydney arrived back in Malaya by RAAF transport and had in his possession a whole set of Wests jerseys and socks for our team.

On the creation of the Wallabies' second team, jerseys were made in exact reverse to the originals, being a white jersey with a black 'V'.

**I as inaugural captain/coach of the Wallabies Rugby Club Malaya
sporting our donated gear from Western Districts Rugby League Club
Sydney at the rugby field, RAAF Base in Butterworth, Malaya.**

A shield was made and Blacky Blackwood made this presentation to Western District Rugby League Club (Wests) Ashfield, Sydney Australia in person, in appreciation for the donation of jerseys and socks. WO2 Blacky Blackwood (the founder of the Wallabies Rugby Club Malaya) is squatting in the front row extreme right.

Competition Three – Malayan North Conference:

This was an interstate competition with teams participating from the following States:

Kedah, Perak, Penang, Selangor and the Commonwealth Forces North (CFN).

CFN was the dominant team in this competition. Our closest rivals always were Selangor State with the Nation's capital Kuala Lumpur, consisting of many British civilians employed in the banking, mining, plantation and other country and state industries which were the mainstays of their state's rugby team. I cannot recall losing a game in my four years (1964 – 1967) representing CFN.

Back Row (L-R): Tasi Woodard, Terry Duggan, Gordon McAskill, Dick Morrissey, Shorty Phillips, Johnny Holman, Tommy Wooten, Billy McDonnell.
Front Row (L-R): Bill Matthews, Bruce Hughes, G. Tait, Peter McNamara, Wally Crust, Brian Leddingham, Bob Heatherington.

140

On arriving in Malaya, I was drafted straight into the CFN Team as a fullback. This photo was taken in 1964 before an Interstate game (CFN defeating Kedah 39-6). I was the only Army member on the team with the rest all being RAAF personnel.

I played in all the CFN teams in the four years when available and captained CFN in 1967. I also played in the annual North Malayan versus South Malayan games as well as the CFN versus Commonwealth Forces South (CFS) games.

From the previous photo, Wally Crust is worthy of mention. On returning to Sydney he captained the Penrith Rugby League team, and also captained City Seconds in their annual City versus Country matches. Many of our team members were of rugby league backgrounds.

In 1966 and 1967 our army unit team won the final of the Base competition; in 1966 defeating an RAF Squadron team and in 1967 defeating Base Squadron (RAAF).

By 1967 I was the captain of three teams being; Commonwealth Forces North in the North Malayan competition, Wallabies Rugby Club in the Penang State competition and our Army Unit team in the Forces Base competition, as well as the coach of the latter two teams.

Our army unit wearing the Wallabies Two's jerseys. Eight of these players also represented the Wallabies' first team and seven of them played for CFN. I am sitting middle row, third from left next to our BC.

In 1966 our unit was replaced by a unit that was raised in South Australia consisting of many 1st and 2nd National Service intake soldiers. Being South Australians, many were Australian rules footballers, who were wonderful athletes. Being through this transition myself I had a busy time converting them in which they excelled. I remained in Malaya with the replacement unit. So, ending my Malayan sojourn and rugby involvement it was back to Australia and into a unit building up for their second tour of Viet Nam ... 1 Field Regiment RAA.

I wish to take this opportunity to relate to Mr M. B. Pestana MBE (the President of the Malaysian Rugby Union) who was a resident in Penang and often visited our games when playing in the Penang State competition on Penang Island. We got to know each other and I was invited by him to do coaching clinics at schools in Penang, which I did when time permitted. I also got to know a few parents carrying out this activity and was surprised to receive a wedding invitation from one of them.

—m—

Early 1968: *"Bombardier Woodard. The Regimental Sergeant Major (RSM) wants to see you."*

The RSM was WO1 Les Kidd, who was a sergeant when I went through the School of Artillery at North Head and he played rugby for the North Head team.

"Bombardier Woodard reporting Sir."

"Come in and sit down Tasi. The reason I want to see you is to ask you to captain and coach the Regimental rugby team this year."

"Yes Sir. When will training commence?"

"Immediately since I have been here some time, I have been earmarking potential players and we will continue adding to the team as new personnel keeps moving in."

So, besides training in a military manner applicable to our battalion supporting role, the rugby training, playing and coaching were in full swing. 1 Field Regiment RAA went through the season undefeated winning the grand final 29-6.

The CO stated, *"Well done Sergeant Woodard."*

1 Field Regiment RAA undefeated Premiers in 1968 in the South East Queensland (SE QLD) Services competition winning the grand final 29-6. Note: Alan Currie (holding the ball) was an outstanding player, who achieved high awards in civilian Rugby League. The captain/coach is centre row, third from the left.

The South East Queensland (SE QLD) Services competition consisted of numerous military units, a RAAF team from Amberley and a Navy team from Brisbane. Our team was a mixture of regular and National service soldiers before the unit's second tour of Viet Nam in 1969. Many National Servicemen were rugby league players, however, conversion to rugby union was no great task with them being young, athletic and a willingness to compete.

One National Serviceman we had who was an outstanding player was Alan Currie, representing East Tigers in the Brisbane Rugby League (BRL). Alan became the Rothmans Medal (Best and Fairest) winner in 1977 within the BRL competition. Alan never served with the unit in Viet Nam as his National Service time would elapse well before the unit's term in Viet Nam expired.

So here I was with back-to-back undefeated premiership teams in 1967 and 1968, in two different competitions in two different countries … one would think is unique. One a civilian competition and the other a services competition … even more unique.

—m—

In early 1969 it was off to Viet Nam so rugby for me was put on hold until 1973. In 1970, back in Australia and with a split unit (two sub-units in Wacol and our sub-unit in Enoggera) I never played rugby for the unit, however, was busy winning a South East Queensland Services basketball competition with our sub-branch on behalf of our parent unit.

In mid-1971 we were reunited at Wacol with our other two sub-units which were building up for their third tour of Viet Nam in February 1972. The regiment did have a rugby team in the South East Queensland Services competition, however, I didn't play as we were still in Enoggera when the season commenced. When we did move to join our unit in Wacol, I watched their inter-unit matches and although they had a very smart backline their forwards were wanting in some basic unit skills.

With another year in Viet Nam it would be 1974 before I would have an opportunity to be involved in a playing capacity and having not played since 1968 realistically, I believed my rugby days were behind me.

In November 1971, at a regimental parade, the CO addressed the parade to inform us that we were to stand down as no more units were being sent to Viet Nam.

For me, the smell of dressing room liniment became stronger. I was appointed captain/coach for our unit rugby team for 1973 and while the competition was underway, I was appointed captain/coach for QLD Army and QLD Combined Services.

In a playing capacity, I played my last game in a Queensland jersey at Ballymore on Tuesday 3rd of July 1973 versus the New South Wales (NSW) Combined Services side (won by Queensland) as a curtain-raiser to Queensland versus the Tonga international team. Little was I to know that by 1980 I would be coaching a few players from that Tongan international side.

Even though I did cease to play at a representative level I continued coaching the Queensland Army and Queensland Combined Services teams up until 1978.

From 1973 to 1978 inclusive QLD Combined Services played NSW Combined Services on fifteen occasions. Queensland won on fourteen consecutive occasions with a block of nine games that NSW failed to score a try. In 1978 we played NSW at Victoria Barracks (Paddington NSW) with NSW scoring their first victory against QLD since 1972, breaking a fourteen-win run. I resigned on returning to Brisbane, however, played and captained unit rugby till 1979.

Queensland Combined Services Rugby Team 1977.
Ex-Internationals within were Epi Bola, front row sixth from the left and next to him
(seventh) ex-Wallaby fullback Bob Brown (v England Test Series). Second from the left
(front row) ex-Souths (Brisbane) halfback Phil Day, perhaps the best halfback in Australian
Services Rugby Union with ex-Manly (Sydney) Bob Dean (fifth front row). In the back
row ninth from the left is Steve Thornton (ex-ACT) who was later to become CEO of
Queensland Rugby Union. Some of these other players were playing A Grade in the Brisbane
competition such as Alan Hudson (Brothers Club Brisbane) back row third from left.

Such was Queensland's domination in Australian Services Rugby I was appointed to be Assistant Coach for Australian Services Rugby Union under Colonel George Newton for 1976, 1977 and 1978.

George in his younger days was an outstanding athlete winning the 100 metres freestyle final in the Olympic selection swimming trials held at the Valley Swimming Pool in Brisbane. He was disqualified for an incorrect turn and never represented Australia at the Olympics. He also represented Queensland Rugby as a prop forward in his pre-army career.

Returning to unit rugby and when in 1973, being a lot heavier and a little older and slower, I moved into the forwards as a prop and enjoyed my rugby like never before unbelievably dominating the front row in Services Rugby. This I put down to having superior body mechanics to most to such an extent I in later life was used as a demonstration model in Australian National Rugby courses as a prop. Humping wheat (at 180 lbs a bag) as a sixteen-year-old was paying dividends as well as filling around one hundred thousand sandbags during my Army career.

During this period 1973-1977 my team won grand finals at Services level though did lose some mainly to battalions whose numbers in strength was almost double to regiments, however keeping in mind they also can only field fifteen players. I learned very quickly if a team can dominate in the forwards, they are the team most likely to win.

In my previous unit at Wacol when in 1976 the CO informed me that the unit, out of petty cash, had nominated me for the first National Coaching course held in Queensland at Enoggera Barracks. The National Coaching courses, coach the coaches, not the players thereby raising the standards of coaches throughout Australia. Upon attending, I was grouped with three Souths Rugby Club (Brisbane) coaching staff that attended. One of these people was Neil Tiny Betts, an ex-Queensland captain and Australian prop. With him were two ex-Queensland reps, one a winger in Ivor Thomas and the other a hooker in Mick Baker. It was through Tiny Betts (also the President of Souths Rugby Club) who offered me a coaching position in Souths that had five senior and three Under Nineteen (now Colts) teams.

When I eventually purchased and moved to a house in Moorooka which was walking distance to the Souths' Club and grounds at Annerley, I took up Tiny Betts and Souths' offer. Thus, began my short coaching career in civilian rugby; a chapter following.

I attended three National Rugby Coaching courses, the first already mentioned where I succeeded in attaining my Level 1. Within a year I was requested to attend a Level 2 - Australian Rugby Coaching course, not only giving coaching lessons on the unit and individual skills but also submitting a paper on subjects on how to improve Australian Rugby overall. My subject related to weights, circuit training and strengthening improvements, and I was pleased to say that I passed Level 2.

With the end of the Viet Nam War (for Australian troops) our National Servicemen had a choice of immediate discharge or seeing out their two-year service, which did pay them dividends. The Australian Army was overloaded with senior NCOs and I was surplus to our unit's establishment and virtually became a full-time jock strapper coaching unit, army and Combined Services, teams.

My BK to me, *"Tasi … report to the RSM at Regimental HQ."*

RSM to me, *"Tasi the CO wishes to speak to you."*

On confronting the CO, he explained to me that our unit had to supply three senior NCOs, one to Mt. Isa (QLD), one to Willoughby (NSW) and one to the Land Warfare Centre at Canungra (QLD).

"You are one of the three that have to be posted. I am offering you the first choice."

"Sir. I shall take the Canungra posting," I replied.

"Thought you would and of course, you won't be lost to SE QLD Services Rugby," he replied. So, in early 1977 it was off to Canungra some thirty miles south of Brisbane.

**Receiving my Australian Army Warrant upon marching
into Canungra, Queensland (extreme right)**

On marching into Canungra, the RSM, a very dedicated and strict infantry RSM called me to his office, *"The Colonel Commandant wishes to see you."*

I was paraded to the Commandant, *"WO2 Woodard for you Sir."*

"Come on in, welcome to the unit and Canungra Tasi." I could notice the RSM's mouth drop open.

The Colonel Commandant was no other than Colonel Colin Khan (Genghis to all except to his face) who I had a rugby alliance in the early sixties.

"Tasi, you are now the unit's captain and coach of the rugby team." Sitting to one side was an infantry major. *"This is Major Lynch. He is the rugby officer. Anything you require, he will get you."*

Following the meeting, Major Lynch asked what I needed. I pulled a page out of the National Coaching manual, *"Here is a plan showing front and side elevations of a scrum machine. I need one asap."*

Now the Canungra Unit has a very large Royal Corps of Australian Electrical and Mechanical Engineers (RAEME) unit that can get anything they require through the system as they build even Vietnamese villages for training purposes.

"Major Lynch here. Your scrum machine is complete. Where do you want it?"

"On the rugby pitch of course," was my reply.

The same afternoon I went down to inspect the machine and yes it was built to specifications as per the manual. We filled up a large number of sandbags to place on the platform and so began, I believe, the most intensive scrummaging training perpetrated on any army unit team.

During my three years at Canungra our team featured in the finals in 1978 and 1979, however, never won the grand final. We were regarded as the best scrummaging team in the competition and on many occasions, I would be on my third prop at the end of the game. Although I admit many of these opposition props were not skilled in the art and were soft and easy and I may add, fragile. On a few occasions, I had opposition props before the first scrum of the game requesting, *"Take it easy Tasi."*

"Yeah right!" Their lack of body mechanics suffered.

Still Going Strong - Participating in a 10,000 m Cross Country race, Canungra 1978.

Retiring from rugby coaching, I let my Level 2 lapse, however I was sent back to a refresher course in 1996 by the then Director of Coaching Queensland, Duncan Hall as Duncan had another assignment for me for the three years of 1996, 1997 and 1998.

A Taste of Civilian Rugby:

While I was still at Canungra, however living at Marsden (Brisbane), Southern Districts Rugby Club asked me to coach their Under 19 Firsts team in 1978. I agreed to this and we did make the finals, however, got defeated in the last minute through a field goal by Easts. I declined to coach at Souths in 1979, however I was requested by President Tiny Betts if I would be interested in accepting the position of Director of Coaching for the club in 1980.

Being involved with the club during the season in 1978, was an eye-opener for me on how the teams within the club were run. I knew if I accepted the position there would have to be a total restructuring within the four senior teams, which probably would not be popular, however it would be a good challenge for me in this category of rugby knowing I had the support of Tiny Betts behind me. This certainly was of a superior level compared to inter-unit services rugby.

From coaching the Under 19s in 1978, I knew I could introduce some new blood, which in turn did emerge a second Queensland player in Danny McIvor and several Queensland Seconds members.

The Souths Club had not been very successful for a long time with their last grand final being in 1957. It appeared to me that to coach in Souths one must have played with the club. It was evident that the club was inbred and I may have been the first coach to be associated with them having never played for them.

1980 – Souths Year of Change:

What a fragmented Club!!! Especially around the A-Grade team, which had three defined groups within it. Firstly, there was an element of the team who had won a grand final in the mid-seventies, I believe it was an Under 19 team and now that some of those players had been elevated to A-Grade, was an independent group. The second group consisted of the Tongans, who on attending training sat outside the clubhouse on the verge of the oval talking amongst themselves. The third group consisted of players who did not belong to either of the first two groups; a total lack of unity.

So, in early 1980 began the restructuring of Souths Rugby Club relating to training and playing, but initially, it was about integration. In my past rugby coaching I was only involved with one team; here existed a huge challenge as under me I had four coaches and teams. Souths did have a 5th Grade team, however consisted of students and players not available for training.

Initially, I had to get the Tongans onside with my way of thinking. I believed they had always wanted to be part of a consolidated team, however, it seemed that except for being very successful on the field of play that they were largely ignored. I approached Sione Mafi with all the respect he deserved, being a former international captain. I sat with Sione and gave him my thoughts on the deficiencies within the club, fully realising Sione was an extrovert when it came to Tongan management, but introverted when it came to Souths' player management as he was only another player. It appeared to me he had no voice or decision-making within the team which was truly a lack of respect for the man's standing. I may add that through the season I often consulted with Sione on how I wished his Tongan players to perform within the team. Sione agreed with me, that for Souths to improve we must have unity.

As the preseason training progressed my relationship with the Tongans, who included Niuselu Fakauho, Saimone Vaea, Sione Mafi, Fa'aleo Tupi and Fatai Kefu, and all ex-internationals, became very healthy.

In 1980, Souths possessed only one Queensland and Australian representative in Andrew Slack, who in 1981 I had a rather disappointing selection fallout with, which is explained in a later chapter.

Club Meeting – Players, Night One:

The Tongans filed into the clubhouse and so did every other potential player wishing to represent Souths in the four senior teams. I had a blackboard set up and following introductions so began the initiation of rugby season 1980. I was pleased to see the club committee in attendance so all could see the direction I was heading. The duration of the meeting took several hours introducing the four-unit skills training set-up and how training for the first month would be conducted not in teams, but as a club. Over that month players' potential, skills level and grading would be ascertained. Individual fitness levels were mainly left to the player, however, all players were made aware that fixed levels would be tested at weekend sessions not during weeknights, where the emphasis is on unit games, unit skills, grid training and individual skills. During this meeting I invited Andrew Slack to accept the position of Club Captain, not Team Captain, as with all State and Australian players, clubs are lucky to get their representative players for four to five games at the club level, a season. Andrew accepted this invitation, a position at the club level in recognition of his international standing.

—⁓∭⁓—

Early season in Brisbane Rugby was the Redcliffe Sevens Competition basically, the Queensland annual sevens where teams from all over Australia are invited. Sevens rugby was not my forte and as one Bruce Hatcher (now QRL Chairman) being of some coaching ability and living within walking distance from Souths I approached him and offered him the position of the Sevens coach. By now I had a good idea of which players would be capable of handling Sevens rugby. I told Bruce I would give him eighteen players (two teams plus) and he would be the sole coach and selector of the final squad. Bruce took the position and dedicated himself to the task.

Souths went through the Sevens undefeated to make the grand final against Randwick from Sydney. Randwick defeated Souths to win the Redcliffe Sevens however, even being defeated gave Souths a huge boost within the playing ranks and it was obvious they began believing in themselves.

—⁓∭⁓—

Early season training was becoming competitive and when I called for a Saturday afternoon fitness player assessment consisting of firstly a 1500-metre race and within thirty minutes an 800-metre race. Unbelievably one Cameron Armstrong (a prop) won both (within his group) setting an example to all their failures and the realisation that they each must lift their game in the fitness stakes.

Everything in all aspects of the training was competitive, both as individuals and in small (five to six) man teams. Individuals did not want to let their teammates down.

Creating a Respected Team:

It had come to my notice that Souths in the past did have a very poor relationship with the referees within the competition, which was a situation that had to be rectified. During a club training evening, all players were sat down and club standards were spoken of. The referee situation was brought to notice and the following rules were laid down:

No player was to mouth off at the referee; the only player to approach and speak to the referee is the Team Captain; even if the referee is wrong, he is right, we all make mistakes; on all occasions, the referee's decision is to be respected and adhered to; this club will not tolerate thuggery on the field of play. It is accepted that especially forwards must always seek physical domination of the opposition, however, it must be carried out within the laws of the game. If foul play is committed on us, retaliation is not to entertained as linesmen and referees will take care of the indiscretion; and we must seek a respected image, one of hard however fair.

Before the season proper I had one of the senior referees from the Brisbane competition come out to Souths on a training evening and with blackboard and chalk available go through with the players the most abused laws of the game. I was astounded at how many players did not fully understand many of the laws of the game. This session served two purposes: To give individual players a better understanding of the laws of the game and to indicate to the referees our club's new approach to the coming season.

The Season Proper Commencement:

With players now allocated to their respective teams, the club was eagerly looking to the initiation of the season commencement. I may add here that the selection panel for teams consisted of myself, A-Grade Coach and Andrew Slack for A-Grade; myself and Coach for Reserve Grade and that combination for 3rd and 4th-Grade, myself and the Grade's Coach. That selection panel stood for seasons 1980 and 1981.

In a nine-team competition, several trophies are presented to the team who leads the competition following the first round which is the Welsby Cup, and who heads the competition at the cessation of the second round; is the Horsley Trophy.

To me it was pleasing to see that five players from the Under 19 team I coached in 1978 had progressed through to A-Grade; being Simon Mewing, Brian Beiers, Danny McIvor, Terry Coyne and Dominic Samios.

Following the first round, two games stood out with one disappointing and one a historic win.

Our historic win was against the Brothers team on their home ground, Albion Park, a win with scores Souths 24 – Brothers 0. This had Frank O'Callaghan, who was *The Courier Mail's* chief rugby writer doing a little research in the archives to later in the week, write in Brothers rugby history, *"It was the first time Brothers had failed to score in a game on their home ground."* Frank (long deceased) was a staunch Brothers supporter.

The second game of note was the second last game of round one. Souths on their home ground entertained royalty with King Taufu Alua Tupou of Tonga on the 15th of June and he watched Souths play GPS who defeated Souths 15-10. This was Souths' first loss of the season and a great disappointment for our Tongan players.

However, disposing of Wests in the final game of round one saw Souths on top of the ladder and winning the Welsby Cup. Souths Magpies lost only one game in the second round, going down to Brothers 16-15 however, retained the top of the ladder position and won their second piece of silverware for the season; the Horsley Trophy.

I may add here that the points for and against were as follows:

First-round was 179 for - 58 against
Second-round was 165 for – 73 against
Total for the seasons club rounds 344 for - 131 against.

Souths A-Grade and 4th-Grade became minor premiers, with 3rd-Grade coming second and Reserve-Grade making the finals.

From the Secretary's Annual Report 1980:

"This is the first time in the Club's history that the four senior teams have all made the semi-finals."

So, to the semi-finals A-Grade: elimination final the University of Queensland versus GPS with the qualifying final Souths versus Brothers. University disposed of GPS in the elimination final and Souths defeated Brothers in the qualifying final to enter the grand final. Brothers defeated University to qualify for the grand final against Souths.

For Souths to win their first grand final in twenty-three years was going to be a huge task. The Brothers club were firm favourites boasting six current Australian Wallabies in an International front row of Tony D'Arcy, Mark McBain and Chris Handy, while the back row boasted Tony Shaw. In their backs at five-eight was the team's rudder in Paul McLean and Australia's top winger in Brendan Moon. Also having Queensland representatives in centres David Logan and Paul Mills and winger Paul Costello.

Two Nightingale brothers in the forwards appeared too much artillery for Souths to handle, which proved a correct assessment. Souths blew a nine-point lead in the first ten minutes with Sione Mafi knocking on a pass two metres from the try line and under the post with no defender in sight. Goalkicker Terry Coyne a few minutes later, missed a penalty goal just off centre, minus nine points.

Brothers then through perhaps the most ruthless forward in Australian rugby, Tony Shaw began to dismantle the Souths forwards by firstly sending opposition back-row forward Simone Vaea to the hospital to have no further part in the game. During this time, the mercurial five-eighth Paul McLean was manipulating his backline to dominance over the Souths backs.

Souths suffered their biggest defeat in 1980, losing the grand final 19-0.

—m—

Following the grand final Souths increased in numbers from one member, in Andrew Slack to three, with the addition of Sione Mafi (No.8) and Danny McIver (halfback) to representative honours for Queensland. Danny McIvor with the Queensland team toured the British Isles and Europe and in early season 1981, he accompanied the Queensland team to New Zealand on a three provincial game tour.

SOUTHERN DISTRICTS RUGBY UNION FOOTBALL CLUB - A GRADE 1980
Winners: WELSBY CUP – HORSLEY TROPHY – MINOR PREMIERS
GRAND FINALISTS

Front Row L-R: Simon Mewing, Neil Betts (President), John Hoyland (Coach),
George Parker (Captain), Andrew Slack (Vice-Captain), Tasi Woodard
(Director of Coaching), Stan Bramham (Manager), Brian Beiers
Second Row L-R: Phil White, Dan McIvor, Jefferey McLean, Peter McLennon,
Cameron Armstrong, Rob Lee, Niuselu Fakauho, Peter Francis
Third Row L-R: Saimone Vaea, Peter Jones, Greg Maloney, George Travos,
Terry Coyne, Sione Mafi
Fourth Row L-R: Paul Reddel, Fa'aleo Tupi, Len Krosschell, Bill Finlay
Absent: Don Townsen, Dominic Samios, John Watson.

A very in-depth assessment was carried out in the off-season period over the 1980 season. One assessment stood out above all others and that was the defensive record of the four senior teams over the season. On our first team meeting of 1980, on the blackboard, I went over the four-unit responsibilities and how if effectively carried out, our defence becomes very hard to penetrate. All coaches were directed to train using the unit skills in their areas of play. Scoring against Souths teams in 1980 the opposition found it hard not only to win but to score.

In the seasons club fixtures Souths A-Grade, Reserve Grade and 4th-Grade had fewer points scored against them than any other team, while 3rd-Grade came in second.

To me these defensive attitudes were a huge plus keeping in mind I was a defensive coach and will always stick by my principles; if the opposition cannot score against you, they will not defeat you.

A Falling Out:

The 1981 season slipped in comparison to 1980 in all grades with A-Grade making the semi-finals. The selection committee stood in 1980 with the A-Grade Coach, Andrew Slack and me as the selectors. Selections for this elimination final were to be my last, due to a falling out with the other two selectors.

On arriving for the selection, I noted that John Hoyland (A-Grade Coach) and Andrew were in deep conversation. The team we were to play in the elimination final was Teachers-Norths who possessed a very good all-round team, however the big danger, who I recognised as perhaps the world's best centre was Michael O'Connor. I was asked by John how I saw the makeup of the backline for this match. I emphatically stated that Andrew must oppose Michael O'Connor as Andrew being an Australian centre and having played with Michael in an international partnership, was the only player we had in our club who could contain Michael O'Connor's brilliance. Andrew was also our best defensive back and the containment of Michael O'Connor was our chance to progress further into the finals.

John suggested that Andrew should be moved into the five-eighth position and our usual five-eight, who I might add had occupied that position all year due to Andrew's absence with Queensland and Australian commitments would be moved to centre. I was emphatic that Andrew must play against O'Connor then I asked Andrew for his input. He agreed with John that he should be selected as five-eight and backline restructure should occur. I argued my case over and over however, both John and Andrew could not be moved with respect to my thinking.

Eventually, in desperation, I asked them both, *"Is this rearrangement your final decision?"*

They both confirmed it was.

I left the meeting with the parting words, *"You two select the team as you see fit. I shall see you next season."*

To this day I believe that Andrew did not wish to directly oppose Michael O'Connor. Andrew will always claim the selection was for team balance, however I will never see it that way.

Game result: Michael O'Connor shredded our backline to end Souths' season.

Andrew Slack some time ago became a member of the Queensland Rugby Hall of Fame and in 2020 was elevated to the Australian Rugby Hall of Fame.

Following me making out the Director of Coaching report for the Souths 1981 Annual Report it was to become my last commitment with Souths in a coaching/selector capacity, as for me 1982 was to be a huge change in my future.

Selection Regrets:

For two seasons Souths possessed an outstanding back-row forward in Gary Swinbourne, whom I believed would be playing in A-Grade with any other team. To this day, I still in not promoting Gary to A-Grade feel l have done this outstanding player an injustice. My reason for not promoting him was because of Sione Mafi and Simone Vaea, both back-row forwards of international representation were ideally suited to complement each other and the other back-row forward in Peter McLennan, who represented Poverty Bay, New Zealand in 1979. I have always pondered over Gary Swinbourne's future in rugby and regret that I never gave him that opportunity of A-Grade experience in 1980/1981.

My only game for Souths occurred when the first-grade props were chosen to play in a representative game for Queensland. Both Reserve Grade props were promoted as with the 3rd-Grade props to Reserve Grade so we became short of props. I volunteered to play 3rd-Grade, as a prop in this capacity I was still scrummaging fit as often in training, I would prop against Souths' front-rowers along with Army and Combined Services in live scrums. I'm glad I was playing 3rd-Grade because as a forty-three-year-old, the pace was down to my speed. The game was against Wests and Souths did win; however, the pleasing aspect of my game was at the completion, I was on my second Bulldogs prop. I may have been the oldest player to have debuted for the Southern Districts Rugby Club.

Rugby Footnotes:

I read Rod Macqueen's book of his life in rugby and he was a very successful coach, firstly with the Brumbies in Super Rugby followed by him coaching the Wallabies to their second World Rugby Cup victory in 1999. Before successes with representative teams, he was coach of a North Shore (Sydney) club side. Rod stated in 1982 upon arriving at the club he formulated the following:

1: All coaches in the grades of the club will identically coach in the same manner so if there is to be promotion and relegation within the grades, players will not be subject to a new team routine. Rod claimed it was his innovation to be followed by other clubs

2: When Rod's club side won the Sydney grand final, he would challenge the grand final winners from Brisbane for interstate club supremacy. He claimed that on his suggestion that the Interstate Club Challenge became a reality.

In reply to reference to #1: In 1980 at the first Souths club players meeting, I stressed that coaching in all four grade teams would be the same so if promotion and relegation occur, players won't be transferred to another team, which possess different playing routines (sadly, I had to have a coach dismissed as he wanted to do it his way).

In reply to reference to #2: Qualifying for the grand final in 1980, Frank O'Callaghan called me and asked, *"Tasi. If you defeat Brothers in the grand final what will your next move be?"*

I replied to Frank (Chief rugby writer for *The Courier Mail*), *"Frank. My first objective would be to challenge the Sydney competition's grand final winner for Australian club supremacy."* Frank did send my statement to press, however after losing to Brothers in the Brisbane grand final the game suggested was never pursued.

I wonder if Rod Macqueen ever learned that there was a rugby coach in Brisbane that had beaten his innovations by two years.

—--m--—

1981 saw my last coaching position with Souths as I did not apply for any further association with the club as 1982 saw a life-changing future in taking my discharge from the Army in February. Being a very keen fisherman, I was to buy a boat, relax and enjoy some very intense fishing. I did become a club follower and did retain a close friendship with the Tongans.

My rugby involvement appeared something of the past in 1981 happy with my lot. I never imagined that some fifteen years later in 1996 I would be sent to a Level 2 Australian Coaching refresher course by the QRU. And from that, a new three-year rugby involvement in a coaching capacity at the state level, and a most enjoyable one, was presented to me. This is a story told in my previous book 'Queensland – Women in Rugby. The first two years 1996-1997'.

A Final Coaching Commitment:

In 1998 I contracted Jeff Morris to build our home in Caloundra. Jeff (now deceased) was deeply into junior sports and was the President of the Caloundra Juniors Rugby Teams with himself being the Coach of the eldest team, the Under 15s. Jeff himself was a former hooker in the Sunshine Coast competition. He was also heavily involved with Caloundra's Surf Club Nippers.

In 1998 Jeff confronted me and this conversation followed:

"Tasi. You coached at Souths Rugby Union Club in Brisbane?"

"Yes," I replied.

"Well Tasi, I am the President of the Caloundra Juniors and coach the Under 15s, could you find the time to come down and help me with my team?"

When leaving Brisbane and moving to Caloundra, I believed rugby was history with me moving on to golf, fishing, and a more social life in retirement. Following a little consideration and taking into account I did want our house to be of the finest quality, I felt stuck between a rock and a hard place.

I replied, *"Jeff, you let me have the forwards, you look after the backs, however, let me take them for team training runs when I request."* Jeff agreed to this.

So off to the Caloundra rugby ground I went, found their scrum machine which appeared to have had little use. And so, began an intensive introduction and coordination in scrummaging, not ignoring other unit skills in line outs, mauling, rucking and support play, a very intensive and condensed learning experience. Such as becoming so superior in scrummaging, that other teams requested and succeeded in having scrums against our team depowered and become a farce.

Coaches are not permitted to approach referees however, during a halftime break an opposition coach went onto the field and started talking to the referee. Well if it was good enough for him then I also wanted a chat. The following conversation ensued:

"Excuse me sir, but following the first scrum, why were scrums then depowered?"

"Well," the referee replied, *"an opposition front row prop asked that the scrum be depowered because their scrum could not compete against your scrum."*

"You mean to tell me that a front-row prop tells you how to referee a game?"

"I object to that. I am responsible for the safety factor of these players and it wouldn't look good for me to have a major injury to a player in a game under my control."

"Referees like you are one of the reasons Australian teams get flogged at the International level in underage competitions."

With that, the referee called over a security officer and requested him to remove me from the field of play, to which I complied. He took my name and I was not to attend future games with the Caloundra Under 15s, however it did not stop me from coaching them.

The Caloundra Under 15s made the grand final, though I never got to witness the game as my wife Ailsa and I had previously planned to spend six weeks in Scandinavia.

After the previous incident, I asked Jeff, who had monthly meetings with the Sunshine Coast Committee, to state that I would voluntarily coach Junior Level Coaches in scrummaging techniques in the off-season.

Arriving home from Scandinavia my phone rang and it was Jeff Morris. *"Tasi, I have been ringing for weeks. Congratulations on being the assistant coach of the first Caloundra team in history to win a grand final."*

In time Jeff presented me with a Caloundra Junior Rugby tracksuit top. He also informed me that he had brought up the subject of the junior teams' coaches being coached in the art of scrummaging and it was rejected. I told Jeff I could no longer be a party to a rugby fraternity that rejected scrums in the game which was an easy exit from any further participation.

"Farewell Club Rugby"

A Pleasant Reward:

At the turn of this century, an Australian medal was struck to commemorate the new century, this being a millennium medal. For Australian sporting achievement, I was bestowed with The Australian Sports Medal. This was awarded for forty-one years of involvement and dedication to rugby from 1957 to 1997 as a player, captain, captain/coach, coach, administrator, and then again in my participation as a coach for the final time.

My initial problem was to find out where it fitted with military medals. Personalities who received The Australian Sports Medal in 2000 for rugby involvement included John Eales, Michael Lynagh and David Campese – I was indeed in good company.

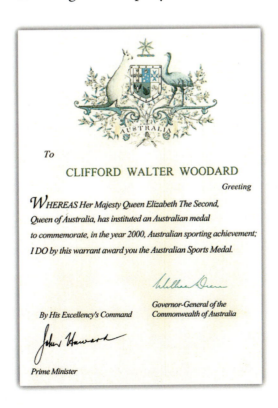

157

NINE

VETERANS AND GOLDEN OLDIES RUGBY

'The Older You Get; The Better You Were'

International Golden Oldies Rugby was initiated in New Zealand by a small group of ex-high profile rugby players who had retired from competitive rugby but still felt the urge to put on the boots and play rugby with and against old friends and teams thus keeping alive friendships and most importantly the social aspect of rugby that I believe did not exist in any other team sport at the time.

Friendships that existed competitively were carried over in a social aspect of rugby where no scores of games were kept and players can leave and return to games when they desired. A colour code of shorts was included indicating age groups, where players of gold and purple shorts were allowed to be apprehended during a game, however, were not to be tackled. This kept elderly greats of rugby involved and honoured for their past services to the game. The greatest aspect of this level of rugby is the social side, where no matter what level players achieved in their playing careers, they had the opportunity to play and socialise with past players of all levels. So Golden Oldies Rugby (GOR) grew at such a rapid rate that it quickly, over a few short years, became an international concept involving tens of thousands and along with that came huge corporate backing.

**Two past high-profile rugby players in (L) Neil Blanchfield and Brian Craies,
who along with Barrie Herring and Tom Johnson were the International
Golden Oldies Secretariat and Foundation Members of the Movement.**

Golden Oldies Rugby was born in New Zealand in the mid-seventies. No doubt, the few ex-high-profile rugby players who initiated this concept could not have visualised their idea would become perhaps the biggest sporting concept on the planet, involving ex-non-competitive teams from all over the world. In 1979 the New Zealand (NZ) organisation decided to put on a festival hosted by the city of Auckland with invitations going far and wide. Of course, New Zealand raised many teams to participate and I believe there was a response from the United States of America (USA) and the United Kingdom (UK) though not on the greater level that there was to be in the future. I believe individuals from Australia attended, who upon arrival were formed into miscellaneous teams.

Such was the support from the USA that in 1981 the second Golden Oldies Festival was put on in the USA being held at Long Beach, California.

The NZ committee to awaken the sleeping giant across the Tasman allocated the 1983 Festival to Australia, hosted by the city of Sydney. This wise allocation certainly awoke Australia with GOR teams springing up all over the country, including the Queensland XXXX (pronounced Fourex) Goldies who were sponsored by Castlemaine Perkins. I did join the XXXX Goldies in 1982, not as a foundation member, but as an early member of the club. I did not proceed to the Sydney Festival but I was to learn this concept had a huge impact on rugby veterans in Australia and no doubt the NZ committee would have been congratulating themselves on their wise decision to give the 1983 Festival to Sydney.

In Brisbane, teams were created from all clubs and many teams from southeast Queensland were formed. A president representing Australia on the Golden Oldies International Board was appointed such to the popularity of this concept in Australia.

In 1984 the South Island of NZ held a New Zealand Festival (just within the country) and the President of Queensland XXXX Goldies, Errol Smith (ex-Easts, now deceased), and I were invited to Christchurch on a look and learn exercise to understand how to run a festival.

I met all the heavies on the committee of the Golden Oldies Board plus the President of the New Zealand South Island Committee who in 1995 was responsible for hosting the International GOR Festival when held in Christchurch. My only blemish on my 1984 visit is that I was admonished for purchasing a jug of beer.

Air New Zealand was now the major sponsor for the International Golden Oldies and passage for me and Errol Smith plus accommodation was taken care of by Air New Zealand.

—⅏—

Such was the growth of Golden Oldies Rugby in Australia, that in 1985 I was appointed Queensland representative to the Australian and International Boards. The 1985 Bi-annual Festival was appointed to England with London being the host city.

Such was the expansion of this concept many corporations were now on board and of course, Queensland XXXX Goldies was sponsored by Castlemaine Perkins. Usually, during these international festivals, teams get to play their three games (Monday, Wednesday and Friday) on different grounds hosted by the rugby clubs. Castlemaine Perkins wished to break into the northern hemisphere beer market. So, on this occasion through allied breweries, Queensland XXXX Goldies was allocated the London Irish ground for the whole festival where Castlemaine Perkins carried out a huge campaign of advertising on their product.

—⅏—

Castlemaine Perkins – XXXX have long been wonderful sponsors of many & varied sporting teams and occasions; usually all things Queensland. I wish to note their continual generous support during my time for the cultural events of Veterans and Golden Oldies Rugby.

Castlemaine Perkins Brewery, Brisbane, Queensland.
Image: *Courtesy of Stephen Fearnley*

The Fitzgerald Brothers, Edward and Nicholas moved from Castlemaine in Victoria to Brisbane and founded the brewery in 1878.

The old joke goes, "Queenslanders call their beer XXXX because they don't know how to spell beer." Their first beer was the XXX sparkling ale. Work continued improving the drop (with the long-standing tradition of X's to indicate the strength of ale) and eventually, it was awarded a fourth X. Simple really ... XXXX (Fourex).

We had in our team one Llewellyn Lewis (the original Wally) ex-Queensland and Australian Wallaby from 1931-1939 at five-eight. Unfortunately, Wally was on the Bill McLean Wallabies tour of the British Isles in 1939 when the day after their ship berthing in England, World War Two broke out, and not a game was played. While we were practising at the London Irish ground a BBC television crew turned up and asked us to form a scrum with a ball passed out to Wally Lewis with him running in and scoring a try. This little play was carried out to perfection with Wally, not respecting his age, diving over the try line to score.

This little snippet appeared on the BBC that night with the mention of Llewellyn Lewis, an ex-Australian five-eight who was a part of a team attending the London Festival. No doubt Wally in his XXXX jumper did his part in Castlemaine Perkins' advertising. It bemused us that it appeared Wally had a great more appeal in England as an ex-International than recognition he received in Australia. Perhaps it may have been his Christian name with a Welsh distinction. Little did we know at the time with his diving act for the benefit of TV, Wally broke his collar bone. No one

161

was made aware of his injury as Wally hid it for the festival duration, however, was noted by his absence in games.

———m———

After the landing of Bill McLean's Wallabies team in 1939, Wally like others joined the Royal Air Force and became a fighter pilot in Spitfires. As we lived quite close together in Moorooka, Brisbane I would often take Wally to Ballymore for big union matches with both of us being QRU members. In his later life while having a cup of coffee at his residence he was telling me of his operations during the closing stages of WWII. He mentioned to me that he and others were flying Spitfires from India to Burma to stop the Japanese advance from Burma into India. The pilots would then be flown back to India to transfer more of these aircraft to Burma. On one particular transfer, his commanding officer took him aside and informed him that his aircraft was fitted with undercarriage cameras and he was to fly over Mount Everest and film it from the air as it had never been done before. The latest Spitfires were the first aircraft capable of flying at that height and so Wally performed the assignment of photographing the top of Mount Everest from the air. He had never previously mentioned this achievement such was the man's modesty. Wally passed away in his mid-nineties at Greenslopes Hospital. Ailsa and I were at his bedside the night of his passing.

———m———

After the game's festival, a dinner was held on the London docks. Such were the numbers involved, which were in the thousands, that the London's newspapers headline the next morning claimed it to be the largest outdoor dinner ever held in the UK's history.

Ailsa and I had hired a vehicle to tour the UK after the festival. Such was the surplus of XXXX leftover at the London Irish ground our car's boot was filled with cartons of beer with directions to just give it away. So, with our suitcases on the back seat and a boot full of beer we proceeded on our way. I think I gave away the last of the beer in northern Scotland at Inverness.

———m———

Now the northern and southern hemispheres had been exposed to GOR. The 1987 Festival was again on in Auckland with the opening ceremony held on Eden Park rugby ground and the closing dinner held in Auckland's Ellerslie racing venue.

Back to the northern hemisphere. In 1989 with Canada's Toronto being the host city, the early bad news was I had a fish dinner and ended up in hospital on a drip for a day and night. I have never eaten fish outside of Australia again. The feature of this festival was the closing luncheon in a park on the Canadian side of Niagara Falls.

———m———

Some Queensland XXXX Goldies at Perth1991.
L-R: Bob Chapman (Brothers), Jeff Willis (Wynnum-Manly), Bob Rex, Ivor Thomas,
Tasi Woodard and Mick Baker (all ex-Souths Brisbane).
Rex, Thomas and Baker were Queensland representatives during their playing days.

Perth, Australia was the host city in 1991 with the feature of this festival being a series of rugby grounds marked out on the huge park in front of Perth City proper and the Swan River. Perth is the home city of the Australian Special Air Service (SAS) at Swanbourne and a team representing the SAS (The SAS Chicken Stranglers) parachuted into the venue.

The first game was on the 31st of May (my fifty-second birthday) and at the start of play, the ball was kicked off by our New Zealand opponents directly into my possession on the run. I was seeking support from my team on my run to the try line, but none came nor did any defence from our opponents. I eventually made it to the try line where both teams surrounded me and sang Happy Birthday. The New Zealand team was allowed to score the next try. After the game the New Zealand team's wives, girlfriends and partners lined up and gave me a stubby each while the team gave me an embrace and kiss. I informed the Kiwis they had it completely wrong, however we all enjoyed the stubbies.

On Saturday two games were played at Perry Park to promote rugby in Western Australia. For one of the games, I was selected to play in a Rugby World XV versus an International Board XV. Our captain for the World Team was former Scotland Captain at six foot ten inches, Bill Cuthbertson and the vice-captain was former Australian dual International five-eighth Phil Hawthorn (now deceased). Other players came from New Zealand, the USA, Yugoslavia, Italy, Singapore, Germany, Cook Islands, Japan, Canada and England.

**Rugby World XV. In an exhibition match versus an International
Board XV played at Perry Park, Perth in 1991.**

The captain of the team is ex-Scotland Captain Bill Cuthbertson (back row fourth from the right) and our Vice-Captain is Australian dual International Phil Hawthorne (front row extreme right) and I am standing directly behind Phil. Bill Cuthbertson (6ft 10ins) was told to squat down for this team photo so as not to make the rest of us look small.

Touch Judges were Jeff Butterfield and Tony Carter both England representatives and the referee was Australian Bob Fordham.

I wish to talk briefly about the Englishman Jeff Butterfield (a touch judge for the above game). I first met Jeff at the 1985 London Festival and did enjoy his company as we became good friends through the festival sharing all things rugby. My next encounter with Jeff was at the 1987 Auckland Festival and it became a reunion with some other NZ committee members, with who I had an Australian/ NZ GOR relationship. I missed Jeff in Toronto, however, in Perth, again many drinks were consumed and rugby matters were discussed and once again resolved nothing. Jeff didn't proceed to Dublin in 1993, however we met again in Christchurch in 1995 where Jeff requested me to march with him and his English team at the opening ceremony. It was at this festival that Jeff gave me a card and on a close inspection, it was an invitation to the Rugby Club of London.

I wish to relate some of Jeff Butterfield's rugby history. Jeff was a centre and played twenty-eight consecutive tests for his country over six years, captaining the English on four occasions. During this period, England won the Five Nations on four occasions and the Triple Crown twice. He toured with the British and Irish Lions to South Africa in 1955 and New Zealand in 1959.

Jeff was born in Yorkshire in 1929 and passed away in 2004. He was just one of many great ex-international rugby players who enjoyed touring the world in a GOR capacity, catching up with many ex-opponents, and enjoying those friendships of the past. I still have Jeff's invitation to the Rugby Club of London in my possession.

—— m ——

Following the 1991 Perth Festival, it was off to Dublin in 1993, drinking heaps of Guinness, telling lies to our guests and listening in turn to their lies, and of course, all harmless and very comical. The year before the 1993 Dublin Festival, the Irish Rugby Union sent out to Australia one of their ex-Internationals in five-eight Michael Quinn. He was to travel around and brief Australian teams on what to expect on their Irish visit. The humour from Michael only left us with no doubt that our visit to Ireland was going to be one of drinking, fun and laughter.

My Wife Ailsa with Ex Irish Five-Eight Michael Quinn at Ballymore 1992.

One of the first things Michael mentioned at our Queensland meeting was, *"Now when you get to Ireland you will notice our currency is called the Punt, and the reason they call it the Punt is that it rhymes with bank manager".*

This bought the house down although left some scratching their heads!

Michael was a great representative of his country and although he played rugby for Ireland he had never played at Ballymore, Brisbane. On the weekend he was in town, gear was found for him and he played a partial Reserve Grade game; his response was, *"Bejesus! I'm glad you never put me into an A Grade game."*

He gave our former Prime Minister Paul Keating a serve as when he visited Ireland all the villagers were made to go out and clean up a cemetery so Keating could visit some long past relatives, the villagers were not happy.

The 1993 Irish Festival hosted by the city of Dublin was a wonderful experience. At our host hotel, sharing a Guinness or two with teammates and locals we were doing a value on the cost of pints, keeping in mind the Punt was approximately the same value as the British Sterling. As pints were costing 2.0 Punts each I said to a local, *"This is quite expensive drinking, isn't it?"* He replied, *"It will be down to 1.6 when you bastards leave."*

That's the Irish. Their humour is to us quite entertaining, however when you analyse their replies, to them it's a straightforward statement, as I quote. In the host hotel, one of our teammates, who was in a *shout* with a local at the bar stated, *"Paddy … your glass is empty. Would you like another one?"*

The reply being, *"And what would I be doing with two empty fucking glasses?"* which had everyone in stitches.

Following the Dublin festival, my wife and I again hired a vehicle and spent two weeks touring Ireland, which was an unforgettable historic sojourn.

Christchurch, New Zealand was the host city for the 1995 festival and Lindsay Parke from Temuka became the festival organiser. Lindsay was the South Island delegate to the Golden Oldies Rugby International Board and he certainly presented an amazing occasion.

Lindsay Parke – Festival Organiser Christchurch 1995.

I first met Lindsay in 1984 when invited to Christchurch with one Errol Smith to a South Island festival to learn the ropes on the organisational procedures of running a festival. Some years later I hosted Lindsay in Brisbane when Brisbane Golden Oldies hosted a festival, in between International festivals in 1988. This was to coincide with World Expo 88 which was held in Brisbane … another story.

At the Christchurch Festival, it was great to see South African teams attending for the first time. One of the more remarkable unions took place during this festival. Cyril Andrews (now deceased) from the Queensland XXXX Goldies met up with an old ex-All Black player residing in Christchurch. They both played against one another in opposing teams in Australia (Australia XV versus All Blacks) during an All Blacks tour in 1946.

This reunion caught the eye of the NZ press and was well published in the daily papers the next day. Cyril represented Queensland on twelve occasions and also represented an Australian XV versus South Africa in the 1937 home series at the age of twenty.

Lindsay had organised the farewell luncheon of the festival to be held in the countryside of a large well-known tourist venue. Nature turned it on as the previous day/night it had snowed heavily at the venue, which was a nice surprise, especially Queenslanders who many had never seen or been in snow. Of course, the reaction was as people stepped off the buses the snowball fights started and became more intense as the amber fluid consumption increased.

Lindsay claimed he was responsible for the snow being available. Well done Lindsay Parke.

Leading up to the festival, Veterans were requested to forward articles to the Christchurch committee to feature in the festival program. I submitted the following. It is not completely my work as I believe it originated from an ex-Australian Rules player long gone. I like the article so I sat down and adjusted it where applicable to identify with our game - Rugby.

ONE MORE FESTIVAL

(Tasi Woodard. Queensland, Australia)

"I'm old and worn, I'm very slow, I can't run like I used to though
I have to play just one more season, don't ask me why you'd know the reason.
If you'd played the game just like mine, and carried the ball across the line
Or set up the try that drew the game, not thinking of the breaks, aches and pain.
I've broken every other bone, my ankle ligaments they've been torn
Knee cartilages taken out, no one can straighten up my snout.
My shoulders suffer dislocation, and Denco Rub with perspiration
Make my clothes smell awfully bad, to play again I must be mad.
My missus, she threw away my gear, but I'll play again have no fear
When I run, they'll all cheer when I'm carried off, we'll have a beer.

My ears have been torn, my heads been gashed, my lips been split, my ribs been smashed.
They put a steel pin in my knee.
I strap my ankle and shoulder; tape and shoulder pads will hold 'er.
My nose was never very nice, Denco Rub kills fleas and lice
Bones once broken mend so strong, why don't you all come along?
And see me running for a try, with blood pouring from my eye
Crash tackling them to stop a run, being trampled on, is lots of fun.
Steadying to kick in silence, crowds will only cheer for violence
We draw the game we're good as any, fun, friendship and fraternity with many.
They cart me off to the hospital
Beer, champagne, a celebration for yet another operation.
My missus says I'll play no more, perhaps she's right; I feel so sore
Come '95 my mates, for me they'll search, and my bloody
oath, I'll see you all in CHRISTCHURCH."

The 1995 Christchurch Festival was my last festival as I withdrew from Golden Oldies Rugby and committed myself to other rugby matters in 1996. Before leaving this social side of rugby I replaced myself from the position of Queensland Delegate to the Australian and International Board with Geoff Phillips from the Easts Toothless Tigers, who was a worthy replacement.

I wish to write further about the two most memorable Veterans Rugby festivals. The first to coincide with the 1988 World Expo hosted by the city of Brisbane, Australia over six months and the third World Masters Games once again hosted by Brisbane in 1994.

During my incumbency, Golden Oldies Rugby teams in southeast Queensland grew from eighteen teams to thirty-two from the New South Wales border, North to Kingaroy and West to Dalby. Individual teams hosted festivals in southeast Queensland three to four a year with many teams travelling long distances for just a one-on-one over a weekend. I attended mini-festivals and on occasions became an honorary member with city teams, travelling to country areas and meeting quite a few Country, ex-Queensland and occasionally Wallaby players.

Golden Oldies International Festivals are ongoing; such is their popularity that they will never die.

"Farewell to Veterans Rugby for me."

WORLD EXPO 88 Golden Oldies Rugby Festival Brisbane, Australia

The World Expo 88 went on for six months so picking the week for the rugby festival was critical, however the All Blacks were playing matches in Brisbane during the week of July 10-17. This made it a *no-brainer* as the two matches, the All Blacks versus Queensland, Sunday 10th of July and the All Blacks versus Australia, Saturday the 16th of July, would be included in the package deal for all Golden Oldies members.

Advertising the World Expo 88 Festival in the Queen Street Mall (Brisbane) during the lunch hour. Some players from the Vintage Maroons team were on display. L-R: David Logan, David L'Estrange, Geoff McLean, Jules Gherassimoff, Stan Pilecki, Llewellyn (Wally) Lewis and Team Manager Tasi Woodard.

Golden Oldies games were played on Monday, Wednesday and Friday. A visit to the World Expo 88 (tickets a part of the package) and a tour to Sanctuary Cove and Gold Coast were scheduled for Thursday. No world festival had a better package on offer than the World Expo 88 Festival. Two All Black matches attracted New Zealand teams like flies to a honey pot with also the opportunity to visit a World Expo. Sadly, more New Zealand teams attended the festival (thirty-two) than all the Australian teams and one team from Papua New Guinea (eighteen from Queensland, two from New South Wales and one from Victoria). Being responsible for the draw I had no alternative but to play New Zealand teams against one another on occasion, however only once during the festival. My other obligation was to raise a vintage Maroons team (below).

Vintage Maroons 1988
Back Row L-R: Mick Freeney, Geoff Richardson, Don Hosking, Peter Horton,
Stan Pilecki, Rick Trivitt, Barry Wood, Geoff McLean, Rod Norris, Paul McLean,
Des Connor, Jack Martin, Tasi Woodard (Team Manager)
Front Row L-R: Ivor Thomas, Mick Baker, Jules Gherassimoff, Geoff Shaw,
David Logan, Bob Rex, Tauto Raulini, Epi Bola
Players Absent from Photo: Chris Handy, Roy Nerichow, David Hillhouse, Richard
Marks, David L'Estrange, Lloyd Graham, Lewellyn (Wally) Lewis, Cyril Andrews
and Lyn Jones – All Queensland and many Australian representatives.

The Program for the Festival Week:

Sunday 10 July 1988:

Transfer to Ballymore for Queensland versus All Blacks match.

07:00 PM Opening function.

Monday 11 July:

09:00 AM Team March Past Ballymore.
10:30 Exhibition Match – Jet Set Vintage Maroons versus The New Zealand Originals. The New Zealand Originals featured many All Black representatives of years gone by including; Keith Nelson, Ross Smith, Grant Batty, John Hotop, Kevin Gimblett, Ken Grainger, Tom Johnson and Joe Kelly. Joe was the oldest Original member at seventy-six years of age (purple shorts) who was being opposed against the Vintage Maroons Wally Lewis who was also seventy-six.

A great confrontation was anticipated as both were having maiden games on Ballymore. A little on this game.

Wally Lewis had the distinction of kicking off the EXPO 88 Festival. Joe Kelly was the recipient of the kick-off and showing he had not lost it, swerved, fended off the defence, side-stepped would-be tacklers and scored his first try at Ballymore and the first for the festival. Wally Lewis not to be outdone by his rival, showing a clean pair of heels and elusive skills replied with his first try on Ballymore. Both seventy-six-year-olds then left the playing arena arm in arm to a huge ovation and no doubt, to enjoy some cool drinks following their Ballymore debuts.

Following the Exhibition Match, all teams were transferred to the respective club grounds for the first round of matches.

Tuesday 12 July:

Free day to explore Brisbane or visit the World Expo.

Wednesday 13 July:

The second round of matches was played at respective Brisbane club grounds.
I may mention that a special Golden Oldies Festival bar was set up at the Waterloo Hotel, where nightly events took place to catch up with old acquaintances and make new ones. Dancing and talent quests were held nightly.

Thursday 14 July:

AM: Teams transferred to Sanctuary Cove
PM: Teams transferred to Sea World and Jupiters Casino.

Friday 15 July:

The third round of matches was played at respective Brisbane club grounds
PM: Waterloo Hotel frivolities.

Saturday 16 July:

AM: Leisure or partake in the Golden Oldies Handicapped Golf Tournament.
PM: All teams transferred to Ballymore for Australia versus All Blacks Test match.
7:00 PM: Final function at Ballymore with a late return by coaches to hotel accommodation deeming the end of the festival. Sunday home.

———

It may be noted that Queensland XXXX Goldies President, the late Errol Smith was also the festival's organiser, backed by a large, dedicated committee, in making the World Expo 88 Rugby Festival such a success.

Perhaps the only disappointment was that Air New Zealand (the official Golden Oldies Rugby carrier) could not get one of the New Zealand teams to the festival until Monday the 11th of July. The team declined to attend.

———

WORLD MASTERS GAMES 1994 Brisbane, Australia

The first two World Masters Games were held in Canada (1985) and Denmark (1989) and it was reported that both events were financial disasters. No country in the northern hemisphere wanted to host the third World Masters Games so why not try the great all-around sporting nation in the southern hemisphere, Australia?

Adelaide was approached - not interested
Sydney was approached - not interested
Brisbane was approached - yes interested.

A delegation was raised in Brisbane representing both team and individual sports, etcetera. Brisbane is a sporting city and having previously successfully run a Commonwealth Games the city possessed all applicable venues to run sporting events of all classes. Now having successfully run a World Expo 88 Rugby Festival our XXXX Goldies committee based at and with their clubhouse on the Ballymore venue had many members, myself included who were Queensland Rugby Union (QRU) members so we approached the QRU committee for a meeting. We explained to them that Brisbane had the opportunity to host the third World Masters Games and with the QRU's support we would introduce Veterans Rugby into the World Masters Games. We could run it all at the one venue Ballymore, which had three grounds and with the games running for a week, we could easily run the concept. The QRU agreed to our proposal, however with one condition, we had to sell their product being of course Castlemaine Perkins XXXX … agreed.

So, with the support of the QRU, a delegation of Veterans Rugby along with other sporting representatives arranged a meeting with the Queensland Events Corporation (QEC) requesting their support for the games. QEC need only supply the sporting venues such as athletic, swimming, hockey, basketball, bike riding etcetera. Even Orienteering was requested and accepted and held in the ranges behind Enoggera Army Base and the Mt Cootha area. Seeing a world event was proposed and run by individuals of their sport, no QEC or Government elements would be involved. Cost-free and without any opposition, we were told we had QEC's total support to proceed. So worldwide advertising began.

Now I can only relate to the rugby portion of the third World Masters Games. Some committee members from the World Expo 88 Festival volunteered to run the concept. Our committee decided to run three competitions with the age groups 30 to 39, 40 to 49 and over 50s. No current representatives were permitted to play. Games were to be played throughout the week with the grand finals of the three age groups to be played on Saturday. Following the three-age group grand finals, we would have a Grand Masters match, Queensland versus New South Wales consisting of ex-Wallaby and State players. My involvement was to raise two teams, one being a Queensland Over 50s team and a Queensland Grandmasters team. The first was easy, letters were sent to all our Queensland Association teams requesting nominations with the emphasis on ex-representative players who were still playing within the Association.

The second was a little more complex, however with the assistance of the QRU contacts (with some personnel living interstate), we commenced to put together a team. New South Wales through their rugby union networks was to raise their State team.

The Myer Centre (Brisbane) was the main sponsor. The event was also sponsored by Travel World, Queensland XXXX, Drake Overload, Crown Paints, Quest, Rugby Products of Australia and Bob Kiri Site Construction.

Amazingly, forty-two ex-Internationals put their hands up to play. Obviously, for both teams, the opportunity for one more interstate contest was too much to ignore as this rivalry will never die. I wish to talk of three incidents of some interest and humour in raising these teams.

Incident #1: Ex-New South Wales and Wallaby halfback John Hipwell had been living and teaching at Mt Gravatt, Brisbane for some years and I extended an invitation for him to play for the Queensland Grandmasters team which he accepted. When the New South Wales selectors got wind of this, unbelievably the exchange became quite heated. So, they said to compromise, seeing Tony Shaw had been working in Sydney for some years for his company, New South Wales would play him. Within a day Tony rang up and demanded a Queensland maroon jersey be put aside for him as he would not be seen dead in a blue one. John Hipwell played for New South Wales and Tony Shaw for Queensland.

Incident #2: When rugby was still amateur any union player switching to rugby league was banned for life from rugby union. In the early eighties when I was Director of Coaching for Souths (Brisbane) and Michael O'Connor was playing for Teachers North (Brisbane), Queensland and Australia, he in 1982 switched to rugby league initially to the St George Club (Sydney) then to Manly (Sydney). Michael was banned from rugby forever.

In 1994 Michael was operating a surf shop in Noosa, Queensland. I rang Michael and put to him on his availability to play for the Queensland Grandmasters team.

He said, "He was banned from rugby and Ballymore."

I asked Michael, "Would you like to play with your old teammates at Ballymore?"

He replied, "I would love to meet and play with my old teammates again."

I smiled and said, "Michael you're in."

Michael O'Connor returned to Ballymore after an absence of twelve years.

Incident #3: New South Wales when seeing the team list after publication queried the selection of ex-All Black great winger Grant Batty. We explained that Grant had been living in Queensland for some years now and was so entrenched, that he was the coach for Brisbane Easts.

New South Wales reluctantly accepted his selection.

The Games:

As team nominations came rolling in, we were surprised to find two Russian teams and a team from Ukraine enrolling. Moving on a little; on the Sunday before Monday's first round of games, we entered Ballymore to find a third Russian team had arrived on Saturday night and having no accommodation booked, slept in the grandstand at Ballymore. Accommodation, registration and with a little adjustment of their age group competition they were made welcome. We had more than thirty teams worldwide for the Masters Games.

All the week's games, which were daily were open free to the public. Due to the crowds, the catering was most profitable and the QRU was making income from the sale of their product. On the Saturday of the three-age group grand finals, followed by the *'Grandmasters'* match Queensland verse New South Wales, admission was $2 for adults and $1 for children, students and pensioners, and $5 for a family. We were overawed as thousands flooded into Ballymore to view the day's four games.

The Over 50s final was between the Queensland team and the Canadian team with Queensland defeating Canada 12–3. The gold medals were presented by the Queensland Governor, Lineen Forde whom I knew is an ex-Canadian.

When presented with my medal, Lineen said, "Congratulations."

I replied, "It's great to be a Queenslander."

She in return with a lovely smile said, "It certainly is."

The victorious Queensland team with gold medals on display after the medal's ceremony. The medals were presented by Queensland Governor Lineen Forde. The Queensland Over 50s team drawn from twelve association teams became the first rugby team to win a gold medal in World Masters Games defeating Canada 12 – 3.

1994 World Masters
The medal bearers and oldest members of each team in the Over 50s
L-R: Anatoli Tumanov: - Russia – Bronze; Clem Marks: - Queensland – Gold
Larry (Dutch) Shultz: - Canada – Silver.

Following the Over 50s final so the format continued with the 40 to 49 final and then the 30 to 39 final. Ballymore had been slowly building up in spectator attendance from late morning. By the time the *Grandmasters* game was scheduled at 3:15 PM, we could not believe the thousands who flooded into Ballymore. Sporting contests between Queensland and New South Wales in Queensland will always attract crowds no matter at what level.

I requested Bob Templeton to attend the following photo of the Queensland Grandmasters team as quite a few of these players were coached under Bob in the late seventies and early eighties. They were proclaimed (by the New Zealand All Blacks management) to be the best provincial team in the world following a Queensland victory over the All Blacks during their Australian tour.

Queensland Grand Masters – 8 October 1994
Standing L-R: Bob Templeton, Stuart McGill (Manager NSW), Tony Darcy, David Cody, Tom Lawton, Nigel Holt, David Hillhouse, Peter Grigg, Peter McLean, Tony Shaw, Mark Loane, Dick Cocks, Grant Batty, Stan Pilecki, Epi Bola, Alex Pope, Tasi Woodard (Team Manager).
Sitting L-R: Chris Roche, Dennis Owens, Tim Lane, Andy McIntyre, Roger Gould, Jeff Miller, Steve Rowley, Geoff Shaw, Geoff Richardson, Mark McBain, David Logan, Michael O'Connor. Absent: Brendan Moon.

Players representing New South Wales were Glen Ella, Phil Crowe, Mick Martin, Brett Papworth, Ken Wright, Lloyd Walker, Phillip Cox, John Hipwell, Tony Melrose, Glen De Vanzo, Geoff Richards, Dominic Vaughan, Mark Harding, John Lambie, David Purll, Ross Reynolds, Simon Poidevin, Peter Fitzsimmons, Steve Williams, Topo Rodriguez, Sean Mooney, Geoff Didier and Peter Lucas.

—⟋⟋⟍—

The game was played in true Barbarians fashion with the emphasis on scoring tries. The pace of the game may have slowed a little, but the skills were still evident. Heard from a Canadian spectator, *"These guys could still represent Canada."*

The game produced eighty-six points much to the delight of the huge crowd. After games functions were held at all levels, new were friends made, old relations revived, and a week to remember.

—⟋⟋⟍—

I can only speak on behalf of the rugby content, however feedback from all other sporting competitions, which relates to a mini Olympics, saw the world's third International Masters Game as a huge financial success on all levels and in particular, the tourism cost-benefit and exposure for Queensland.

The world was watching as four countries applied to host the fourth World Masters Games with the USA being successful in its bid and Portland in Oregon being the host city.

It would be remiss of me not to mention the organisation committee in the rugby aspect of the games.

Convenor: Michael O'Callaghan

Members: Mark Asprey, John Barry, Artie O'Connell, Salty Eckel, John Hand, Col McInnes, Roy Nerichow, Bob Rex, John Simpson, Ivor Thomas, Gary Thornburn and Anita Wilkinson.

And a big thank you to the twenty-one referees.

—m—

Swedish Rugby:

How many Australians would know rugby is played in Scandinavia?

While still living in Brisbane a casual chat in a rugby office turned out for me representing Australia in a world side against a Swedish team to celebrate fifty years of rugby in Sweden in August 1994 to be played in Stockholm. The qualifications to represent were that all players had to be fifty years of age or older, still had to be participating in Veterans rugby and of course their availability. I qualified easily and was asked if I wish to be involved and represent Australia's participation. Ailsa and I love Scandinavia as we had been on two tours before travelling Scandinavia quite comprehensively, especially Norway, Denmark and Finland. As with other Scandinavian cities we love Stockholm so off we went leaving Brisbane Thursday night to Singapore, Copenhagen then on to Stockholm arriving Saturday afternoon for the Saturday night match (daylight to almost 11:00 PM).

On arrival at the playing venue, I was approached by the World Team Manager, *"You Tasi Woodard from Australia?"* I confirmed his question.

"Which side of the scrum do you play on?"

I replied, *"That I usually play on the loosehead side."*

"Well the French prop was here first and he insisted he plays on the loosehead side."

I replied, *"That I've had and would play on the tighthead side of the scrum no problem."*

So, our front row consisted of a Frenchman, our hooker on introduction confirmed that he had represented Southland (NZ Otago) and me, an Australian. A lot of countries were represented within the team, including England, Wales, Ireland, Scotland, Italy, Norway, Germany, South Africa, America and Argentina.

Our captain and the full-back, a Norwegian, was quite tall and athletic and I did become surprised at his talent in that position (another cultural rugby surprise - Norway rugby).

At the beginning of the game, Sweden was awarded a scrum. On scrum engagement I detected no power coming through from the Swedish scrum and my initial thoughts were, "Shit! This is soft." Their halfback put the ball in the scrum on our tighthead side and the ball remained momentarily in the centre of the tunnel. I wasn't sure if we should let them win their scrum or not (being friendly) however I said to my hooker, *"Want it?"*

"Shit yeah!" was the reply and as there was no power coming through from the opposition scrum I with my outside foot funnelled the ball back under my hooker's feet.

After the match, my hooker said, *"I represented Southland for the best part of a decade and can remember winning one tight head. I play in Sweden and I win seven in one game. They will never believe me at home."* Such was the deficiency in body mechanics in scrummaging, rucking and mauling by the Swedes, it became a very soft game.

By half time we were leading twenty-something to nil. I suggested during the break that our team should ease off a little and let them score a couple of tries as I felt the game could get out of hand score-wise. The team consented to my suggestion. Not to be humiliated, Sweden did make a comeback and the final score became a respectable 36-18 win for the visitors.

A huge photographic event took place after the game followed by a much larger engagement, mainly a seafood buffet with copious amounts of refreshments. Around midnight we were shuffled off to the most popular pub in Stockholm, which was ironically named the Boomerang Hotel - unbelievable. Such was the popularity of the drinking hole many of the patrons imbibed on the footpath surrounding this quite large establishment. I was ushered through the crowd to meet the hotel manager. Lo and behold she was a Tasmanian and she explained to me that all employees at the Boomerang Hotel were female backpackers only from New Zealand and Australia.

Following several more days of celebrations, I was requested to remain in Stockholm for the following weekend as Stockholm was the host city for the annual European Tens Rugby Festival. Needing to flee this continuing rugby fest celebrations and dry out I declined the offer, so Ailsa and I moved on to one of our favourite Scandinavian destinations, Norway. I left Stockholm with my playing jersey, a European Tens Rugby jersey and a Swedish plaque, which is mounted in my bar. One of the more enjoyable rugby events I've ever had the pleasure of participating in.

Sweden's National Over 50's Rugby Team

**Invitational International Over 50's Rugby Team consisted of players from
England, Wales, Scotland, Ireland, New Zealand, Australia, Italy, Germany,
USA, Spain, South Africa, France, Norway, Denmark and Finland.**

179

Left: After game presentations were made. L-R: Team Captains from
Norway, Sweden, myself (Invitational International) and the USA.
Right: They love their Rugby in Sweden; here the Player
of the Match (not I) gets his just rewards.

TEN

MY SPORTING CAREER

*"Bombardier Woodard. You are good at everything;
however, you will be a champion of nothing."*

So I was informed by my CO, a Lt. Colonel, not happy about seeing me stay in camp while the unit left for military exercises, which were usually at Tin Can Bay or Wide Bay, Queensland. I often remained at camp as I was involved in unit, task force, interservice or interstate sports. However, I must say the armed services do emphasize physical fitness, for individuals and especially their involvement in team sports. My CO was right, although I was up with the best at the service level, I never became a champion at any.

The Australian Army presented many sporting opportunities and participation was strongly urged by them. During my service career, I became involved in a range of sports from the most popular to the more orientated. My involvements included athletics, basketball, orienteering, tug-of-war, cricket, volleyball and badminton but the most consuming was rugby, where I had a constant involvement (excluding 1969/1971) in the twenty-six years of my service career from 1957 through to 1982.

1: My Illustrious Cricket Career

I never played competitive cricket outside of services competition. I was an all-rounder, a fair medium-pace bowler which was the stronger of the two disciplines, as I was a very average middle-order batsman. I considered myself a pretty ordinary cricketer so the following should make most readers feel better about themselves in such circumstances.

My only Representative Game - a Disaster:

During my time in the Army Wednesday afternoon was a designated sports day and individual units would play against each other in a competition applicable to that sport. In the early 1960's I was selected in a GOC's XI to play against the current Queensland Sheffield Shield side at Duncan

Oval in Enoggera. On arriving at Duncan Oval, the two teams were each split in half and then amalgamated to no doubt balance both teams.

I was pleased to be selected in the side that also had West Indian fast bowler Wes Hall in it however, it did not prevent me from being bowled for no score in a *golden duck* performance by another Queensland quick in Sandy Morgan. When it became our turn to field, I was given the ball and was quickly replaced after being smashed for twenty-six runs in two overs, not to bowl again during the match. So ended my only rep match in cricket no doubt having a line drawn through my name for a future GOC's XI.

A Memorable Win:

Later in 1965, I was captain/coach of the Wallaby rugby team in Malaya stationed at the RAAF base in Butterworth. Outside the airbase situated on the Malacca Straits and just north of Penang Island was located a servicemen's Boat Club. There were not many boats but a great and relaxing drinking hole for off-duty occasions and following rugby games on base. It was our favourite watering hole to rehydrate.

This boat club certainly had more members than our rugby team and on one occasion during a session, it was suggested the Boat Club should play the Wallabies team in a social game of cricket. Of course, who knocks back a challenge when mid-session of a social indulgence, so a game was organised for the weekend.

The Boat Club team won the toss elected to bat and scored one hundred and twenty-two runs all out. Sadly the Wallabies rugby team was dismissed for ninety-six runs. Back to the Boat Club, just the beautiful environment on the ocean makes one thirsty! As the night wore on with one team boasting of their magnificent victory and the other lamenting of their unlucky loss a rematch was organised however, the rematch was to be played for a keg of beer with the loser paying. Once again not one to back down on a challenge the return match was organised for the following weekend with much higher stakes.

The Wallabies batted first and this time we did manage to score a little over one hundred. Wayne Hall is my vice-captain in the Wallabies, who is RAAF personnel and a very good all-rounder in sports. Wayne and I opened the bowling. He took six wickets for four runs and I returned the figures of four wickets for six runs and with two byes the Boat Club were all out for twelve. An early ambush on the keg, which is a true account of the game.

I can now relate to another cross-code cricket contest. Moving onto the mid-seventies I was the captain/coach of the Regimental rugby team and after the season (both interunit competitions) the unit's Aussie rules team challenged our rugby team to a cricket match. Not only did the rugby team win, but I also contributed forty-nine runs, which was the highest scorer from both teams, and in taking three wickets was awarded the *Man of the Match*. This story doesn't stop here.

Some thirty years later (about 2006) now long retired from the army, living in Caloundra in Queensland, and at the ripe old age of sixty-one years took up golf and became a member of the Caloundra Golf Club. Upon joining and immediately after attaining a handicap, I automatically went into the veterans (over 50s) competition and soon got to know and play with a regular foursome. Now one of the foursomes was Dennis Greinke, who in his younger days was an outstanding opening batsman playing for Valleys, a club in the Brisbane Cricket Competition. Dennis was also in the Queensland Sheffield Shield cricket squad however in ten years he told me he never received a first XI cap.

One day during a round of golf the subject of cricket came up and I related to Dennis about the game described above saying, *"Dennis during a cricket match I was on forty-nine, the highest score I had ever achieved and the bowler came in delivering the ball. I hit it with the full face of the bat with the ball going to go back over the bowler's head, surely for four. The bowler proceeded down the pitch on his follow-through, leapt high into the air and fair dinkum the ball stuck in the ends of his fingers of one hand high over his head. I never scored a fifty in cricket,"* I sadly related.

"I know exactly how you feel Tasi," replied Dennis. *"I got out for one hundred and ninety-eight once."* Back to the golf game.

A Long Though Well Played 100:

I had to include this as I did achieve a ton in 2018 through a donating capacity, which started in 1962 and took me fifty-six years to complete. I was sent a thank you card of recognition and invited to attend a breakfast with my wife Ailsa by the Australian Red Cross. This was held at the Mooloolaba Surf Club in 2018 to recognise my ton.

I know I had donated more times than recognised as I was still in Malaya when Australia committed to the Viet Nam War and blood was becoming an urgent necessity. Malaya was a close neighbour to Vietnam and we were called on to donate blood regularly there. Whereas in Australia they request giving whole blood every three months, in Malaya we were donating every six weeks. I do not remember the number of donations I supplied, however, I do know that I have recorded a *100 + … Not Out.* So ends the highs and mostly the lows of my cricket career.

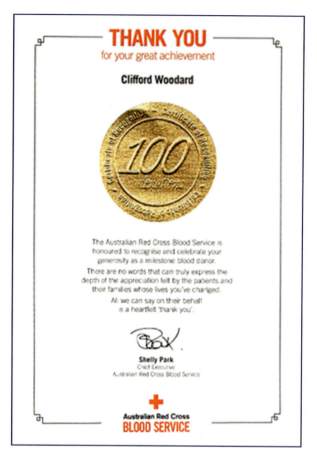

2: Australian Rules Football

Being born on King Island (Tasmania), my elder brother and I were indoctrinated into the only football played there, which was Australian Rules. Initially, King Island had three teams Grassy, Currie and Norths. Though following WWII, a Soldiers Settlement Farming Scheme had been put aside for veterans at Mount Stanley thus as their population grew a fourth team was raised.

Grassy colours were green with a gold 'V', Currie adopted Essendon colours being the famous black with the red 'V', Norths were maroon with a gold 'V' and Mount Stanley wore the Richmond colours of black and gold. My brother played for Currie while I enlisted with Norths. Our biggest event for the week was the Aussie rules match eagerly looked forward to it on Saturday mornings followed by the A-grade game. My football virtually ceased on moving to Tasmania until I attended the Ulverstone High School and represented against other schools on the northwest coast and Circular Head. On leaving school as a fourteen-year-old and gaining employment on the Tasmanian Government Railway (TGR) at Smithton, I played for Trowutta (in the Circular Head minor competition). At fifteen years I played my first senior game for Smithton, the senior competition in Circular Head, which was a four-team competition consisting of Smithton, Stanley, Forrest and Irishtown.

**As a fifteen-year-old I played in my first A grade match for Smithton
in the Circular Head competition; myself front row far right.**

I left Smithton and moved to Launceston and through workmates, I played for Rocherlea in the East Tamar competition up until I joined the army.

After joining the army, I learned that other football codes existed (I had previously heard of soccer through my father) however was oblivious to the codes of rugby and rugby league. When I left the recruit training battalion (Kapooka, New South Wales) and transferred to North Head in Sydney I found the Australian rules players posted and training at North Head. As it was their nearest club, they all played for North Shore in the Sydney Australian Rules competition. I fitted into the North Shore side in 1957 which in that year was experimenting with the sixteen-a-side competition which was eventually axed.

North Shore team in 1957, myself standing far right. Note sixteen-a-side only.

When posted to Brisbane in 1960 I had a close friend whom I had played Aussie Rules in Sydney with. He was originally from Brisbane and his local team in the Brisbane competition was Windsor (later to become Windsor-Zillmere) and he successfully talked me into playing for the club. These were the last games of Aussie Rules I played as I was well and truly converted to rugby by the army in Sydney from 1957 onwards.

I take this opportunity to pay a tribute to my older brother Richard (Dick) Woodard who excelled in Aussie rules. Dick was by far a superior player to me, who earlier in his career following his move from King Island, Tasmania did not take him long to be an outstanding player in the Northwest Football Union (NWFU) competition. From his early days in the NWFU, he was invited to Melbourne in the off-season to trial with Victorian Football League (VFL) clubs. He had offers from Collingwood, Essendon, South Melbourne and Carlton, however being a country boy, he utterly despised the 'big smoke' and vowed, *"I will never leave Tasmania to live in that environment."* So, Dick spent his days in Tasmania playing at all the levels of representative football that the State had to offer.

I left Tasmania at seventeen never to return permanently and rugby became my forte. I know in my mind, that if my brother had ever converted to rugby, he would have excelled as a five-eight. He was an athlete who possessed all the skills for that position; fast, a magnificent stepper, outstanding ball skills and could kick off either foot.

Dick was aged only sixty-three when I attended his funeral in May of 2000. I had only seen him twice in forty years, so his old football team members from the many Tasmanian club sides who attended his passing, when introduced to me were a little more than surprised, *"We didn't know he had a brother, who did you play for?"*

In answer, I could only state, *"You wouldn't understand"* and left it at that.

Our eldest sister Veronica kept a scrapbook on Dick's football career in Tasmania. It took me all day to read through it before I could appreciate and realise his outstanding sporting career playing Australian Rules. I am glad I left Tasmania as I would have been known as that other Woodard.

3: Athletics

I was a reasonable 400-yard sprinter. Although not fast, I could run at my top pace over that distance without waning, and almost always caught and passed my opposition in the final fifty to sixty yards such was my endurance. The most memorable races I was always selected for were the mile medley teams, consisting of 1 x 800-yard runner, 1 x 400-yard runner (myself) and 2 x 200-yard runners. I could never understand why this race was ever dropped from athletic meetings and especially the Olympics as to me the mile medley was an exciting relay race involving runners in different distant categories.

4: Basketball

I only took up basketball at service level to keep up a standard of fitness during the off-football season. At service level we were not playing against the sport of giants however, I was always a defensive player as I had exceptional aerial ball skills and anticipation. This I can put down to my upbringing in Australian rules which benefited me greatly, however, my failure in the sport was that I was never a very good basket shooter.

Following our unit's withdrawal from Viet Nam, a gun battery and HQ Battery from the regiment was relocated at Wacol and our gun battery was posted to Enoggera. Our unit was located right next to the huge gymnasium at Enoggera and as I was the senior NCO in our fractured and rebuilding unit, held two PT sessions a day; first thing in the morning and the last period of the day.

Having an element of basketball players within our small numbers I entered a team from within our battery to represent the regiment in the Southeast Queensland Services basketball competition. I'm neither an outstanding basketball player nor a coach, however amongst our ranks and the last of the National servicemen was a Victorian who was by far the most outstanding player in the whole competition and could score from all over the court. In every game we played, he would shoot up to 60% of our points. The Victorian and he alone won the grand final as all we had to do was gain possession and get the ball to him. I believe that the grand final in 1971 could have been my last competitive basketball match.

In later years my eldest son took to this sport and by far excelled my capabilities, not only as a player but also as a very successful coach. Even though considered short, Norman played representative basketball at junior and senior levels and during this time, after gaining his Australian Coaching Accreditation coached representative teams also at both the junior and senior levels within State and National competitions and events. Just like his old man he enjoyed a taste of international play at the 2005 World Masters Games in Edmonton, Canada. Upon his return, he commented, *"It was a great experience and wonderful fun. Even though I have been a part of a team in winning six Australian Masters gold medals it was quite humbling against the might of the Americans, Canadians and Europeans in not being able to win a single game."*

5: Tug-of-War

In services sport, tug-of-war was and perhaps still is a high-rating team sport. Army team sports are encouraged and during my time tug-of-war was competitive within the unit, between units and even at the interservice level. In finalising a tug-of-war team a lot of emphases is put on many key factors including weight, strength, coordination and endurance and much of the training existed where it would be one on one competition. I excelled in factors where others failed. I was neither heavier nor stronger than a lot of my competitors vying for a place in the eight-man team, however, I had endurance and this is where I excelled. More importantly, as I was later to learn in my latter rugby career, I possessed outstanding body mechanics. These two factors alone elevated me to a point where on many occasions, much bigger men were pissed off with my ability to outgun them at one on one tug-of-war. I succeeded within the unit, against units, and advanced to represent Army at interservice. I found tug-of-war was character-building, not only as an individual but more so at a team level.

A Tug-of-War Team
Teams have the shortest at the front and tallest at the rear.
The army team at Wacol in 1962 (L-R): Tex Laxton, Ken Buhman, Dick Kanga, Laurie
Thompson, Ron Thompson, Tasi Woodard, Rex Taylor and Buck Rodgers. Coach – Pat Squib.

Other sports including volleyball and badminton I played only at an inter-unit level more for fitness benefits, however, I did enjoy the competitive spirit of the unit. Orienteering was not only a fitness challenge but also tested one in military map reading which I enjoyed and taught at the unit level.

Ah … The Army life is great for allrounders.
"Good at everything, however a champion at nothing."

ELEVEN

SPORTING ODDITIES

This chapter consists of memorable content of sporting greats, events and incidents that I happened to be fortunate enough to witness, have had some involvement with, or attended during my life experiences.

1: Outstanding Greats of Their Game

Rugby League:

At the age of seventeen, I was posted to North Head, Sydney from Kapooka. Among my fellow young soldiers was a friend in Don Watkins, a Sydney-bred man whose parents lived at Randwick. One weekend at the School of Artillery he asked, *"Have you ever seen a game of rugby league."*

"No!" was my reply, *"But since joining the Army I have heard of it."*

"Well," Don replied, *"I want to take you to the Sydney Cricket Ground (SCG) not far from home to see a match then come home for dinner."*

So Don escorted me to the SCG to watch my first game of rugby league which just happened to be St George (The Dragons) versus Wests (The Magpies). Don was explaining the game to me as one specific player took my eye, who was just carving up the opposition.

I asked Don, *"Who is that number three?"*

"That's Reg Gasnier."

The Immortal Reg Gasnier.

Premierships 1960-1965
NSWRL Player of the Year: 1960, 1962, 1965
NSW Rugby League Team of the Century
Australian Rugby League Team of the Century
Kangaroo Tours: 1959-60, 1963-64, 1967-68 and as Australian Captain in 8 Tests.
So watching my first game of rugby league I was to witness one of the all-time greats and I will always remember his outstanding exhibition of running rugby league.

Gasnier was nicknamed Puff the Magic Dragon and The Prince of Centres for his high-quality play and so deservedly an Immortal.

Australian Rules Football:

As mentioned in another chapter, either in 1965 or 1966 the Geelong Australian Rules team came to Penang, Malaya for their after-season tour and played a RAAF team at Butterworth. The Geelong team was led by and captained by the great Polly Farmer. Fortunately, I was in a position to see the game and witness another great champion from a different code.

The magnificent Polly Farmer flying high for a big mark.

Farmer was a revolutionary player and an inspiration to generations of indigenous footballers. In 1953, at the age of eighteen, he played the first of 176 games for East Perth and in 1956 he won the first of three Sandover Medals awarded to the fairest-and-best player in the West Australian Football League (WAFL).

Farmer then travelled east and played 101 games for Geelong, captaining the club from 1965 to 1967, winning a premiership medal in 1963 and establishing himself as the finest ruckman to have played the game. He then returned to play for West Perth. Farmer was named best and fairest in ten of his nineteen seasons of football, earning the accolade at each of the three clubs where he played. As well to his three Sandover Medals, he was runner-up for the Brownlow Medal when playing at Geelong and was named to the All-Australian team on three occasions.

2: David Foster

Whilst talking of greats I need to mention David Foster, a unique personality in his chosen sport. Following Australian rules, woodchopping is one of the next popular sports within Tasmania. The timber industry in Tasmania was a massive business having thousands employed within it. For most Tasmanians growing up with an axe in their hands from a very young age was a part of the family chores which was initially on the home wood heap.

Tasmania has produced many State and Australian champions holding the majority of world records between them. One specific family from the 1950s and 1960s was the Youds with seven brothers and six of them axemen. Merv, Doug, Rex and Ray held almost all the world records between them in the different categories of competitive woodchopping. Their father was also a well-known axman, who unfortunately was killed in a timber industry accident.

International meets are arranged mainly between the countries of Australia, New Zealand, the USA and Canada. Australia dominated these events with many of the team members being Tasmanians. I had the opportunity to meet and spend some time with the great David Foster, who is considered one of the all-time greats of woodchopping and a legend within the sport.

My sister Veronica, who was married to Ted Keen (both now deceased) lived all their married life in Latrobe. Ted had chopped competitively for a few years and considered more than average started competing against the best such as the likes of David Foster, who he knew quite well. David was appointed to run the Tasmanian Axemens Hall of Fame and Museum of the great axman through their history, with the museum situated in Latrobe on the northwest coast of Tasmania. On visiting my sister in Latrobe earlier in this century I requested them to take my wife Ailsa and myself to the Axemens Hall of Fame. When we arrived at the museum Ted introduced me to David and we went into rather a long discussion on the subject of woodchopping. David Foster is a very large man, six foot five tall and weighing some twenty-three stone and the greatness of this man is he's the only sportsman in the world to have won a thousand (yes one thousand) championships in his given sport. This occurred at 3:15 PM on Thursday the 16th of April 1998 at the Royal Easter Show in Sydney. David's wife Jan informed me since 1998 up until our meeting had won quite a few more and was still very competitive.

I had watched David chop on numerous occasions and where great axeman would be handicapped twenty-two seconds, such was his greatness that his handicap in some events went out to thirty-six seconds and he would still win. It may be noted that David's father George was the World Champion of Champions in 1970.

—⋙—

I feel the following introduction by R. F. Edwards in the book *The Power of Two - The David Foster Story* should be quoted in this book.

"David Foster is arguably the greatest sporting champion the world has ever seen, in any sport in any era. With each blow of his wood chopping axe, he produces more power than the world's greatest hammer throwers, with the balance and poise of a Nureyev, the agility of a gymnast and a delivery speed three times faster than that of Muhammad Ali in his prime, which is why David Foster has been the World's Champion Axman for an unprecedented twenty years.

A giant in his chosen sport he is also a giant amongst men, of immense stature and power with appetites to match an infectious lust for life. David is a living legend in the wood chopping world and a much-loved icon in his native Tasmania."

Left: David was presented the Order of Australia Medal by Sir Phillip Bennett in 1991. David was also awarded the Australian Sports Medal in 2000 and the Centenary Medal in 2001.
Right: David is hard-hitting the 300-millimetre standing block at Footscray, Victoria. He set a new world record with 12 blows in 28 seconds.

My wife Ailsa throws out a challenge to the great David Foster. David would not accept the challenge.

3: Rugby Union - 2 GR8 8's

During my military and civilian rugby experiences, I was fortunate to have had a relationship with two great ex-International No.8's, one within the services and the other while being Director of Coaching with Southern Districts Rugby Union Club, Brisbane.

The Federation of French Rugby (FFR) each year names a World XV team and during the seventies named each of these players as a No.8 in their selected World XV in consecutive years. I talk of the much-loved Fijian Epi Bola Waqatabua (shortened to Epi Bola) and similarly, Sione Mafi Pahulu (always known as Sione Mafi).

Epi Bolawaqatabua:

Epi first represented his country in 1963, being Fiji's 171st Internationally capped rugby player and is equal sixth with most matches as a captain for his country being twelve from 1969 to 1973. These were against Australia (1972), New Zealand Māori (1970 and 1973), Papua New Guinea (1969), Samoa (1963), Solomon Islands (1969), Tonga (1963 and 1972), Wales (1969 in Wales and Fiji in 1963 and 1973) and New Zealand (1970). Epi Also coached Fiji.

In 1964 Epi attended the University of Queensland, Brisbane as a dental student. Some years later when Epi and I were involved with rugby he related to me, when the University team commenced training in early 1965, I attended the session and I was asked, *"What position do you play?"*

I replied, *"No.8"*, then was told to find another club as Mark Loane is the No.8 here!

Epi went to the Brothers Rugby Club and became their No.8 and he would have been delighted to be a part of the Brothers team that defeated the University team in the grand final in 1966, thumping them 36-9. From there Epi captained both Brothers and the Queensland team.

During the mid-seventies, Epi became a fully qualified dentist and joined the Australian Army as a dentist and rank of Captain. Although based at Enoggera, he had surgery at Wacol Army Camp (1 Field Regiment RAA) and visited our unit once a week. As I was the captain/coach of the unit team he asked me could he represent the regimental team in the midweek all Services and Police competition. I was also the coach of the Queensland Army and the Queensland Combined Services teams, so I wanted his rugby service.

Epi eventually captained the Queensland Army and Combined Services teams. When I became a coach in the Australian Services Rugby Union (ASRU) from 1976 through to 1978, he also became captain of ASRU.

He eventually retired from the Army and worked for the Queensland Government as the flying dentist for all of the Cape York Peninsula. I would receive postcards from Cape York places I had never heard of. Epi purchased his dental surgery in Cairns, North Queensland and when visiting, I would stay with Epi and his lovely wife Manu.

Sadly, Epi passed away in Cairns on the 24th of May 2018. Epi was selected in the Brothers Brisbane Team of the Century. On one occasion while staying with Epi in Cairns, he gave me the following photo. This was taken at Brothers Rugby Club in Brisbane of Brothers players who had been International captains.

Brothers players who have been International Captains.
L-R: Tony Shaw (Australia), Epi Bola (Fiji), John Eales (Australia), Paul McLean (Australia), Rod McCall (Australia) and Des Connor (New Zealand and Australia).

Sione Mafi:

Sione was Tonga's 151st Internationally capped rugby player. He debuted against New Zealand Māori at Christchurch on the 16th of August 1969. Sione was ranked seventh with the most matches as a captain for his country being eight from 1973 to 1975.

In Australian Rugby's biggest upsets in history, Tonga captained by Sione turned the first Test hiding around to defeat the Wallabies and square the 1973 series. Sione scored two tries in the history-making match-winning 16-11 in a boil-over.

In the mid-seventies, the Brisbane-based Souths Rugby Club, brought to Australia some of this Tongan International team to bolster their team within the Brisbane competition, including Sione Mafi, Fa'aleo Tupi, Fatai Kefu (father of Queensland and Australian No.8 Toutai Kefu), Niuselu Fakauho and Saimone Vaea.

I first met Sione when I became Director of Coaching with Souths in 1980. I had the greatest respect for Sione and his Tongan players and did cement a very healthy relationship with them. It did not take long to realise he was the mouthpiece for his people and the large Tongan community treated him respectfully as their unofficial mayor and leader.

In 1980 with Queensland's No.8 Mark Loane spending time in South African Rugby with Western Province Sione did represent Queensland in Mark's absence.

Sadly, Sione passed away with his funeral being held on the 22nd of December 2010 at the Tongan Park Uniting Church, South Brisbane. I wondered why the service was to commence so early at 9:00 AM and found that this Tongan funeral was to take four hours. A front pew was reserved for me and Mick Baker (ex-Queensland and Souths hooker and also the player Souths sent to Tonga to recruit the Tongans). Sione's coffin lay on the floor in front of our pew with the lid open and Sione looking at his best. It was a full house with the Tongan community in attendance. Such was the respect for the man that the Tongan players who were in Sione's team that defeated Australia were flown in from Tonga. They were dressed in national tradition, which looked impressive. A Tongan children's choir performed and believe me, all Tongans when singing are so harmonious. A representative from Tonga's winning team in 1973 spoke for quite some time on behalf of their team.

The Australian Rugby Union had requested Geoff Richardson (ex-dual International) and the Australian five-eight during that 1973 match to attend and respond. Geoff is a very well-educated man and spoke highly of Sione and his team and was well applauded for his presentation. Following the funeral, we travelled out to the Souths Rugby Union Club where it was great to have a few drinks and catch up with the Tongans who previously played for Souths.

I still have in my possession the Order of Service for Sione's funeral however, I cannot understand a word of it as it is all in the Tongan language, though a lasting memento to a great person, Tongan and rugby player.

I feel fortunate and honoured to have had a very special relationship with two great players from South Pacific countries.

4: Perfection

Having attended three National Coaching courses under the ARFU and being involved as a rugby coach periodically from 1960 to 1997 in both services and civilian rugby, I consider myself well credentialled to recognise the outstanding and greats of the game.

From a coaching point of view, it does not take long to identify the weaknesses of players. Once noted, I would direct them to practice in these areas, while still maintaining and refining their strengths. This not only developed them into better players but also enhanced the strength of the team. There is no such thing as the perfect player however, there are many who almost arrive at the zenith of perfection and one player who in my opinion I believe rises and stands above the rest in the perfection stakes is Michael O'Connor.

Michael played for Queensland and Australia during rugby's amateur period then turned his hand to rugby league. In those days, if a player turned to a professional career such as rugby league, then his name amongst the hierarchy became a dirty word to the extent, that he would be banned from all rugby venues. Michael's rugby career included twelve tests for Australia and now was over by the age of twenty-two when he joined the St George Rugby League Club in Sydney before moving to Manly, also a Sydney club within that competition.

The great dual International Michael O'Connor.

When I became Director of Coaching with Souths in 1980, Terry Doyle around the same time became CEO of Queensland Rugby Union and we struck up a friendly relationship and did travel on rugby tours together.

In the early eighties, I was at Ballymore and dropped in to have a coffee with Terry and the conversation went thus, *"Tasi. Have you heard the bad news of Michael O'Connor's defection to rugby league?"*

"Terry. The rumour has been around for some time," I replied.

"Well it's official; he's gone and he's mad."

"Why do you say he's mad Terry," I asked?

"He will never make it," was Terry's reply.

"Terry, Michael is the most skilled player in either code and he will be the next dual International," I stated.

"No! He will never make it," was Terry's final say on the matter.

The following year after Michael's League debut he was selected in turn for the Sydney City versus NSW Country match, the NSW State of Origin team and as an Australian Rugby League International. I recall one State of Origin match, the headlines read 'O'Connor 18 – Meninga 2' as

Michael O'Connor scored all of NSW's points. Following his success in Rugby League, Terry Doyle insisted I never mention the topic again of Michael O'Connor.

After being barred from rugby union I invited Michael back to Ballymore to represent *Queensland Grand Masters* versus *New South Wales Grand Masters* as the final rugby match of the third World Masters Games (Brisbane 1994) where between the two teams forty-four ex-Internationals were involved.

It is recognised that there are twenty-two individual skills in the great game of rugby and Michael came close to mastering them all.

5: An Early Meeting with a Future Australian Captain

During the mid-eighties, I was land clearing in Upper Brookfield, Brisbane and maintaining two other properties for the owners of EGR Plastics. Located at Salisbury in Brisbane, EGR are the initials for Edward the father and his two sons Greg and Rod, who came from Victoria and set up the company. All three were staunch Australian Rules supporters and I believe foundation members for the then Brisbane Bears, which later became the Brisbane Lions.

Rod owned the property at Upper Brookfield which there was a rather large hill. So he had the top of the hill demolished to build a large house and later added a swimming pool and tennis court to it. While involved with ground maintenance I was also land clearing it from rubble and hillsides over quite a time.

I was working the day Rod's wife Jenny, a very attractive English lady came home with their first child. After alighting from a taxi Jenny called me over, *"Tasi. Come over and see my baby."*

I ceased work and went over to accompany Jenny as she pulled back the baby's shawl and exposed the boy. *"This is my son"*, she proudly announced.

After admiring the baby for some time, I stated, *"Jenny, we might be able to make a rugby player out of him."*

Jenny being very English replied, *"He may well be a soccer player."*

Knowing his father Rod and family were staunch Australian rules fans, my suggestion would be third in the possibilities of a potential football code player.

Jenny and Rod's baby grew up to be the captain of the Queensland University rugby team, the Queensland Reds, leading them to their 2011 Super XV championship against the Canterbury Crusaders and finally the Australian Wallabies. The baby was James Horwill.

6: Great Rugby Athletes

There comes a time when rugby produces some outstanding players, however periodically along with above-average players there emerge great athletes. In my association with rugby, above all others, two outstanding rugby athletes come to mind. Both ex-Australian Captains, one a forward and one a back.

I refer to lock John Eales, arguably Australia's greatest lock and centre Jason Little, who was known as the elegant centre.

John Eales:

At school, John played rugby, cricket, basketball and athletics, showing promise in all of them. His cricket was good enough to keep Matthew Hayden out of the First XI and he spent two years in the rugby First XV.

In 1990 his first year of club rugby, John won the Rothmans Medal as the best and fairest player in the Brisbane competition. John made the Queensland Team in 1991 (now twenty-one years of age). Wales was his first opponent and to the surprise of everyone, Queensland won 35-24. Ironically, his first Test match was against Wales where he paired in the second row with his clubmate Rod *Slaughter* McCall. John went on to play 97 matches for Australia (86 Tests) and 112 matches for Queensland.

Some of John's records read:

Most successful Test Captain in the history of Australian Rugby;

Captained Australia on 60 occasions (55 times in Test matches) the most as a forward;

Scored 173 points for Australia, only one of twelve Australians to score 100 or more international career points and the only forward to do so;

Is the highest-scoring forward in test rugby history;

Retired as the most capped lock forward in world rugby (86), with 84 Test appearances in that position (his other 2 Tests were as a No8);

By 1999 he was only one of five players, which included Dan Crowley, Tim Horan, Jason Little (all Queenslanders) and Phil Kearns to win the Rugby World Cup on two occasions, there are only twenty-one players who have achieved this to date since its inception in 1987;

Is one of only 21 players to have represented the Queensland Reds in 100 or more state games;

Scored a total of 402 points in the Super 12 competition for the Queensland Reds with no forward scoring more points than John in the competition's history;

Nobody was the nickname bestowed upon John Eales by the rugby world, because as they say nobody's perfect, which the majority always witnessed when he played.

Along with John Thornett, he was entitled to be respected as The Captain of Captains.

Jason Little:

Jason was a product of the Darling Downs, a regional area in Queensland and at Toowoomba Grammar School he showed that he was an exceptional all-around student-athlete. Jason spent two weeks in Los Angeles representing Australia at the World Junior Athletics Championships, also played in the Australian Under 17s Rugby Team and was an outstanding cricketer.

In junior athletics, Jason represented Queensland in the Interstate Schools Athletics Carnival which was hosted by Western Australia. At fifteen, he won the high jump for Queensland at a height, that would have won him a bronze medal at the Rome Olympics.

Toowoomba had never won the GPS (Greater Public Schools – but refers to elite Private Schools) cricket title until Jason was at the school and then won it twice.

A teacher at the school told him at this critical period of his life, *"Well to be perfectly honest Jason, I think you're a better cricketer than you are a rugby player and I believe you've got a better long-term future in cricket than any other sport."*

Fortunately, Jason ignored this advice going on to become one of Australia's greatest centres and in his partnership with Tim Horan, who was also a product from the Darling Downs, was respected throughout the world. Jason's first test for Australia was in France however his first test on home soil was at Ballymore versus the South African Boks.

I had become good friends with Jason's parents Ray and Pat and before this test match, they had called me from the Darling Downs and arranged to meet me at Ballymore (as I was a QRU member) as they were bringing Jason's grandmother with them whom I had never met.

At the same time as this match, the Australian Cricket Team was playing an Ashes Series in England. On arriving at Ballymore and meeting his grandmother I said, *"You must be proud to be seeing Jason representing Australia in Rugby?"*

Her first words to me were, *"He should be in England playing Cricket."*

Jason played 92 matches for his country (75 Tests) and those who saw him in action marvelled at the rhythm of this gifted athlete and as such was known as the elegant centre. At test level he was a natural, playing with fluidity and grace either at inside centre, outside centre or wing and all equally well. Jason captained his country.

Jason Little makes a break with John Eales in support during Australia's 53-7 Test win over Argentina at Ballymore, Queensland in March 1995.

7: Great Foresight

In the late eighties, the Brisbane-based Souths Rugby Union Club brought five teenagers down from the Darling Downs. The players Tim Horan, Jason Little, Damien Smith, Brett Johnstone and Garrick Morgan all went on to represent Queensland and Australia.

With locals Tom and Rob Lawnton, Dan Crowley and Toutai Kefu, Souths dominated club rugby in Brisbane for many years. Club history records that Souths' front row of Rob and Tom Lawnton along with Dan Crowley represented both Queensland and the Australian Wallabies.

8: South America with the Queensland Reds

1989 saw a four-week tour by the Queensland rugby team to South America, which included seven matches.

John Connolly was appointed Queensland coach in 1988 and the South American tour was his first with the Reds. This was the first time I met John following his appointment, who later was to become the Wallabies coach.

The visit to South America was a March preseason tour, which consisted of many new faces in the Queensland squad. The itinerary consisted of six provincial games in Argentina and one game in Santiago against Chile. The game versus Chile became a very political affair, which ended up a fiasco, however, the visit to Chile was one of great interest and highly educational.

Departing Sydney on the 1st of March by Aerolineas Argentinas Airlines we endured a direct fourteen-hour flight to the Argentine capital. On our second night in Buenos Aires, we had a beef night in a well-known restaurant where to our surprise a huge beast was rotating on the spit in the window. Now the main entertainment in Argentina is the evening meal, which does not commence until after 10:00 PM and will carry through to the early hours of the morning. We sat down at huge wooden tables where the entertainment began with wine and entrees.

Frank Burnett (the CEO of Castlemaine Perkins - Queensland XXXX) who was with us on tour and I became very good friends, and he urged me to get into the wine. The empty wine bottles were replaced immediately as would water carafes in Australian restaurants.

I told Frank, *"Wine took a toll on me and if I was to overindulge, I would suffer for several days."*

"This will not act on you Tasi," was his reply. So reluctantly I indulged and the later the night became the more of the wine passed over my lips.

The meal was very generous with large lumps of beautiful beef that kept being replaced on our table as it was consumed, including testicles as nothing is wasted. I cannot remember returning to our hotel however later on in the morning when I awoke, I was waiting for the headaches to start, though the terrible mouth taste was absent and remarkably I was feeling fine. When Frank later asked how I felt, I told him I could not believe my healthy state. *"Why is this?"* I asked.

Frank explained that in Argentine they do not add preservatives, colours or additives into their wines.

Later to my surprise with inflation so rife in Argentine, one could purchase wine for bottom shelf prices at $0.60, middle-range $0.90 and top-shelf wine for about $1.20 a bottle. Needless to say, I became a wine buff for the next month purchasing top-shelf wine by the carton for travel. I may add that Argentine beer is also a very nice beverage. While on the subject of Frank Burnett; no matter where and when we arrived at game destinations, our favourite drop of XXXX beer was on hand - great organiser Frank.

Sights we saw in Buenos Aires included the Family Crypts all of thirty acres in central city (for the rich only) and La Boca being the port. Spanish traditions are inherent within the city of some twelve million, closing down from 10:00 AM to 2:00 PM for siesta. It's hard to imagine a big city with so many people and hardly anyone to be seen during this period with shops closed and the electricity turned off.

A feature in the city is the liberator General San Martin Square. Statues of General San Martin are in every city in Argentina and also in Chile. He liberated South America from the Spanish in the early 19th century over twelve years with huge armies that were always growing bigger with the liberation of the continent.

What Christ the Redeemer sees when looking down on Rio de Janeiro.

Following game one at Mar Del Plata it was off to Rio de Janeiro for four days, flying from Buenos Aires to Rio via Sao Paulo, the city with the biggest population on the continent being some sixteen million. Of course, we did all the touristy things in Rio including up Corcovado Mountain to the monument of Christ the Redeemer.

We caught two cable cars to get to the top of Sugarloaf Mountain and on looking back to Rio, the city geographically is a beautiful city, however at the time appeared to lack City Councils as down in the city proper it was quite filthy.

L-R: Myself, Frank Burnett and Chris Handy with ladies. I captioned this photo, *'I only caught one this big.'*

**Left: The beautiful aspect from The Lagoon with Sugarloaf Mountain in the background.
Right: Chris Handy with 1.2 million cruzados for the cost
of lunch - approximately AUD 600 at the time.**

Following another game, it was off to the Iguazu Falls on the Argentina side. From the plane on the approach, you could see a huge amount of mist rising out of the jungle, due to the collective forces from the falls. The falls are spectacular and one can walk amongst them on the Argentina side and look down on them from the Brazilian side. The falls are part of the Parana River, which the three countries of Argentina, Brazil and Paraguay border.

**The Iguazu Falls is a spectacular series of powerful individual waterfalls.
This photo is taken on the Brazilian side where you can view the extent of the falls.**

Back to Buenos Aires then onto beautiful Mendoza for the game Queensland versus Cuyo.

Mendoza is at the foot of the Andes where General San Martin raised his army and crossed the Andes liberating Chile then onto Peru and Ecuador for their liberation following Argentina 1822-1834. Whereas we flew into Mendoza we crossed the Andes by bus. The road followed the route forged by General San Martin's Army early in the 19th century.

Liberator General San Martin Square – Buenos Aires, Argentina.

Reaching the heights of the Andes we did experience a light snowfall. Arriving in Chile's capital Santiago on the 9th of March our hotel overlooked Military Square, the Presidential and Government headquarters.

Our view of Military Square from lodgings at Hotel Carrera.

Our visit to Chile saw us exposed to two controversies; one political and the other sporting.

The Political Controversy:

In 1970 the US organised the assassination of Chilean President Salvador Allende, who didn't believe in the holy objectives of American foreign policy. The US replaced Allende with Augusto Pinochet, which led to mass kidnappings, detention, torture and murder to which even today some thirty thousand Chileans, who disappeared during his presidency have unknown places of finality. Pinochet, in the typical style of a dictator with the total support of the Army, ruled with the point of the bayonet or bullet and a massive army of the secret police. The Chilean public suffered with hardly a family not suffering from a member's disappearance. After suffering from his dictatorship and brutal regime for years, Pinochet promised the Chilean people free elections on Saturday the 11th of March 1989. Well here we were in the centre of Santiago on the 11th of March 1989 with the city teeming with armed military and Armoured Personnel Carriers (APCs) and from our hotel, you could observe machine gun post on top of the high-rise buildings, which overlooked Military Square and Government HQ.

Armed military in Military Square in front of the Government HQ with the Presidential House in the background.

It was in this building where the former President Allende was ruthlessly machine-gunned to death. The armed presence was obvious on walking around the city. There were no civilian protests or uprisings or may I add, elections.

The Sporting Controversy:

Even though South Africa was still in international sporting exile a group of South African rugby players, on invitation was permitted to arrive in Chile to bolster and represent Chile against the Queensland side. We were looking forward to the match as we were aware among them were some world-class players. John Breen, Queensland's Team Manager welcomed and liaised with the Springbok (Boks) players only to learn that they intended to run on and play all seven players from game initiation. This concerned John a little so a call to the ARFU (Australian Rugby Football Union) back in Australia was warranted. The ARFU said they would speak to the government on the subject and get back to him. Because of the time difference no doubt back in Australia, rugby administrators and politicians were being pulled out of bed to go over this international sporting matter concerning South African rugby players. After a while, John received a call back stating that seven rugby players constitute a team (as in seven a side) and he was informed to tell the Bok players that only six members can be on the ground at any one time however, they were permitted to rotate the players.

The Boks refused to bend, *"Seven or none"* was their demand.

So, another call by John to Australia relaying the Boks stance was made.

The call-back was by the ARFU after a quick liaison with the Government. *'No!'* was the answer, *"only six players on the ground at any one time."* This ultimatum was relayed to the Bok players who in turn reiterated, *"It was all or nothing."*

So, nothing it was and the game became a complete shambles with Queensland defeating Chile from memory, 72-0. However, the opportunity to see some of Chile was worth the trip.

We received the news that President Pinochet sacked the Chilean Rugby Union administration on Tuesday the 14th of March.

—⁂—

Another incident that was almost a disaster was being told over and over, *"Only eat boiled vegetables with your meat, definitely no salads."* One of the touring party (not a player) overlooked the caution and became seriously ill. He stayed in bed all the next day and by the following day was a mess, weak and *non-compos mentis.* We called the doctor and after examination and a rather nasty injection in the butt, informed us that if it had not been treated, he would have been dead within twenty-four hours. Lesson to potential travellers to that part of the world; only eat boiled vegetables. The member could not remember his visit while in Santiago. We were hosted by the Australian Ambassador to Chile on our last evening in the capital and yes XXXX was available - thanks again, Frank.

—⁂—

We visited Valparaiso, Chile's Naval Base before catching Air Chile and flying south down along the Andes, which is the world's longest mountain chain and it was impressive observing the small, however active volcanoes along this mountain chain.

Above: Valparaiso, Chile.

A visit to Puerto Montt and Vares completed our Chilean tour then it was back over the Andes by coach and ferries, crossing three magnificent lakes high in The Andes before landing and being transported to the Bariloche (Argentina) ski fields, which were very European in appearance.

**The Puerto Montt Trio, Roses Cantina in Puerto Montt, Chile. 13 March 1989.
I am the musician on the left playing the phantom harmonica.**

Salta Town Square.

A flight to Buenos Aires (BA) was followed by another flight to northern Argentina to Salta, just south of the Bolivian border for Queensland's next match. A strange arrangement with air movement in the country is that you cannot fly directly from city to city in Argentina. All flights must return to Buenos Aires and then to your next destination.

Following games in Salta, Tucuman and Parana it was back to Buenos Aires for the final game of the tour versus Buenos Aires itself. I was surprised at the quality of rugby in Argentina's provincial teams; in fact, Tucuman was the current provincial champion.

To date, Queensland had won all six matches. Sadly, Queensland had their tour blemished with a loss to Buenos Aires 20-21. Queensland scored three tries to nil, converted one try and kicked a penalty goal. Buenos Aires had an outstanding goal kicker and replied with seven penalty goals. Without being biased, Queensland was robbed by being penalised out of the game. On one occasion Queensland had a scrum on the BA goal line (five-metre scrum) and as Queensland had the BA scrum going backward, Queensland was penalised for collapsing the scrum – Unbelievable!!!

I talk of this game mainly because of the after-game reception. When it was the captain's turn to speak Queensland Captain (and Australian lock) Bill Campbell's first statement was, *"To the referee … you are a fucking cheat."* You could have heard a pin drop. Bill went on to deliver the rest of his speech.

Later on, in the evening while breasting the bar, the referee approached Bill Campbell and after getting his attention spoke. *"Mr Campbell, I am sorry how you feel about the match today however, tomorrow you will get on an aircraft and return to Australia. Myself, I have to live here."*

On our last night in Buenos Aires, we were hosted by the Australian Ambassador to Argentina at his residence. Yes, XXXX was available, thanks again Frank. If I could have my time over again, I would seek higher education and attempt to crack the Australian Diplomatic Corps after being hosted by the Australian Ambassadors in both Chile and Argentina.

Before we left Argentina, news drifted through to us that Tim Horan (not on this tour) had been selected to play for Australia versus New Zealand. Tim was one of those rare selections of representing his country before his state.

In flying home, we left Buenos Aires on 30th March 1989, south to Rio Gallegos to refuel, then to Auckland and over the ditch to arrive in Sydney the next day.

At home in Brisbane, an invitation from Frank Burnett arrived, stating;

*"Cocktail Party at Mayfair Crest Hotel
Tuesday, April 11, 1989, 6:30 PM
For the ladies who stayed at home during the QRU Argentina Tour"*

John Connelly and I, who both live on the Sunshine Coast, Queensland, meet and enjoy breakfast following the Dawn Service on ANZAC Days.

ANZAC Day 2019 John Connelly & Tasi Woodard
RSL Sub-Branch, Kawana Waters Surf Life Saving Club.

9: The Padre, Rugby and Me

One meets all types of personalities when involved in rugby however, an unusual friendship occurred during my services rugby career.

Battalions carry a Padre at the unit level and being a large unit (over six hundred personnel) the Padres would travel into areas of conflict with them. This particular Padre I am writing about is Father John Tinkler. John served in Viet Nam with the battalion he was attached to, and after getting to know John he does break down when referring to the soldiers he passed their last rites onto in Viet Nam. He also consoled the wounded through all of their various conditions.

John was the only minister that I have ever known and even with myself being a non-religious person, we became friends. How did I come to know John Tinkler? He is the only man of the cloth whom I met that played rugby.

Tinks as he was commonly known by all ranks was admired by everyone and a very popular person. Whenever we played against each other, Tinks being a hooker for the battalion and myself being a prop for the regiment, he would always say before the first scrum engagement of the game, *"Now Tasi. Don't do anything today that God wouldn't approve of."* Within five minutes he would be rucking the crap out of one of my players laying on the ground during a ruck. Amen.

To this day Tinks and I keep in touch mainly at Christmas time. He is a practising Minister in Moama on the New South Wales and Victorian border.

10: Ties

Tie #1:

In 1981, while I was the Director of Coaching at Souths in Brisbane, the All Blacks toured Australia for a three-Test Series plus games against New South Wales and Queensland between the Test Matches. During that period the QRU allocated a club side to host the All Blacks following the NZ versus Queensland match on a rotation basis. So in 1981, Souths were the host club and the All Blacks were transported out to the Souths Clubhouse following the match.

Later in the night, I proceeded to the Souths' toilets to relieve myself of our sponsor's generous donation. When standing at the urinal I was joined by an All Black player and while we both stood there enjoying the relief, I noticed he was looking at my chest.

My first thoughts were, *"What's this bloke on about?"*

He became aware of my concern and asked, *"What's that tie you're wearing?"*

I replied, *"A Five Nations tie"* which I had secured some years earlier in the UK.

He replied, *"I have never seen one of them. Nice tie."*

I said, *"You can have it for yours!"*

So, there we were standing at the urinal exchanging ties.

The following year Stu Wilson (All Black 1977 – 1983) became the first winger in their history to captain their National Team.

Tie #2:

While escorting a Veterans Team to New Zealand our hosts from Wellington put on a function at the Wellington Yacht Club for us. During the evening, when silence was called for their committee to thank us and proclaimed, that they had a presentation to make. I was called forward and a little old lady was standing there with an All Black tie in her hand. She is a sister of Ivan Vadonovich (three Tests for the All Blacks and their Manager from 1967 – 1972) and she wished to present me with Ivan's All Black tie.

I explained that I was honoured by the proposed presentation, however, I was reluctant to accept it as it was her family and country's heritage. There was a very large Māori standing behind me and he lent over my shoulder and said, *"Take the fucking tie."*

I accepted the tie thanking all for their generous gift.

I have Stu Wilson's and Ivan Vadonovich's All Black ties displayed in my bar.

11: South Africa - 2000 Tri-Nations Series

"Pack some good gear Tasi as we will be attending some official functions by the South African Rugby Union (SARFU)" - as I was informed by Terry Doyle, the CEO of the QRU. So off to South Africa for the Tri-Nations 16th – 28th August 2000.

On arriving in Johannesburg, we were driven to Sun City to stay at the Palace of the Lost City. Sun City is about a three-hour drive northwest of Joburg. The Palace is described as one of the most outstanding and luxurious hotels in the world and I can confirm their claim.

Above: (L) Entrance to the Palace of the Lost City. (R) Adorned with exquisite mosaics.

Above: (L) The hotel foyer has a life-size elephant sculpture. (R) Inside the foyer.

The resort has an incredible Valley of the Waves one of the world's most amazing water theme parks where there is jet skiing, windsurfing, water skiing and body surfing by the means of artificial waves. The resort also has two 18-hole Gary Player designed golf courses and at night-time, one can take in a star-studded spectacular show, enjoy a meal at one of the many gourmet restaurants or try your luck at the large casino.

Saturday - 19th of August:

An early morning tour of the Pilanesberg game reserve, home to the Big Five which is the leopard, lion, elephant, rhino and buffalo. We mixed with four, though unable to locate a leopard, but viewed many other animals in the game reserve.

We were transferred back to Johannesburg and moved into our hotel at Sandton. We were transferred to Ellis Park for the Tri-Nation match, New Zealand versus South Africa, which was won by the 'Boks' thus eliminating the All Blacks from the Tri-Nations series.

Between Sun City and Johannesburg, we were treated to a dance troupe at Hartbeespoortdam in northwest Transvaal.

Soweto – A Lifetime Experience:

Soweto is situated only fifteen kilometres south of Johannesburg with a floating population of between two to four million people. The population, as explained, was hard to determine as a continuous flow of human movement poured into South Africa from the northern countries Mozambique, Zimbabwe, Botswana and Namibia. The Shanty City was unbelievable with dirt streets, housing consisting of pieces of tin and timber, with no electricity or running water; the whole place just screamed with poverty.

A typical street in Soweto.

We were told not to give the children any gifts as we would have hundreds of wanting gifts also. We were invited into one family's home and as I sat on a makeshift chair, I noticed a young girl shyly glancing at a biro I had in my shirt pocket. The whole small house consisted of one room with an earthen floor, a small stove, table, and cupboard with rolled-up beds stacked in one corner however, the home was clean and tidy.

On talking to our hosts about their existence it became apparent that there was no government assistance for their welfare and day-to-day living was a survival experience.

I thought of the billions of dollars made available to Aborigines on an annual basis and thought, *"Wouldn't an exchange program be a cultural shock for both civilizations?"*

Before we departed our host, I removed my biro and passed it on to the little girl in a concealed transaction and she immediately hid it in her flimsy clothing. It may have been the first writing implement she ever owned and I only hoped it contained an ample amount of ink in it. It was a biro from our hotel so another would be made available for me.

We walked and drove around Soweto City and were treated to a nice lunch besides sightseeing this very unusual place, which is only fifteen kilometres from Johannesburg.

A Little History of Soweto:

In January 1976, the Department of the Bantu Education decreed that all black schools had to replace English and teach courses in Afrikaans instead, the language of their oppressors.

The first explosion took place in Soweto on Wednesday, the 16th of June 1976 as approximately ten thousand students marched through the dirt streets protesting against the Afrikaans decree. Unknown to the marchers, hundreds of policemen armed with tear gas canisters, rifles and shotguns had formed a barrier. When the students reached the barricaded street, they stopped but continued waving placards. The police opened fire and continued firing.

A photograph had been taken of a 13-year-old with his forehead shattered by a bullet, who was picked up by another youth and carried into a nearby yard. The image of the lifeless boy in the arms of the youth, his face blazed with anger, hate and defiance made headlines around the world.

"You are now standing exactly on the street where the massacre occurred," we were informed.

The riots continued by other schools in defiance and when October rolled around the official death toll of students stood at four hundred, the unofficial figure was estimated to be twice that. Where we were standing was Freedom Square and the Hector Peterson Memorial, where the first students were shot.

Not all the housing in Soweto are tin shanties as during our travels we stopped at Winnie Mandela's home.

Another historic feature about Soweto is that it has the only street in a city anywhere in the world where two Nobel Peace Prize winners lived; being Nelson Mandela and Sir Desmond Tutu.

—⟋⟍—

Leaving Soweto, we visited a gold mine where we experienced descending underground by an active gold extraction shaft. It seemed an eternity being lowered by the lift some four hundred metres; however, we were told that the shaft did descend to just over sixteen hundred metres making it the deepest mine shaft in the world.

—⟋⟍—

Terry Doyle visiting Winnie Mandela.

Departing Johannesburg, it was off to Cape Town to be met by Theuns Roodman, the CEO of Western Province Rugby. Western Province Rugby and Queensland Rugby are sister unions with Theuns Roodman and Terry Doyle sharing a great relationship. Theuns gave us a vehicle and driver on behalf of Western Province Rugby to go wherever we desired for the duration of our four-day stay in Cape Town. However, that evening we were to be entertained at Newlands Rugby Park by Theuns with a braai (BBQ) and a tour of Newland's Rugby Park. It may be noted that housing exists at Newland Park for the CEO and other working park members.

Following the braai, Theuns escorted us to the President's Bar within the complex for a few refreshments. I mentioned to Theuns that the glass I was drinking out of was quite exquisite being embossed with the Springbok. *"It is yours as a souvenir,"* he replied. It now sits in our kitchen cabinet.

The magnificent Newlands Park Stadium, Cape Town, South Africa.

Not only is Newlands Park Stadium a magnificent rugby stadium, but Cape Town is also perhaps the most beautiful city in South Africa.

A full-day tour along Cape Peninsula to the Cape of Good Hope Nature Reserve which extends along forty kilometres of coastline and leads to Cape Point, where two oceans, the Indian and the Atlantic meet. In the nineties, my wife Ailsa and I stayed with friends in Perth and spent some time in the Margaret River area of Western Australia. We visited the meeting of two oceans there, the Great Southern and the Indian, and at the time the latter was a much more violent collision of two great oceans.

We visited the historic University town of Stellenbosch, home of the late Dr Danie Craven. Stellenbosch is a rugby University and unbelievably we drove past at least a dozen rugby pitches.

Daniël Hartman Craven (11 October 1910 – 4 January 1993) was a South African rugby union player (1931–38), National Coach, National and International rugby administrator, academic, and author. Popularly known as Danie, Doc, or Mr Rugby, Craven's appointment from 1949 to 1956 as Coach of the Springboks signalled 'one of the most successful spells in South African rugby history' during which the national team won 74% of their matches.

Statue of Doc Craven with his faithful dog.

While as a player Craven is mostly remembered as one of rugby's greatest dive-passing scrum-halves ever, he had also on occasion been selected to play for the Springboks as a centre, fly-half, No.8, and full-back.

As the longest-serving President of the South African Rugby Board (1956–93) and Chairman of the International Rugby Board (1962, 1973, 1979), Craven became one of the best-known and most controversial rugby administrators.

Visits to Seal Rock at False Bay and a cheetah farm at Spear outside Stellenbosch were visited. The area is also a wine-growing area and a visit to Groote Constantia where we enjoyed sampling the product from the Cape's oldest wine farm. A day at leisure in Cape Town situated at the foot of Table Mountain confirmed Cape Town is the safest the most beautiful city in the Republic.

Thursday - 24th of August:

Transfer to Durban, the capital of KwaZulu-Natal.

On Friday after taking in the lovely residential area of Durban we took a historic tour driving inland to the spectacular Valley of 1000 Hills and a Zulu Kraal. Mixing with the tribal people it was here that I was offered three Zulu maidens for the price of eleven cows being thirty-three cows for the three of them. Unfortunately, I had no cows in my possession.

Left: All mine for thirty-three cows
Right: A statue of Mahatma Gandhi is prominent in Pietermaritzburg

We continued to Pietermaritzburg which was the provincial capital of the Union of South Africa in 1910 and visited the railway station which was used in the film Gandhi. Lunch was taken at DumuZulu or Shakaland where we had the opportunity of experiencing Zulu culture including tribal dancing. Before returning to Durban we visited battlefield sites where British, Boer and Zulu conflicts took place and treaties were signed.

Friday - 25th of August:

Now in Durban, it was time to spruce up with the good gear Terry told me to pack before leaving Queensland. In the finest hotel, we were invited to attend a function presented by the South African Rugby Union on the eve of the Tri-Nations final, Wallabies versus Springboks. The hierarchy of SARU was in attendance. While enjoying pre-dinner drinks and nibbles I asked Terry, *"Who was that large gentleman in the centre of a threesome deep in conversation?"*

"That Tasi is the past President of the SARU, Louis Luyt, who ran the World Cup here in South Africa in 1995".

"Gee. I would love to meet him Terry," I suggested.

"Tasi, unless you want to talk in millions of Rand or big business no one gets an audience with Louis Luyt; him being a business tycoon and also a politician," was Terry's reply.

Oh well, nothing to lose and so with a drink in hand I approached his group. Louis's audience moved away and I presented myself to him stating I was from Queensland. Louis was extremely interested in Queensland and obviously, its rugby. Louis called for a tray of nibbles and more drinks as we moved into a fairly in-depth conversation, which went for some twenty minutes. This was only broken up by the request for all to take in welcoming speeches by the hierarchy of the SARU.

Terry confronted me and asked, *"What did you two talk about for so long?"*

"Just Queensland and rugby," I replied.

"Bloody incredible!" was Terry's last comment on the subject.

—◆◆◆—

On Nelson Mandela being elected President of the Republic, Louis Luyt unsuccessfully ran for the position of Vice President.

—◆◆◆—

Following a wonderful evening and the obligatory speeches by the upper crust of SARU, who on more than one occasion we were informed, that following tomorrow's clash Australia would remain unsuccessful in winning a Tri-Nation series. We were escorted back to our residence in the early hours of game day.

—◆◆◆—

Saturday - 26th of August 2000:

Game Day – Tri-Nations final between Australia and South Africa at Kings Park, Durban. Before the match, we had been invited to a large corporate marquee for lunch, no doubt through Terry Doyle's contacts and presence. This pregame lunch goes for some hours as the game was not played until 5:00 PM and we were to return to the same venue for the aftergame function and dinner. I may add that these functions were prepaid for as we were guests. These corporate lunches are the norm in South Africa before test matches and the pre and after-game functions dwarf Australian social aspects of the game, as rugby is South Africa's national sport.

Pregame function seated left to right; me, Terry Doyle and our South African host. Standing: Sydney couple Margaret and Geoff George.

The Game:

Kings Park Stadium, Durban holds 52,000 spectators and for the Tri-Nations final it was certainly packed. It is a very steep stadium as when seated the heads of the spectators sitting in front of you are at the level with your knees. Now Springbok (Boks) supporters certainly can give opposition supporters a verbal working over and, on some occasions, not at all friendly. We, who were wearing Australian (Wallabies) apparel endured the banter for the majority of the game with the Boks leading by two points as the siren sounded for the game to be over however the Wallabies had been awarded a penalty on the sideline in the Boks half just before full time. History shows that Stirling Mortlock converted the penalty from the sideline with the Wallabies winning their first Tri-Nation series by one point. Now it was our turn to reciprocate with some verbalisation!!!

Back to the corporate tent with us exhibiting much jubilation and the large crowd of Boks supporters a little despondent. Once again, the meal was excellent and we were allocated beer tickets, which when produced at the bar you were given a refill. Now the Boks supporters were not in the mood to further their losing experience so when their meals were consumed, they were very complimentary in coming to our table congratulating us on the Wallabies' win and giving us their beer tickets. This became a very regular occurrence and before long in the centre of our table stood a mountain of beer tickets. Such was the pile it was certainly beyond us to dispose of them in a night's indulgence, however, help was forthcoming.

When Channel 2's broadcasting commitments were complete their team consisting of Gordon Bray, Chris Handy and Simon Poidevin joined our table and helped us to try and expend our gifted tickets. The exercise was beyond our capacity and so by closing time and I may add quite merry, with us being the only remaining guests, we had to depart the venue still with beer tickets on our table.

Sunday - 27th of August:

Last look around Durban, not feeling all that smart with a PM departure from Durban to Johannesburg then a 7:50 PM departure from Joburg to Perth, a short stopover then onto Sydney with a 7:00 PM (Monday 28th arrival); a 9:15 PM departure from Sydney for arrival at Brisbane.

A very tired traveller arrived home, however experiencing a very historic and I may add adventurous sightseeing tour of the Republic besides making some lifelong friends.

I had become very good friends with Geoff and Margaret George, who live in Mosman, Sydney and on several occasions stayed with them to attend rugby lunches and Test matches, upon their invitation. Wonderful people.

A Note on Terry Doyle:

In the obituary column on the 24th of September 2011 the headline read:

"Rugby Unions great communicator, Terry Doyle was appointed the code's first full-time Chief Executor, where he held the position of CEO from 1980 for sixteen years and lifted rugby union in Queensland to previously unthought-of heights. He was a born promoter."

Terry was a driving force when South Africa emerged from the sporting wilderness and the then Super 6 competition was increased to a Super 10. It later became a Super 15 rugby competition played between New Zealand, South Africa and Australia's provincial teams. One of his brain waves was to introduce bonus points to encourage running rugby, which now even extends to the Rugby World Cup. Terry was Australia's representative to draw up the Super Series and Tri-Nations draws. Despite his contributions, Terry left the QRU in 1996.

Terry was born in 1946 and passed away on the 12th of September 2011 survived by his wife Denise, and children Michael, Camille and Madeline.

The Great Communicator Terry Doyle with children in Soweto.
RIP Terry; an outstanding man and friend.

12: Last Say on Rugby

Finally, in my Rugby involvement I will name my Queensland squad from the 1960s to now, keeping in mind I was out of Australia from 1964 through to 1967 (inclusive) and from 1969 to 1970.

These selections always create disagreements; however, I am prepared for any backlash. I have chosen a twenty-five-man squad.

My Queensland Selection

1: Tony D'Arcy	9: Des Connor (Capt.)	16: Jeremy Paul
2: Tom Lawton	10: Michael Lynagh	17: Dan Crowley
3: Andy McIntyre	11: Brendon Moon	18: Stan Pilecki
4: Bill Campbell	12: Tim Horan	19: Rod McCall
5: John Eales	13: Michael O'Connor	20: David Wilson
6: Tony Shaw	14: Ben Tune	21: Will Genia
7: Jules Guerassimoff	15: Roger Gould	22: Paul McLean
8: Mark Loane (V/Capt.)		23: Jason Little
	Coach: Bob Templeton	24: Geoff McLean
		25: Toutai Kefu

Two players, I wish to make special mention of:

#1: Jeremy Paul – He was born in New Zealand, moved to Australia at a young age in 1991 and was considered a Queenslander, however he never pulled on a maroon jumper. At seventeen Jeremy was the hooker for Easts (Brisbane) when they won their first grand final. Ex-New Zealand great, Grant Batty as Easts Coach told me he pleaded with the Queensland Retention Committee to place him in the Queensland squad, however they were blind to his potential.

After starring for the Australian U21s in 1997, Jeremy was snapped up by the ACT Brumbies where he played one hundred and twelve games for them and seventy-two appearances for Australia. In 2005 he won the John Eales medal for Australia's best player. This was the first time a hooker had ever won the coveted medal. Jeremy Paul was the best hooker in Queensland that never represented his State.

#2: Geoff McLean – In his mid-twenties, Geoff was playing for Queensland Country against the visiting England team at Rockhampton (Queensland) when he shattered his leg. It was deemed that badly that amputation was a possibility and it ended Geoff's career. As a winger, he was built in the mould of Tony Shaw, raw-boned, fast and brutal. Geoff could have been the greatest of the McLean clan unfortunately his potential was cut short by a horrific injury.

13: A Bit of Rugby League

On forming up a new Field Artillery Regiment in the Australian Army in 1960 and then being transferred from Sydney as a member of this new unit and now a young married member, the Army found temporary accommodation for my wife, son and me at Wynnum Central (Brisbane), in a massive old Queenslander in which had been converted to four units.

No sooner had we moved in when one of the other unit tenants introduced himself being the five-eight for the Wynnum Manly team in the Brisbane competition one Kenny Prior who later was to play for Brisbane in the Bulimba Cup competition.

When Ken learned I had some Union experience behind me he said, *"Get your gear. You're coming to training with me."*

I may add here that the only people in Australia who were permitted to play both Rugby and Rugby League were Service Personnel as from the mid-fifties on Service Personnel were in and out of Australia in South East Asia on military matters and as Service Personnel only played Rugby competition in Australia on Wednesday afternoons if you wanted to play weekends it was with a civilian team.

So off to training with Wynnum Manly, I went with Ken and being somewhat impressed with my ball skills they immediately positioned me as the inside centre, which was my rugby union position. It was early pre-season training and I had played some trial matches for Wynnum Manly when the Army allocated my family married quarters out at Wacol Army Camp, which ended my brief introduction to rugby league.

It wasn't until sometime later that I found I had been in the company of some very outstanding league players in Lionel Morgan a winger and the first Aboriginal to represent Australia at the International level. As previously mentioned, Ken Prior played for Brisbane in the Bulimba Cup. Harry Muir a fullback from the Northern Territory could kick field goals from inside his half and Bill McDermott, another aboriginal also played Bulimba Cup League for Brisbane as an outside centre. Here I was as the inside centre with Bulimba Cup players on each side of me, at five-eight and outside centre, and an international winger. I was surrounded by league royalty but was cut short of further exposure by being transferred out to Wacol.

While moving in and out of South East Asia I did play for several teams in the Brisbane Commercial League (second Division) mainly Normandy and The Brook.

Returning from Viet Nam and being in a split unit, our sub Unit was stationed at Enoggera and the other two sub Units at Wacol. As Enoggera was close to the Grange, I ventured out to train with the Brothers Rugby League side in 1971. Again, I was given several early-season trial matches in the A Grade side as a second-rower, however when the season proper began, I was in Third Grade. The problem existed when military exercises took place and I was away for one to two weeks, and with the no train – no play ruling in place, I was more often than not relegated to Third Grade. I continued to play for Brothers in 1972 again mostly in Third Grade due to being absent for prolonged periods.

My last game for Brothers was in the 1972 knock-out final against Easts at Lang Park. Unfortunately, we were defeated 17-16 where I scored thirteen points myself – a try and five out of the six goal attempts (tries were three points then). Following our loss and when sitting in the dressing room, a Brothers' official sat beside me and said, *"If you had kicked that other goal we would have won."*

I grabbed my jumper put it over his head and replied, *"Stick this up your arse."* Yes … it was my last game for Brothers. A notable player for Brothers in these two years was a twenty-year-old by the name of Wayne Bennett.

—⁓—

This wasn't to be the end of my rugby league career as in late 1972 I was approached by several men, who played for The Brook (Brisbane Commercial League). I had played with them during my time home from South East Asia when the Captain/Coach was ex-Valleys five-eight Des Mannion. I was offered quite a deal of money to captain/coach The Brook for the 1973 season so I accepted the offer.

The Brook within their playing ranks ex-Internationals previously had Col Weir, Arch Brown, Queensland and Parramatta star John Gourlay and another star in Kev Tyack, who later played for North Sydney. Unfortunately, The Brook did not have those quality players for 1973. This year I was also the Captain/Coach of the Queensland Army and Queensland Combined Services Rugby Union Teams, however, nothing clashed as I was unhindered in juggling the two positions. Services Rugby during the weekdays and Rugby League on night times and weekends.

Now Rugby League is a pretty simple game and so I only concentrated on four factors during the preseason and the following competition. The four factors I concentrated on were;

increasing everyone's fitness level, raising the individual's skill levels, team support play, and effective positional areas in defence.

———— w ————

Following is an extract from the Commercial Rugby League Year Book 1973:

"The Brook RLFC

Present Coach T. Woodard was this year's Queensland Combined Services Captain (and Coach) and has had a run of success winning the 'Craven Filter Shield' and the 'Bill McLeod Trophy'. They are now one point away from taking out the minor premiership. The Brook has a well-balanced side and is now poised for grand final honours."

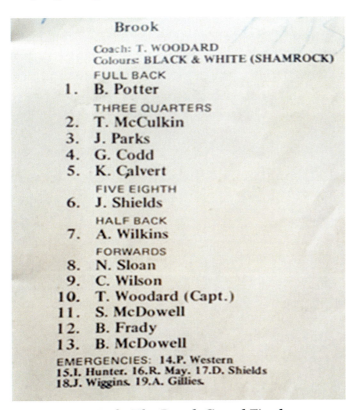

Brook

Coach: T. WOODARD
Colours: BLACK & WHITE (SHAMROCK)

FULL BACK
1. B. Potter

THREE QUARTERS
2. T. McCulkin
3. J. Parks
4. G. Codd
5. K. Calvert

FIVE EIGHTH
6. J. Shields

HALF BACK
7. A. Wilkins

FORWARDS
8. N. Sloan
9. C. Wilson
10. T. Woodard (Capt.)
11. S. McDowell
12. B. Frady
13. B. McDowell

EMERGENCIES: 14. P. Western
15. I. Hunter. 16. R. May. 17. D. Shields
18. J. Wiggins. 19. A. Gillies.

Left: The Brook Grand Final team as per the program
Right: The Brook Captain/Coach Tasi Woodard.
The Brook became minor premiers and won their maiden grand final in 1973.

———— w ————

In 1974 I was invited to captain/coach the North Ipswich Rugby League side in the Ipswich competition by the President of the club, Dud (Dudley) Beattie, who was a part of the famous Ipswich, Queensland and Australian front row of Parcell, Kelly and Beattie.

I was placed on an incentive payment, so the higher in the competition the team achieved the more payment I received. I convinced several of The Brook players to transfer with me, which included Jim Parks, who was eventually selected for the Queensland Country side.

North Ipswich were non-achievers in previous years and failed to get to the finals. In 1974 Norths ended up in the top four only to get defeated in a knockout semi-final after having our hooker sent off within the first ten minutes of the game – we lost that semi by two points, though a very healthy bonus still landed in my lap.

In later years a little halfback in Alfie Langer came from the North Ipswich Club.

Much later when living in Caloundra on the Sunshine Coast I ran into Dud Beattie and he confirmed he had been living in Caloundra for some years. Unfortunately, Dud passed away in 2016.

Following my 1974 playing/coaching rugby league in Ipswich I was strongly advised by the Army that my coaching efforts should be aligned with Services Rugby, so ended my rugby league association forever. But not without making many new friends from the league fraternity and having played semi-finals with two clubs and winning a grand final with another.

14: Crocodile Hunter

Many great yarns have been created since the initiation of the State of Origin (Queensland versus New South Wales) Rugby League in 1980. This in my opinion is perhaps the best of all I wish to share with readers; Crocodile Hunter – Enjoy.

'On his recent tour of Australia, the Pope took a couple of days out of his itinerary to visit the wild outdoors of Northern Australia on an impromptu safari. Deep into the bush, beside a river, safe inside his 4 x 4 Pope mobile his entourage came upon an enormous commotion.

They rushed to see what it was all about and upon approaching the scene the Pope noticed a hapless man in the river, wearing a New South Wales Blues jersey, struggling frantically to free himself from the jaws of a twenty-foot crocodile.

Almost immediately a speedboat containing three men wearing Queensland Maroon jerseys roared into view from around a bend in the river. One of the men aimed and fired a harpoon into the croc's ribs, immobilizing it instantly. The other two reached and pulled the cockroach from the river and using long clubs, beat the croc to death.

They bundled the bleeding, semi-conscious man into the speedboat along with the dead croc and then prepared for a hasty retreat when they heard frantic shouting from the shore. It was of course the Pope. He summoned them to the riverbank.

When they reached the shore, the Pope went into raptures about the rescue and said, *"I give you my best Papal blessing for your brave actions. I had heard that there is a racist xenophobic divide between Queensland and New South Wales, but now I have seen with my own eyes that this is not true. I can see that your societies are true examples of racial harmony and could serve as a model on which other nations could follow.”* He blessed them all and drove off in a cloud of dust.

As he departed, the harpooner turned to the other Queenslanders and asked, *“Who was that???”*

“That,” one answered, *“was his Holiness the Pope. He is in direct contact with God and has access to all God’s wisdom.”*

“Well,” the harpooner replied, *“he doesn’t know much about croc hunting! How’s that bait holding up ...”*

15: Olympic Venues

I can confirm that I am a sporting addict and will admit that I am a couch potato throughout the Olympics. So during my overseas travels, if I was staying in a city which had hosted an Olympics, I ensured I went out of my way to tour these sporting venues. They became unforgettable memories, commencing with my visit to the venue of the modern Olympics, which was Athens in 1896.

Athens, Greece:

Following the Dawn Service at Gallipoli and a tour of the Greek Islands in 2001 our small group tour finished in Athens. As my wife Ailsa and I had time in Athens and it was open to the public, we naturally visited the Olympic venue of the modern Olympic Games of 1896.

Naturally, I proceeded intending to walk a lap of the historic arena however we had in our group a Victorian who was some ten years my junior and when standing on the starting line he said, *“Come on Tasi let’s have a 400-metre race”*; being one lap. Even though we were dressed casually, I’m not one to turn down a challenge so I accepted his invitation. He took the inside lane and gave me lane two, so as we were standing side by side, he had an advantage from the start.

I was a mediocre 400-metre runner in my younger military days so this race was not new to me. On his call of *“Go,”* he took off like a greyhound and in the first two hundred metres had a lead of some thirty metres on me. My immediate thought through my past experiences was unless he was supremely fit, he would not be capable of maintaining that pace. Following the first two hundred metres, I noticed he was starting to fatigue and over the next one hundred metres I had run him down, passed, and drew away from him. After passing him and now ten to fifteen metres in front I transferred from lane two into lane one, thereby winning by some twenty-five metres.

When he crossed the finishing line exhausted, he said, *“You would have been disqualified for changing lanes.”*

I thought, *“Poor losers those Victorians”.* So at the ripe old age of sixty and in such a historical place, my last 400 metres race was run.

Athens has since hosted another Summer Olympics, which was in 2004.

Panorama of the Panathenaic Stadium which was the main venue, hosting four of the nine sports contested at the original games in 1896 ... the scene of my last 400-metre race.

Seoul, South Korea:

With all Olympics, like many people I watched the Korean 1988 Summer games on television. However, when visiting the venue I was quite surprised at the size of the complex as on the television screen it gave me the impression of being much larger. It was a pristine site and a beautiful Olympic venue. The philosophy of the games was for world unification, which was truly illustrated through symbolism such as the World Peace Gate.

The World Peace Gate.

There are always extraordinary feats and stories that prevail from Olympic games and just one of the many that came out of 1988 was that Indonesia gained its first medal in Olympic history when the women's team won a silver medal in archery.

Helsinki, Finland:

Even though Helsinki was initially allocated the games in 1948 it was held in 1952. This came about as London was to host the Olympics in 1944 however, due to World War Two those games were cancelled and so given the 1948 games, which pushed Helsinki back to 1952.

Fortunately, I had a friend in Helsinki and had an invitation to call him on our Finnish arrival. My wife Ailsa and I arrived on a Friday afternoon and following a phone call, my friend Rauno Eskola planned to meet us at our hotel the next morning for a Helsinki guided tour.

Rauno asked what we would like to see in this very interesting city. *"Firstly, the 1952 Olympic venue,"* was my reply.

In Olympic history, there were two eras when Finland possessed the world's most dominating middle to long distant runners, mainly Paavo Nurmi during the 1920s and Lasse Viren during the 1970s. Inside the venue's museum, they had testimony to both of them, by playing a continuous film highlighting many of their Olympic gold and World record racing achievements, which had me amazingly absorbed.

Alongside the Paavo Nurmi statue at the entrance to the Olympic Venue.

Munich (Bavaria), Germany:

Two incidences came out of the Munich Olympics in 1972; one a tragedy the second a phenomenon. The tragedy was the massacre of the Israeli Olympics team members by Muslim extremists and the phenomenon came in the package of a fifteen-year-old Australian swimmer by the name of Shane Gould.

At that time Germany was still split in two, and it had become obvious that the East German women competing in both athletics and swimming had a huge advantage over all other competitors by something other than natural talent and ability.

Still, Shane Gould competing in the pool against the East Germans won three gold medals, breaking World records in the 200-metre (m) individual medley (IM) as well as the 200 m and 400 m freestyle. She also won the silver in the 800 m freestyle and bronze in the 100 m freestyle swim, which she admitted was her greatest disappointment. Arguably Shane Gould could be acknowledged as the greatest freestyle swimmer male or female of all time by simultaneously holding all the world freestyle records, 100, 200, 400, 800, 1500 m plus the 200 m IM all at the age of fifteen.

The great Shane Gould.
Shane retired from competitive swimming at the age of sixteen.

While in Munich a visit to two other venues of historical note was where the British Prime Minister Neville Chamberlain met with Hitler and other prominent dignitaries then returned to England and stated, *"There will be peace in our time"*. The second venue was a prison in Munich, where Hitler was interned in 1933 never to be released.

Montreal, Canada:

Montreal, Canada held the Summer Olympics in 1976. Sometime after this, we were spending some time in Montreal so a bus ride out to the Olympic venue was a must. A lift to the top of the very high observation deck gave us a wonderful outlook back to and over the city of Montreal some ten kilometres away.

**Montreal Tower, part of the city's Olympic Stadium and
formerly known as the Olympic Tower.**

After taking in this very special viewing it was off to explore the main arena and other sites. When attempting to enter the swimming venue I was met at the main entrance by a security guard wishing to know my purpose for entry. I explained that all I wanted to do was view the swimming complex. He explained that the venue was off-limits to visitors as Madonna was inside doing rehearsals for her upcoming Montreal concerts. I explained that I was from Australia and I was not interested in Madonna nor would I attend a concert featuring Madonna even if I had free tickets. All I wanted to do was look over the swimming complex. No amount of pleading allowed me entrance. I am no fan of Madonna.

Sydney, Australia:

The 2000 Summer Olympics (officially known as the Games of the XXVII Olympiad and commonly known as Sydney 2000, the Millennium Olympic Games or the Games of the New Millennium) was the second time the Summer Olympics were held in Australia, and in the Southern Hemisphere, the first being in Melbourne, Victoria, in 1956. These were also the second Olympic Games to be held in spring and to date the most recent games not to be held in its more traditional July or August summer slot of the Northern Hemisphere.

Pre games' all-day tour of the Olympic complex in Sydney was a day well spent for an Olympic games follower. No site I had previously visited could compare with this magnificent venue, an ornament that Sydney, New South Wales and Australia should be justifiably proud of.

The IOC President at the time, Juan Antonio Samaranch stated that the Sydney 2000 Olympic Games *"Were best games ever."* A large part of this was due to the community spirit.

**Fireworks and the Sydney Harbour Bridge during the closing ceremonies
of the 2000 Summer Olympic Games in Sydney, Australia.**

Brisbane, Australia:

At the time of writing this book Tokyo, Japan is hosting and alive with the events of the 2021 (deferred from 2020 due to the Covid-19 pandemic) Summer Olympics. Paris after holding the games in 1900 and 1924, has been allocated the event in 2024 and Los Angeles (LA) will present them in 2028. This will make LA the third city following London and Paris to host the Summer Olympics on three occasions (1932, 1984 and 2028).

I live in southeast Queensland and just before the opening ceremony of the Tokyo Games, the small new world city of Brisbane was confirmed as the host of the 2032 Summer Olympic Games. So on this occasion, I will be looking forward to exploring it in my backyard.

16: Conclusion

In conclusion, I look back over the past and likewise with military personnel, quite a few rugby greats have passed on. I have been most fortunate in being associated with some and in an era when many of Australia's most outstanding have graced the pitches not only in Australia but globally.

For an individual who never heard of or witnessed rugby until I was seventeen, I thank all who took part in my education. Although not reaching the ultimate in this game (no Wallaby Warrior here; referring to the WWI great -Tom Richards, the only Australian ever to play for the British Lions) I may say that there is no sporting fraternity like the rugby fraternity.

Through rugby, I have made friends and still keep in contact with those friendships locally, around Australia and overseas. From someone born on King Island, no one could have foreseen my future with this great sporting concept.

TWELVE

SEEING AUSTRALIA

Like many seniors who have travelled extensively in our case all around the planet for thirty years and have been in and out of every capital city in Australia however never seen Australia itself. Getting weary of twelve-to-sixteen-hour international flights with many hours spent at various airports in foreign countries awaiting connecting flights finally my wife Ailsa and I agreed we had had enough and I am sure like many decided to explore our own country which in retrospect has much to offer unlike nowhere else.

A Trip to the Daintree

Our first sojourn was a drive from home (the Sunshine Coast, Queensland) to far north Queensland and in particular to visit the Daintree. It took several weeks to arrive at the Daintree as we took in most places situated along the vast Queensland coastline including a flight over to and several days' stay on the then beautiful Dunk Island. Since our visit sadly it was destroyed by a cyclone and even now has not been restored.

Beautiful Dunk Island before Cyclone Yasi.

233

My reason to visit the Daintree was for years I had been in and out of the great rainforests in the Malayan highlands in a military capacity and had read of the Daintree as being one of the oldest rainforests on earth. In addition to that point, it is only one of two in the world, where the rainforests run down to the ocean. In comparison, it was a disappointment as the Malayan rainforests are more lush, voluminous and spectacular.

The mouth of the Daintree River, Queensland.

A local on the Daintree River, Queensland.

Several days spent at the Silky Oaks Resort in the Daintree was an outstanding experience with the resort situated on a crocodile-free, clear, running water river made it so idyllic. A drive south and an overnight stay with friends at Cairns was followed by a two-day drive back home.

Darwin – 24 Hours

On one of our last returns to Australia from Scandinavia via Singapore, our aircraft's next port of call was Darwin, Northern Territory and since I had a sister living there whom I had not seen in some twenty years, a two-night stay with her in Rapid Creek, Darwin was an opportunity not to be missed. Alighting from the aircraft at 2:00 AM was like stepping out of a refrigerator into a furnace. We spent what little night-time left laying on a mattress under a ceiling fan. As we only had one full day in Darwin our host thought it appropriate to take us out to visit a crocodile farm. Well, the

Northern Territory humidity does make you thirsty so a stop at the well-known watering hole of Humpty Doo was good thinking indeed. We never did get to that crocodile farm and we returned to Brisbane the next day.

—m—

Western Australia – Two Good Weeks with Two Great Friends

An old ex-serviceman and close friend of mine Reg Miller (refer to One last Parade in Chapter Seven) had been pestering me for years to come and stay with him and his wife Tracy in Perth, Western Australia. As Ailsa had never been to Perth a fortnight in the west sounded like a good idea. Reg took a two-week holiday from work and hired a bungalow in a very exclusive resort in the Margaret River area. He and Tracy were wine buffs, so over the next week, we dined at every well-known winery in the Margaret River.

We did visit the coastal area where the Great Southern and Indian Oceans meet and the clash of these great oceans on the day was spectacular. The bungalow where we stayed was in a state forest (the bungalows were no nearer than one hundred metres) and walking through the bushland observing the wildlife proved very exhilarating before breakfast. All the trees had their botanical name tags attached and Ailsa and I had to have a photograph taken standing under (fair dinkum) a *Snotty Gobble* Tree.

On return to Perth, we then caught a ferry to Rottnest Island for a few days' stay. Before going home Reg and Tracy took us north to Yanchep Sun City (now known as Two Rocks) which was a marina and large housing development built to host and defend the America's Cup won by Australia in 1983. Of the sites considered for the contest (Mandurah being the second location), the Royal Perth Yacht Club decided on Yanchep.

—m—

Cruising Cairns

Back to Cairns for a five-day Cairns to Cairns cruise, which took in a visit and a half-day stayover in Cooktown then onto several deserted islands in the Coral Sea in which to explore. Onto Lizard Island where we laid up overnight. The next morning for those active enough, we walked up Cook's Hill where he sought after and detected a passage through the Great Barrier Reef to the open sea. He needed to source such a route after the repair of his ship at Cooktown following his near-disaster grounding on the Great Barrier Reef some months prior in the late 1770s.

Cooktown, Queensland.

Departing Lizard Island, it was off to the outer Barrier Ribbon Reefs, the last reefs before the continental shelf. We anchored up, and gear supplied, swam amongst these pristine reefs which spoil you for any visits to the inner reefs. We anchored up and swam in three of these ribbon reefs which included a two-night layup. It was then back to Cairns, spoilt forever in snorkelling any other Australian coastline.

Loving Lord Howe Island

During the 1980s Ailsa and I decided to visit Lord Howe Island and spent Christmas and the New Year there. Even though a small island it has a lot to offer either by walking or by bicycle. There are no car hires. Spectacular may be a fitting description. It possesses the most southern coral reefs known and on one beach named Neds no fishing is permitted however, you can don snorkel and flippers, wade out ten metres and it is like swimming in an aquarium among the tame and curious marine species. We spent many hours often at Neds Beach.

We stayed at one of the old and historic pioneer establishments, The Pines. Offshore a few kilometres stands The Pinnacle, an impressive two hundred and fifty-metre sheer cliff that stands like a sentinel off the eastern side of Lord Howe. We did a light aircraft continuous circuits around The Pinnacle so close that one could almost touch it, one could see the bird nests quite plainly, such as its security, it is a bird's haven.

The Island is the home of the Kentia Palm, which is its main export sending its seeds to all points of the compass. Kentia Palm is not found as a native elsewhere on the planet though plenty can be seen on the island's nine-hole golf course, which was quite challenging for a novice like me.

Lord Howe Island was discovered in the early nineteenth century by a British ship on its return journey to Australia after depositing a ship full of convicts on Norfolk Island some nine hundred kilometres northeast. It had never been settled by humans; such is its isolation. Small aircraft from Sydney or Brisbane is the island's connection to Australia. It is situated between the two cities (approximately six hundred kilometres from either city) and is administered by the New South Wales Government.

The small airfield (width of the island) was constructed by the Australian Army Engineers during WWII and before that, one could only visit using a flying boat or ship.

Such was our affection for the island we revisited two years later in the same time frame of Christmas Eve until New Year's Day. During this visit, I climbed Mt. Gower with a guide. This little excursion took eleven hours. Upon reaching the summit of Mt. Gower the guide unlocked a metal trunk extracted a book and I entered and signed my name in it. Something from me will always remain on this magnificent island isolated in the southern Pacific.

This photograph of Mounts Lidgbird and Gower was taken from Mt. Eliza while I was climbing it. Rabbit Island sits in the middle of the bay, a leisurely swim to the island and back was a good start to the day before breakfast. I later climbed Mt. Gower on Christmas Eve 1987.

Tasmania

There have been several trips to Tasmania, to attend funerals, visit relatives and general touring of the state. You could never tire of exploring the area because of its history and the variety of scenery it offers. Due to Tasmania's size, you can travel from any point in the state to anywhere else during a daylight drive.

There is no other area on the Australian mainland that compares with the island's diversity. You could easily believe, that millions of years ago, following the continental break up and the drift of Gondwanaland, the South Island of New Zealand and Tasmania could have been the same. Geographically they are very similar with the only difference being the mountain ranges on the South Island are much larger.

There have also been trips to my birthplace of King Island. On one of the occasions, I was a bearer for my last uncle, a WWII veteran. Another time I delivered a photographic display of my four uncles' military history from WWII to the island's museum, as they all were born on King Island.

The Northern Territory and Dreamtime

Darwin Again:

The call of the north engaged us again, so off to Darwin we went. Ailsa had been studying a street map and no sooner had we moved into our accommodation, she informed me that we were within a few blocks of Paspaley's, a world-renowned pearl distribution office. Following a very long selection process and discussion exercise, we left Paspaley's with the bank balance somewhat lighter, however a very happy wife with a prized possession.

Day One: A historic walking tour of Darwin took place being informed that Darwin's initial name was Palmerston. We learned of the early pearling industry dating back to the 19th century and its toll on the divers is well preserved. It also detailed the Japanese bombing of Darwin over some eighteen months during World War II and the havoc that Cyclone Tracy created in almost devastating the city in 1974. A very informative history lesson.

Day Two: This day saw us off on an all-day tour to Litchfield a popular tourist destination. The most interesting for me was the area of Rum Jungle, approximately one hundred kilometres southwest of Darwin. This was the site for Australia's first large-scale uranium mine officially opened in 1954, supplying the US and British nuclear weapons programs. The site closed in 1971 and the area had almost been reclaimed by nature.

I am standing in front of an anthill in Litchfield National Park. Further, into the park we stopped to look at square miles of anthills (which looked like a huge cemetery) with all the hills built precisely magnetic north.

Jabiru:

We had a three-week itinerary in front of us so the next day we travelled to Kakadu and took up residence at Jabiru the home of a current active uranium mine called Ranger.

The following day by four-wheel drive (4WD) it was off to Jim Jim Falls following the 4WD excursion it was into an aluminium boat upriver to the spectacular falls. Many freshwater crocodiles were observed, which reinforced the many signs warning people not to swim. No matter what language one spoke there was no mistaking the signs showing a crocodile with a human in its mouth encircled by a big red ring with a red line across it. The following day it was off again by 4WD, though on this occasion it was a few kilometres of rock hopping (no tracks) to our destination of Twin Falls. Following lunch, we enjoyed a lengthy swim in a (so we were told) safe area free from any danger. Both the falls on the Arnhem Land escarpment are icons of the world heritage listed Kakadu National Park.

Arnhem Land - One:

Permission must be sought to enter Arnhem Land. Upon crossing the East Alligator River we marvelled at stunning billabongs and towering escarpments on the way to the aboriginal village of Injalak. We were in a small group with one being a young German, and on driving for a few miles we could see this huge plateau rising in the distance. Our guide explained this Arnhem Plateau was the size of Switzerland, you could see his mouth drop open and shake his head in disbelief. Arriving at Injalak we were met by the aboriginal tribal elder who I got to know quite well. He later explained to me the reasons for becoming a young tribal elder as his people did not accept his father to be the tribal elder so skipped a generation, his position being passed down from his grandfather. He took us on a long walking tour that included walking up a large boulder hill which was several hundred metres tall and looking back down on their village one way and sitting down looking north was just miles and miles of savannah-like country with a heat haze shimmering out to the horizon. We just sat there quite mesmerized, just spellbound by what we were viewing, saying nothing, I felt I was close to understanding and acknowledging what Dreamtime to aboriginals meant. I felt that something within me was out there!

Finally, my host told me that when the rains came during monsoon season, all in front of me would be filled with fish, barramundi, turtles and crocodiles. I remarked, *"There would be plenty of barramundis to eat?"* He replied, *"No! That's white man's tucker, we eat the turtle."*

From my army training, during daylight, I can tell the direction using my watch and the sun I pointed and said, *"North."* He seemed quite taken aback and nodded repeating, *"Yes. North."*

Sometime later he asked, *"Do you want to see my father?"* I answered, *"Yes. I would like that."* *"Come with me,"* he gestured and with that, I followed him a little downhill then crawling under and past huge boulders supporting one another we came upon this skeleton.

He said, *"My father. This is where he wanted to rest on his death."* Some hours later returning to Injalak I learned what I had been gazing out over, feeling a touch of Dreamtime, was the Minkinj Valley. Arnhem Land is the only place in Australia where the territory is under and controlled by the past tens of thousands of years of native culture, however there is a police presence available for more serious crimes.

Arnhem Land - Two:

Following two days back in Darwin, it was out to the airport onto a small aircraft, no bigger than a small car, flying along the south-eastern shore of Melville Island in the Timor Sea then onto the Coburg Peninsular situated in the Arafura Sea, to Seven Spirits Bay. The Coburg Peninsular is northern Arnhem Land and the closest part of the Australian mainland to Indonesia.

Before landing on the small gravel airstrip, the pilot had to buzz the water buffalo off the strip and then while landing, negotiate the buffalo's droppings. On coming to a standstill in front of six large upright posts with a corrugated iron roof which boasts a huge sign … Welcome to Seven Spirits Bay International Airport. We were picked up by a 4WD and transported through a close country bush track to Seven Spirits Bay. We alighted from the vehicle and before claiming our luggage the driver lined us up and had us facing the bay stating, *"The first thing I must warn you is, that if it lives in the water and can kill you it's in there. No swimming!"* That evening still facing the water before the evening meal we observed the bay and yes, it was all in there. Seven Spirit Bay is located on the tip of the Coburg Peninsular overlooking the azure waters of the Arafura Sea. It is remote, far from civilisation with no radio, television, or phone reception. The lodge complex houses the restaurant, bar, library, reception, meeting room and swimming pool. Guests are accommodated in individual habitats with two queen beds and all self-contained facilities with large ceiling fans and screened ceiling-to-floor louvred windows.

In its early history, the British attempted to settle the area of Port Essington, however, due to the stifling heat, crocodiles, mosquito-infested areas, and during the dry monsoonal season, the lack of rain and fresh water, the area was abandoned. I believed this happened in the early 19th century and the settlement lasted less than a decade. The remains (foundations) of the hospital still exist and Ailsa and I walked to it after breakfast one morning perhaps a kilometre from the lodge. Departing the beach, we followed a track about four to five hundred metres inland to see the foundations which to our surprise were quite large. From the library, we learned that any British personnel from Port Essington who was interred never returned to the settlement. On our return to the beach, we were confronted by a rather large water buffalo standing across the bush track. Having spent six years in Southeast Asia and having a reasonable association with water buffalos I very slowly approached him. He initially stood his ground however as I reached him almost within arm's length he reeled away and disappeared into the dense bush. Another prominent feature in the marsh areas around the lodge were the many crocodile slides, being their tracks from the mud into the water. The area was active with water buffalo, deer and wallabies, all crocodile tucker which brought them from the water during darkness.

It is believed that trading between the Arnhem Land aboriginals and Indonesians had been carried out over thousands of years and the Indonesians had introduced two types of water buffalo to the bay, with one type not seen in any other part of Australia. Much of the flora in the area is of southeast Asian origin and can only be credited to importation by Indonesian traders.

Farewell to Seven Spirits Bay, Arnhem Land back to Darwin then home to Caloundra. Yes, there are parts of Australia unique to this continent that does not exist anywhere else in the world.

Kangaroo Island

To the other end of the continent with a stay with friends in Adelaide then by light aircraft to the island's airport Kingscote, a pickup by our host and then a transfer to the Southern Ocean Lodge, a little celebration for our forty-second wedding anniversary. Renowned as Australia's Galapagos and brimming with diverse wildlife and spectacular landscapes, Kangaroo Island is a place of extraordinary contrasts. The Southern Ocean Lodge faces the Great Southern Ocean overlooking Hanson Bay, sitting upon huge limestone cliffs, with nothing but ocean between here and Antarctica.

A half-day signature experience was a spectacular introduction to Kangaroo Island's wildlife, maritime heritage, stunning coastal landscapes, Cape Du Couedic Lighthouse, remarkable rocks, Admirals Arch and a unique fur seal colony were some highlights. On another excursion, we visited Seal Bay, which is home to Australia's third-largest colony of Australian sea lions. It is only the second place on the planet where you can tour the beach amongst these wild animals. This colony extended for a kilometre or more along the beach and it was impressive to see some returning and some leaving for their extended journey out to sea.

A further visit was to Australia's largest koala bear colony and sanctuary, and on this island, the numbers are in the thousands. Following overpopulation, they are shipped back to the mainland and resettled into a natural environment.

Our five-day stay was most memorable and lasting. Sadly, in January 2020 a huge bush fire engulfed Kangaroo Island destroying many properties including homesteads and sadly burnt to death many wallabies, kangaroos, and koalas by the thousands being poor tree-dwelling animals with just nowhere to go.

This unfortunately was the greatest setback in the island's history. It was sad to see as photographed from the air the destruction of the Southern Ocean Lodge consumed by the wildfires.

Cruising the Kimberley Coast 2010

"Tasi. I've just come back from cruising the Kimberley Coast. Do it before you die," was a phone call from an old friend, who could not emphasise enough the extraordinary magnificence of the venture.

Ailsa was not interested so I called Coral Princess Cruises and booked myself to sail from Darwin to Broome on their smaller ship, which carries a maximum of thirty-five passengers from the 30th of April to the 10th of May 2010. On gaining access to my room I found a letter welcoming me back for my second cruise with their company and in an ice bucket, a bottle of wine. On departing Darwin we sailed overnight into Joseph Bonaparte Gulf and I committed to writing daily notes on this trip.

The Coral Princess off the Kimberley Coast. We were on the Explorer
which when not in use is attached at the rear of the vessel.

The *Explorer* was used for river cruising and land exploration.

Saturday 1st of May

King George Falls:

Entering the King George River one can only admire the vertical cliffs. Our final destination was King George Falls at the head of the river which splits into two separate waterfalls. Here we got into inflatables, donning wet weather gear and got a close-up view of these magnificent falls.

King George Falls.

Sunday 2nd of May

We sailed overnight and following breakfast, boarded the Explorer and visited Hathaway's Hideaway with their large ancient aboriginal middens. These were found at the entrance to several sandstone caves and we were able to explore the inner sanctums. Leaving here we visited Winyalkan Island and viewed a small Gwion Gwion (previously known as Bradshaw) rock art site. In the afternoon we alighted at Wary Bay on Bigge Island, to witness the fascinating art of Kaiara figures of the Sea Wandjinas (cloud and rain spirits from aboriginal mythology).

Kaiara figures of the Sea Wandjinas.

Returning to the Coral Princess we departed at 1700 hours en route to Prince Edward Harbour.

Entrance to Prince Frederick Harbour.

Monday 3rd of May

Arriving at the above harbour we were treated to spectacular scenery dominated by rock formations, which geologists claim, as are all the rocks of the Kimberley, are more than 400 million years old.

Spectacular and unusual rock formations over 400 million years old.

At this location, passengers had the opportunity to fly by helicopter across the Mitchell Plateau to the Mitchell Falls in a series of steps along the Mitchell River.

As I have seen Niagara Falls from both the USA and the Canadian sides (several years apart) and spent some three days in and around the Iguazu Falls from both the Argentina and Brazilian sides and seen some spectacular falls in the Norwegian fjords, an aerial photograph of the Mitchell Falls did not excite me. Those not visiting the falls spent half a day touring the Hunter River by the *Explorer* and seeing the wildlife including cruising crocodiles. Overnight we moved onto Careening Bay and the Prince Regent River.

Tuesday 4th of May

A short journey on the Explorer over to Careening Bay and a piece of history. Captain P. P. King careened his boat HMC *Mermaid* on this beach for repair. He etched the boat's name and the date 1820 into a huge baob (Australian baobab) tree which even now is quite legible. Later that morning the Coral Princess entered an area called Whirlpool Point. It was a great experience standing on deck and viewing these extraordinary whirlpools in the ocean.

The afternoon saw us in the Explorer cruising this majestic river to the King Cascade Falls which was the scene of a tragic event, the death of Ginger Meadows.

King Cascade Falls.

Tragedy at King Cascade:

'Ginger Faye Meadows was born in Charlottesville Virginia, USA on 30 March 1962. Described as a vivacious extrovert, a love of travel and adventure brought her to Fremantle to enjoy the America's Cup, at the age of 24. When the partying was over, she scored a job as one of five crew aboard the luxury motor cruiser *Lady G*, returning to the east coast via Australia's top end.

On 29 March 1987, the *Lady G* anchored in the vast scenic bowl of the St George Basin. The skipper suggested the crew take a run in the tender up to King Cascade to replenish drinking water supplies, shower and enjoy the wilderness scenery. At the cascades the crew did their own thing: some explored some lazed. At 1130 it was high tide. Stylish in their bikinis Ginger and the Aussie chef Jane Burchett, foolishly swam from the tender, now tethered on a long line from the rocks. Swimming to the spray-cooled base of the cascades, they found themselves waist deep on a ledge, their backs against a solid rock wall.

"Crocodile," yelled skipper Bruce Fitzpatrick from the top of the cascades. The girls trapped screamed for help. Jane had the presence of mind to remove the shoe and threw it at the rapidly advancing four-metre reptile. The crocodile was briefly nonplussed at the impact. Ginger, in panic, dived in

and swam frantically for the boat. She only got a few feet. In a lightning grab, the crocodile seized her by the hips and both vanished underwater. The horrified skipper next recalled:

"Then she came back up clear to about her waist with her hands in the air and a really startled look on her face … she was looking right at me … but she didn't say a word."

After that, nothing but bubbles came up. Ginger's camera, bag and blouse lay in the sun on the seat of the *Lady G's* tender. Her stunned shipmates went into shock. Tomorrow would have been her 25th birthday.

The Aftermath:

A telex to Broome police from the *Lady G* alerted the world. A media frenzy ensued. Two small cabin cruisers with search parties were immediately dispatched from the iron mining settlement of Koolan Island. Among those aboard was Koolan's sole police constable and retiree Vic Cox: a former crocodile shooter on the Kimberley Coast in the 1960s. It would be the 31st of March before *Penguin* and *Voyager* could reach the Prince Regent River. Statements had to be taken aboard the *Lady G* from her four devastated crew.

Vic Cox correctly predicted that Ginger's body would be found in mangroves near the cascades, for saltwater crocodiles like to store their victims and return to eat at leisure. Sure enough at 1345 Cox located the now armless torso, face down. The remains were put into two body bags, wrapped in tarpaulin and lashed to the foredeck of the *Penguin*. The search parties later anchored for the night, some 15 kilometres west of the cascades. On at least two occasions that evening, three-metre crocodiles tried to leap aboard the foredeck to grab the remains. Rather than risk any further incidents, the *Penguin* team got the vessel underway and headed for the open sea.

Early on 1 April, the body was transferred to the customs launch *Jacana*, which then motored at high speed the Koolan Island. The medical officer there immediately ordered that the deteriorating corpse be chilled. It was next flown to Broome's morgue, where a jet-lagged, estranged husband had the grim task of confirming her identity. It would be 13 April, before the tragic cargo left Perth Airport for burial at Ginger's hometown in Virginia, USA.

A coronial inquest on 21 August cleared the *Lady G's* skipper, Bruce Fitzpatrick, of any blame for the tragedy.'

[Source: Hugh Edwards (1988). Crocodile attack in Australia, Swim Publishing, Sydney.]

Wednesday 5th of May

Hanover Bay, Camden Harbour, Sheep Island and Samson Inlet:

We visited Sheep Island which was the final resting place for at least ten people from the failed settlement at Camden Harbour. Sheep Island was the site of the first burial of a white woman (Mary Pascoe) in the Kimberley. Mary and John's daughter was the first child to have been born in the settlement. I wandered over to the baob tree and found the headstone that marks Mary Pascoe's grave. The baob itself is inscribed with now illegible details and a walk among the gravesites finds most of them now as unmarked stony mounds overgrown by thick vegetation.

The inscribed baob tree is the site of the graves at the failed settlement on Sheep Island.

A scenic cruise into Samson Inlet where we viewed more aboriginal art. The day ended with a sunset barbecue on Wailgwin Island before returning to the Coral Princess. En route to Samson Inlet, we passed Kuri Bay, which is the site of the largest pearl farm in the world (Paspaleys). It produces 500,000 pearls worth 200 million dollars annually.

Thursday 6th of May

Montgomery Reef and Red Cone Creek:

Montgomery Reef is an expansive 400 square kilometre reef that is exposed during low tide. We arrived at low tide and walked over a section of the reef. Runoff in small waterfalls is continuously falling off the reef, which had been pooled before the receding tide. As it is exposed twice daily it does not possess the coral colours of the Great Barrier Reef however must have been a shipping hazard during early exploration. In channels between reef sections, we observed a lot of marine life, sharks, stingrays and barracuda. Following lunch, we travelled by the Explorer up Red Cone Creek and falls. For those capable, a sheer climb up a thirty-metre cliff face by ropes allowed us to enjoy a leisurely swim in a deep and slow-running creek.

Friday 7th of May

Raft Point, Talbot Bay and Horizontal Falls:

Raft Point has been a significant place for the local aboriginal people in particular relating to their seafaring lifestyle. Parker King observed groups of aboriginals on wooden rafts departing from and returning to a prominent point of land. John Lori Stokes aboard HMS *Beagle* also made the same observations as P. P. King and was responsible for naming it Raft Point. It was noted that the aboriginals used the tides in their favour when venturing out to the nearby islands.

He called these aboriginals the tide riders.

At Raft Point we went ashore to visit a significant Wandjina art site then preceded in the Explorer for a scenic cruise around Steep Island.

In the afternoon the *Explorer* departed for a scenic cruise of the upper waterways of Talbot Bay wherein zodiacs we surfed the Horizontal Falls. This freak of nature is due to the tides running through small gaps in the cliffs to large like lagoons then only having small apertures to flow out from. The tides along the Kimberley Coast rise and fall over twelve metres surpassed on the planet only by those in Nova Scotia, Canada. Raft Point has the largest concentration of baob trees on the Kimberley Coast.

Saturday 8th of May

Iron Islands, Nares Point and Crocodile Creek:

We were now travelling in The Buccaneer Archipelago, which was named by the King in commemoration of William Dampier's visit on the *Cygnet* in January 1688.

The *Explorer* put us ashore on the Iron Islands and when you pick up a rock, the reason becomes very obvious for their name. Returning to the *Explorer* we make our way down the canal past Koolan Island and see the iron ore mine face of Yampi Sound at close quarters. It is the only iron ore mine that extracts the material below sea level. It was explained that the iron ore seam was of such a high quality that they just keep following the seam and mining it.

Following lunch, we cruised across to Crocodile Creek, climbed a ladder and enjoyed a freshwater swim. The extraordinary experience from this swim, myself being a reasonably strong swimmer is that the deeper one swam down into the water surprisingly became noticeably much warmer. Following our swimming excursion (third on tour) it was onto the majestic beach at Nares Point for sunset drinks and a beach walk before heading back to the Coral Princess which then departed for the Lacepede Islands.

Sunday 9th of May

A partial extract from Buccaneer William Dampier in January 1688:

"New Holland is a very large tract of land. It is not yet determined whether it is an island or a main continent, but I'm certain that it joins neither Asia, Africa nor North America."

AM: Morning exploration of Middle Lagoon near Emeriau Point.

PM: With fishing gear supplied I joined some males in the Explorer to troll around Talboys Rocks, which is a large undersea bommie where the pelagic fish are plentiful. The fish were abundant and I enjoyed catching the largest golden trevally I have ever caught in Australian waterways, though like all the others, the catches were released. I was somewhat upset when the fishing expedition concluded though the Captain's farewell drinks were enjoyed on the top deck followed by a luxurious farewell dinner.

Monday 10th of May

Disembarkation 0800 hours at Broome:

Several days in Broome, flight to Darwin then to Brisbane.

I saw much of the Kimberley Coast, however, the region had me curious to return to see more of the Kimberley by land. Several years later my wife Ailsa and I did take on such an adventure. I thank my old friend (now deceased) for suggesting to me I should partake in this journey while able.

—⁓—

Touring the Kimberley Country 2011

Even though tired of long air travel to foreign countries it still is a five-hour flight from Brisbane to Broome. In 2011 and accompanied by my wife Ailsa, we set off to see (more in my case) the Kimberley than you would see on a coastal expedition, which is a journey worth undertaking. We had an overnight stay in Broome as we had a flight the next morning to Kununurra, which was to be our base for the next week. Even though we arrived at the end of the monsoonal season, there were still volumes of water running and the depressing humidity caused one to continuously sweat, so the ceiling fans were on 24/7.

Kununurra is a reasonably sized town situated on the Ord River which runs into the Cambridge Gulf and is the source of the great Lake Argyle. A walk around Kununurra showed us that a sizeable aboriginal population existed and the children, with their smiling faces, were a source of friendship.

A little history of the Ord River Dam is necessary for the existence of Kununurra. By the 70s the Kimberley had become huge beef cattle stations. In early planning the country was divided into pastoral leases of up to 1,000,000 acres, the largest became the Victoria River Downs consisting of some 6.4 million acres or 10,000 square miles. The early Kimberley exploration was initiated in an 1882 venture by Durack/Emanual who had been given credit for the initiation of the cattle industry in the Kimberley.

Introduction:

A reference to the white settlement of the Kimberley is best historically described by Pasty Millet in her book *'The Durack of Argyle'*, a summary of a pioneering venture and the years 1852 - 1950 in Kimberley, Western Australia.

'The area chosen by white men for their pastoral empires ended 40,000 years of aboriginal occupation. For an ancient race content within a sheltered and serene environment, the arrival of the white man came as a cruel awakening. They found themselves powerless against winds of change that blew from all directions without warning or meaning, dispossessed of the land of their belonging, Aboriginal people found themselves trapped between wanting a place within the new order yet unable to abandon the precepts of their forebears.'

The above just refers to the East Kimberly area keeping in mind the extensive Kimberley region is three times the size of England and situated in tropical north-western Australia, the Kimberley district is statistically divided into Broome, West Kimberley, Wyndham, East Kimberley and Halls Creek bounded by the Ord River Valley on the east, the Fitzroy River Valley to the south and the Timor Sea to the north and northwest, the area consists of a great plateau of pre-Cambrian sandstones interspersed with volcanic rocks. The terrain varies greatly as does the rainfall varying according to monsoonal wet and dry seasons. One cannot convey the outstanding splendour of an ancient landscape, for many explorers the sheer beauty and infinite variety of the country defied description and even as they suffered and died, they had no complaints about the drama of the setting. Today in the burgeoning tourist industry travellers came from afar to catch a glimpse of untamed scenery as fantastic as can be found anywhere in the world.

Brief background of the Duracks:

Patrick Durack was born in Scarriff, County Clare in 1834, the eldest of eight children. The Duracks were among many struggling tenant farmers held to an existence of poverty by the unjust tax laws of the day. When an adventurous branch of the family set out for New South Wales and a brighter future. Letters of encouragement to his father Michael saw him follow them in 1854. Patrick made some money on ovens goldfields and purchased his first small shareholding. By the end of 1855, he had managed to purchase 273 acres in the Goulburn, NSW area followed by another 240 acres south of the town. In 1862 he married Mary Costello, an Australian-born daughter of an Irish family. He had stocked his properties with the growing demand for beef during the gold rush years. In 1863 with his brother Michael and brother-in-law John Costello, he set out with horses and cattle to establish a property in southwest Queensland, which proved disastrous due to drought.

Despite the setback the sanguine Duracks and Costello's still considered the parched country needed only a good season, deciding to give it another try. By 1867 Mary Durack had produced another two sons Michael and John. In Burke the Costello's had suffered hard times, the two families resolved to again join forces and proceed to a big permanent water hole John Costello had discovered on Mobel Creek just over the Queensland border once again. They stayed only long enough to recuperate and set up a supply depot before a further pilgrimage northwest into the good pasture country of Coopers Creek establishing the Durack and Costello Holdings.

Between them, they pegged claims to some 17,000 square miles of land between Kyabra Creek and the Diamantina River. It was a wondrous thing for Patrick Durack to contemplate that his properties covered an area almost the extent of his native country. By 1877 his cattle had increased from 100 to about 30,000 head. Always on the lookout for more dependable land, his attention was caught by a report from the explorer Alexander Forrest of excellent prospects in the Kimberley district of WA. In partnership with his friend Solomon Emanuel, he financed and organised an expedition to make a firsthand assessment.

The Durack/Emmanuel Kimberly exploration 1882:

The Durack/Emmanuel expedition departed Brisbane, QLD for Darwin, NT in 1882 led by Patrick Durack's younger brother Michael, who was one of Queensland's most experienced bushmen. Others in the party included Tom Kilfoyle, John Pentecost, James Josey and Tom Horan, who were also tried men along with a raw recruit in Emmanuel's twenty-year-old son Sidney, who would prove himself as hardy as the rest. Two territory aboriginals Pannikin and Pintpot later joined them. They departed Brisbane with twenty-three horses and supplies to Darwin then onto Cambridge Gulf. Phillip Parker King's chart of the coast was drawn over sixty years earlier, and yet the only guide available. Two to three weeks of hard travelling inland through rocky gorges and over precipitous mountains. They followed up four major rivers which they named the Pentecost, Durack, Dunham and Bow. A sweeping valley between high ranges was noted by Michael for its pastoral possibilities. The surrounding scenery was even by dramatic Kimberley standards, stunningly beautiful as he wrote to his wife, *"If one were to paint this country in its true colours, I doubt it would be believed. It would be said that the artist exaggerated greatly, for never have I seen such richness and variety of hue in these ranges and in the vivid flowers of this northern spring."*

The journey stretched beyond their supplies, the party lost many horses and the rest so weakened they could not carry their riders or the provision packs. Reaching the coast six weeks overdue the exhausted group was dismayed to find their ship had given them up and sailed away. They were rescued by a pearling lugger. On their return to Brisbane, the travellers declared the natural resources of the Kimberley were worth a sizable investment. The country was divided into pastoral leases of up to 1,000,000 acres and with a few strokes of a pen, the Emmanuels became heirs to the vast floodplains of the Fitzroy and the Duracks to the rolling basalt downs and craggy quartzite ranges of the Ord. Patrick Durack signed the Kimberly holdings over to his sons. During the next decade, a series of great cattle treks bought into existence and industry which became for half a century virtually the only active on over 40,000,000 acres of leasehold.

Argyle Floods:

In 1922 are protracted wet season caused the Ord River and its tributaries to rise as never before on record to the verandahs of the property Argyle homestead. Two years following the Kimberley suffered a prolonged drought. Argyle, for many years the only place in East Kimberly that justified the name of a home in its having been lived and cared for by the womenfolk of the original pioneers.

Towards an Ord River Dam:

The Kimberley continued susceptible to mercurial markets and unprecedented drought while these conditions were not shared by the west Kimberley region where floods added to the setbacks. A great portion of the state north of the 26th parallel had led successive governments to examine the possibility of an Ord River dam. In 1958 the state received a grant of £5 million from the Commonwealth government for northern improvement and the Ord River scheme was put forward as a priority. Planned over three major stages the initial work on the Ord project involved the construction of a diversional dam, the development of 30,000 acres of irrigable land on the Ivanhoe Plain and the establishment of a town. A townsite was selected in 1959. Mary Durack put forward the name Kununurra, which was accepted. This is the word applied by the local Miriwoong tribe to a section of the river.

Rescuing Argyle Homestead:

In 1969 the orders scheme subcommittee charged with appraising the tourist potential of the Ord region suggested the fine old homestead on the Durack property had great historical significance and should be preserved for prosperity. As the water backing up behind the Ord Dam to form Lake Argyle would inundate the property, it was proposed that the homestead be moved to a higher site. Work began on dismantling the homestead for storage before reconstruction. It was estimated it would take two wet seasons from the completion of the dam to submerge the vacated homestead. By July 1972 the fertile valley of the Ord was covered by the new inland sea, nine times the size of Sydney Harbour. The Miriwoong people were relocated to the Kununurra reserve.

The museum with a portion of Lake Argyle in the background.

Argyle Homestead Museum:

For two years the stones taken from the old homestead and numbered for reassembly remained in storage at Kununurra. Reconstruction work began at a place above the shores of the dam some sixteen kilometres from the original site. Period furniture, articles and equipment with photographs were gathered and assembled for display. Items long treasured by the Durack family were donated. The Durack headstones rescued from the flood were placed within the homestead boundaries with other headstones of pioneers also finding a prominent position. On 23 June 1979, the Argyle Homestead Museum was officially opened. So much for a history lesson on the Kimberly however, to understand the Kimberly one must be aware of its history to appreciate it.

253

Touring the Kimberley 17 May 2011:

On our first full day in the Kimberley, we had planned to visit the Argyle Museum situated at the Argyle Dam by vehicle, which was a fifty-kilometre ride. On the way out we stopped at a bridge over a very fast-running river with rapids. A driver explained this waterway was at the overflow end of the Argyle Dam and an artificial river constructed in one giant semicircle diverted the overflow back into the Ord River below the dam. Although by May the wet season had concluded, a lot of water was still running off. Alongside this bridge on the flats were numerous crocodiles looking upriver. Large barramundi caught in the overflow then ensuing rapids would drown and the crocodiles would swim out, retrieve their lunch and return to the flats. No hunting for these crocs. Our driver informed us, that during the heart of the wet season the volume of water coming down from the overflow in a twenty-four-hour period, would be equivalent to the volume of the Sydney Harbour. The mass of water of the Argyle Dam just went on and on and we visited the area where by water they generate their electricity.

A further ride brought us to the Argyle Homestead Museum and a history lesson. One can only take their hats off to the early explorers and pioneers, who were mostly from Irish stock, and the harsh times endured.

Following the dam inspection and more history, it was onto a river barge along the Ord River for our return trip to Kununurra some forty-five kilometres north. With the Ord River Dam at Lake Argyle and again the dam at Kununarra it was explained to us that the 45 - 50 kilometre of water between the two dams contains the highest density of crocodiles in Australia as for them there is no escape from that portion of the Ord River. The density is reportedly one crocodile per hundred metres stretch of water. Some distance down the river we stopped for afternoon tea at a safe area where some short exploration of the landscape was enjoyed. Further downstream we slowly glided into a large bat colony, infested in the overhanging trees by bats and by crocodiles in the water. It was a breeding colony and the crocodiles just waited for the baby bats to fall from the branches; one might say for crocodiles - a drop-in lunch.

Just at dusk, we motored into the broadening reaches of the river at Kununurra and at this time of the month, we could observe easterly the rising of the full new moon and westerly the setting of the sun, both reflecting on the waters of the Ord River.

The Argyle Diamond Mine 19 May 2011:

A flight from Kununurra out for a day visit to the Argyle Diamond Mine. On landing at the mine's airstrip and awaiting our transport to the mine proper it was explained to us that on the 1979 discovery of the rich alluvial diamonds an airport was hastily built (where we had just landed) for quick access into the area. Our guide explained that way this landing strip was sited within the surrounding area could hold up to $300 million of diamonds. The Argyle diamond mine is enormous and no matter where we observed as we were guided around, we could see huge trucks transporting their loads to the filtering sheds. On arriving our first introduction for our visit was, *"Under no circumstances was anyone to pick up anything."*

This photograph shows a portion of the huge Argyle Diamond Mine. Sixty thousand acres were resumed from a one hundred thousand acre cattle property, by the Western Australian State Government when diamonds were discovered in this area.

As the place was under full surveillance and if anyone was detected picking up anything they would be apprehended at the main gate by the meanest looking *bastard* in Australia with a glove on his big hand. No one picked up anything. Following a guided tour around the complex we pulled up where the truck maintenance area was situated, these trucks are gigantic and ladders are built externally onto the truck's frame just to have access to the cabin of the vehicle. The largest diamond to date found in the mine was extracted from the treads of the massive tyres of a vehicle that had been brought in for maintenance. Following a self-service lunch from the mine's canteen area we were taken to the on-location jewellery shop where all grades of diamonds were on display. Each visitor was given a small case enclosed diamond gift as a reminder of their visit. So ended an education about the Argyle Diamond Mine, which is deeply isolated in the vast Kimberly area.

The Bungle Bungles:

Several days later it was back into our air taxi for a return flight to the Bungle Bungle Range in the Purnululu National Park. This flight takes the best part of an hour flying over the vast Lake Argyle also the Argyle Diamond Mine. One can only truly digest the size of Lake Argyle when flying along its length. On passing over the Argyle Diamond Mine our pilot pointed out to us the mine's boundaries, which encompassed approximately 600,000 acres in area. This land was seized by the

Western Australian state government on the discovery of diamonds, taken without compensation to the station holders of the 1,000,000 acre property leaving the property holders with an estate of only 400,000 acres.

The Purnululu National Park and the magnificent Bungle Bungles.

Onto the Purnululu National Park and the Bungle Bungles. The pilot before landing at their airstrip flew us through quite a few canyons of these most impressive, beehive-banded sandstone formations. The airstrip is situated near Picaninny Creek where we alighted for a basic meal and another well-enjoyed history lesson. On leaving, our pilot once again flew us over and through this large unique area of the Kimberley. Once seen, never forgotten although I must say most impressive from the air.

So ended our Kimberley sojourn however I must state only a small portion of this huge area. We returned to Broome for a few days' stay at the impressive Cable Beach Resort before a flight back to Brisbane and home.

The Whitsundays

Besides driving in and out of Airlie Beach we had not yet seen the Whitsundays. So a bus ride to Brisbane, a flight to Hamilton Island and a transfer to the Reef View Hotel with a room overlooking Catseye Beach found us standing in the sunshine looking out to sea. We spent four days and nights seeing all Hamilton Island had to offer including the Sports Club, Marina Village, shops, restaurants and bars.

They do have an interesting small zoo on the island which does possess one huge crocodile. We visited the most impressive yacht club which is the home base of the many times winner of the Sydney to Hobart Yacht Race *Wild Oats*. During our stay, we were fortunate to get a very up-close inspection of this great ocean racer. On one occasion we enjoyed a half-day Whitehaven Beach tour which was a special attraction. We left by launch at Hamilton for a three-day/night stay on Hayman Island, Australia's iconic private island resort nestled at the northernmost point of the Whitsunday archipelago. Within this private island resort, stylish elegance reflects the harmony of nature with beautifully appointed accommodation set against the backdrop of the Coral Sea. Finally, by launch we returned to Hamilton Island for another night's stay, catching our aircraft back to Brisbane the following day.

A Little Bit of Victoria

We certainly picked a bad time to see a little of Victoria, in mid-July, however, settled into our Melbourne accommodation for a few days.

One of my desires when visiting Australia's second-largest city was to do an in-depth tour of their great stadium the Melbourne Cricket Ground (MCG) which I had never been to. I walked from the Central Business District (CBD) through a huge park took in Captain James Cook's cottage then crossed several main roads to enter the impressive stadium grounds. An outside circuit of the stadium admiring the impressive sporting statues of not only some of their great Australian rules players of history but also of some great Australian cricketers and athletes of world renown. On entering the stadium there are continuous group tours. I attached myself to one consisting of Indian tourists with myself being the only outsider in this group. The tour of the stadium covering its past sporting history is well covered including a chair painted in a different colour to all the surrounding chairs depicting the longest six ever hit on this ground by a Victorian in Simon O'Donnell.

The Indian tourists got excited when we entered the cricketer's player station. It was explained to us that this is where the batting side sits waiting their turn to venture to the crease and the seat where the next batsman due in sits awaiting the fall of a wicket.

The question was asked, *"Did Sachin Tendulkar sit here?"*

"Yes" replied our tour guide, *"Any batsman in next sits here."*

257

All the Indian tourists had to have their turn in sitting in the seat. Then it was on to the honour boards, which displayed the names of those that have either scored a century, which had Sachin's name recorded and the bowlers who had taken five wickets in an innings, during international games at this venue.

Regarding some of the logistics of the venue, we were shown the vast kitchens where some two hundred cooks would be employed to field an attendance of some 90,000 plus spectators. Through the changerooms of the Australian rules footballers where they would prepare for a game, we were allowed to walk onto a selected part of the stadium's turfed area. To stand on the playing area and complete a 360 degrees slow turn is when you grasp the immensity of this great sporting venue.

Of course, we were lectured on it being Australia's first Olympic games venue in 1956. That year is fixed firmly in my mind as I passed through Melbourne in 1956 on the initiation of my army career. As I had purchased an all-day ticket, it allowed me to explore their large and impressive sporting museum, which is the greatest in Australia and as such would challenge the world. Although it mainly concentrates on their great past Australian rules footballers it also includes other sports and great sporting identities of international fame. A feature that surprised me most was the number of Olympic games medals and associated photographs and details of the events, which had been donated to the museum. If you are a sporting buff and in Melbourne, put aside a day to absorb the sights and history of this majestic sporting colosseum, which was my most impressive memory of the city. On the way home, I walked out to the War Memorial to visit the statue of the great Australian, Weary Dunlop.

An hour train ride to Geelong, which was the first visit for either my wife Ailsa or me. We hired a car to explore the surrounding area and had dinner with an old army veteran, now a holder of a Member of the Order of the British Empire (MBE) whom I had served with. At that time he was an infantry captain and I was a WO2, his 2IC. After a few days in Geelong, Ailsa and I agreed that if we were to reside in Victoria, this would be our area of choice.

We then ventured the tourist trek along the stunning Great Ocean Road and its lovely towns and sights with overnight stays at Apollo Bay, a seafood village embraced by tranquil beaches followed by Port Fairy, which is a picturesque coastal town with a historic riverfront port and a thriving arts and food scene. From here we travelled north into the heritage-listed Grampians National Park (Gariwerd) for a several-day stay at Halls Gap, where unfortunately torrential rain set in. Three roads were closed to our north and the east, so our only way out was by backtracking south to Dunkeld onto the Glenelg Highway to Ballarat. There remained a continued deluge of rain and the mid-winter weather at Ballarat is cold and windy.

On leaving home I was still swimming, though definitely no swimming in central Victoria during winter. The next day's drive was to the Melbourne airport to return us to Brisbane, then home to Caloundra, the Sunshine Coast where swimming was again a feature of my weekly routine.

Across the Ditch

Having spent three tours in Scandinavia with my favourite in that part of the world being Norway I could just never keep out of their incredible and beautiful fjords. Talking to some friends about their majestic features one remarked that the equivalent in the southern hemisphere is located in the southwest of the South Island of New Zealand (NZ). This I had to see as I love these great natural features. Now my seafaring tourist line by sea, the Coral Princess within several months just happened to be departing Wellington (NZ) for a tour down the east coast of the South Island culminating in sailing into four sounds. I booked my passage and like on a previous trip, found a welcoming bottle of wine on the bedside table for this, my third tour with them.

A couple of days in Wellington and a walking tour of the city, once again visiting parliament house the Beehive in which some years earlier, I had been a guest of the speaker of the house for several hours one afternoon... another story. Wellington is a very impressive city situated on Cook Strait and as you often hear, is very windy at times.

Departing Wellington on the Coral Discoverer in the late afternoon we anchored up in a bay overnight on the north of the South Island where the next morning we did a walking tour in a part of Long Island. Proceeding south we pulled into Kaikoura and boarded a whale-watching boat. It was enjoyable spending several hours admiring these great sperm whales who reside near Kaikoura as these seas possess a two thousand metre deep trench just offshore. Following that experience and learning how they can descend to those depths, remain there for some time, and then surface again is an amazing feature of these denizens of the deep.

Sailing south our stopover the next morning was at Akaroa, east of the city of Christchurch on the Banks Peninsula. We had a half-day staying in beautiful Akaroa and I may say if one in my dotage had to live in NZ, Akaroa would be my home. It has a remarkable history. In the 1700's it was discovered by the French who left half its crew there to sail back to France, arrange a fleet to return and establish a French settlement. The British now aware of this operation sailed a small fleet to Akaroa and proclaimed it as a British possession by raising the Union Jack. Streets in Akaroa do have French and English names while both French and English flags are flown from different premises. Also whilst taking in the town sights I came across a War Memorial erected in the early 1920s which claims to be the first War Memorial erected in the southern hemisphere following the Great War of 1914 – 1918. Such history for a lovely town and setting.

An overnight journey saw us next morning enter Port Chalmers and alight in Dunedin. Dunedin is another historic city built in the early gold rush days and through their wealth, almost everything was imported from Scotland regardless until the goldfields waned. A day was spent in this city of the south which has New Zealand's most prestigious university, and I believe was erected from the plans of the Glasgow University in Scotland. Following a bus tour of the city, we were given a few hours to explore the CBD before boarding to resume our southern journey. Our next stop was Anchorage at Stewart Island for half a day and a three-hour walk to see the wonders of the planet's most southern temperate forest. Stewart Island was named after the British ship's captain who discovered it was an island, as decades before this Captain Cook had sailed under it and believed it to be part of the mainland. Leaving Stewart Island although my journey to date had been one of great interest and history, my main interest lay next. The first sound we entered was Dusky Sound, followed by Doubtful Sound into Thompson Sound and finally north to Milford Sound, which concluded our tour by sea.

A historian told us that most of New Zealand's earthquake occurrences commence in this area, then transfers upwards to and across Cook Strait then up the east coast of the North Island. While touring the sounds you could notice previous large mountain slides down the cliffs into the sounds creating small islands, which in turn became home to a variety of seals and birds. Some islands of long ago formation then began to grow their vegetation. One could also determine the age of mountain slides with some still obvious however revegetating while later slides had not yet commenced that process.

In one of the sounds, we landed and took note of cement plaque where Captain Cook stayed for some months commencing to plot latitudes of the earth. Longitudes were simple pole to pole however latitudes were a much more complex issue. No wonder Captain James Cook is regarded as perhaps the greatest seafarer and navigator of all time. Alighting at Milford Sound, we travelled by bus to Queenstown, New Zealand's greatest tourist area, followed by a several-hour stopover at Lake Te Anau, which is the largest of the southern glacial lakes.

**Glacial lake, Lake Te Anau looking back to Mitre Peak in
Milford Sound, South Island New Zealand.**

Flights from Queenstown to Brisbane are direct and as Queenstown was the end of the tour and is such a wonderful tourist area, I stayed for three days to take it all in, including jet boat rides. My curiosity now satisfied I can state the difference between the great fjords of Norway and those of New Zealand. For thousands of years, the fjords have been waterways between villages and towns with very little wildlife however majestic. The sounds of New Zealand are also majestic however covered in wilderness, in most cases inaccessible and possessed a large variety of wildlife. Both are strikingly magnificent features of nature.

South Australia 2018

Excluding two previous military reunions, our South Australian ventures to date had only been to Adelaide and Kangaroo Island, so we decided to explore more of what the state had to offer. Since it had been a while, we spent four days in Adelaide where we met and shared good company with old friends and indulged in several sightseeing tours. Amidst all the information that was shared with us, you can understand why Adelaide is known as the city of churches. I spent half a day at the impressive new Adelaide Stadium, strolling from my hotel over the footbridge and taking in the history of the outer grounds before entering this most outstanding sporting venue. The facility hosts Australian rules football and Test cricket and at the time of writing the first of the rugby league State of Origin series 2020, which even being huge underdogs, was won by Queensland. After this stay, it was time to pick up our car and head north.

We ensured we spent several days in the Clare Valley staying at the country club and visiting many wineries, a favourite being the Skillagalee Winery where an impressive history of the estate and the region was given to us. We proceeded north for a two-day stay at Port Augusta, which like most of the country we were driving through, sadly needed some good rains. Motoring down the Eyre Peninsula on the Lincoln Highway to Cowell at Franklin Harbour, we arrived at our final destination Port Lincoln staying in the large prestigious Port Lincoln Hotel overlooking the beautiful harbour. After five days in Port Lincoln and its surrounding areas, we left our car at Port Lincoln and flew over the Spencer and Vincent Gulfs for our connecting flight in Adelaide back to Queensland.

IN CONCLUSION

As a child, I can remember when men raised their hats, opened doors and pulled out the chairs for women. Children never interrupted adults' conversations and spoke when only spoken to. We adored our parents and obeyed them at all times. Further to this we also respected our teachers and the police with youth crime and theft being non-existent.

Playing outside was mandatory and desired by us, and all children had their indoor and outdoor chores to be completed daily with discipline at all times being the norm. Families sat and ate their dinner at a table together, never commencing to eat until Mother had sat down, then requested to be excused when leaving.

Christmas lunch was probably the most important meal of the year with us gorging ourselves, then to finish with the pudding and perhaps finding a threepence or sixpence piece. Only Dad would ever find a two-shilling piece, though the the possibility of finding the big payout always existed. Every child only received one present, however we were thrilled about accepting our gift.

I can remember when politicians were elected to serve the people and upon leaving school, everyone had a job, while national service was compulsory.

Nowadays after every monthly Returned Services League (RSL) meeting our vintage have a few beverages and more often than not the discussions would turn to our upbringing and early life, our youth and life's history in general. Strangely all tend to agree that our generation being the late 1930s to the 1950s was the lucky generation and does not have a great deal of confidence for the future of young Australians in today's society. Collectively we feel Australians are losing their identity, mateship and belief in their fellow man with decades of politicians' wayward immigration policies and the ever-increasing rate of crime, drugs and terrorism. Yes, we believe we were fortunate in becoming Australians in the latter part of the first half of the 20th century.

"Australia may be the smallest continent; however we are the only continent without foreign borders."

Up until recently, we used to boast such a statement, however power crazy state premiers have divided Australia by building walls and diminishing the unity we once shared. The Federal Government has to look at dismantling State Governments, expanding themselves and strengthening the local Councils. All this could be done on the $40 billion it costs this great country to run the State Governments annually.

"Unite Australia Again."

—◆—

With the passing of my first cousin Allan Woodard in August 2020, I now have arrived at the top rung of the Tasmanian Woodard's ladder, the last of our generation. However, I wish to add that some early life observations still exist, as I still open doors and pull out chairs for women.

—◆—

TWENTY-FIFTH ANNIVERSARY

THE REUNION

The author's first book 'Queensland Women in Rugby, The First Two Years 1996 – 1997' was released to mark the twenty-fifth anniversary of this outstanding team, which during the years was by far the most successful sporting team, male or female, in Australia. The anniversary and subsequent book launch were held at The Caxton Hotel, Brisbane on the 3rd of September 2021 during The Vintage Reds Annual Luncheon. In the following photograph are some of the thirty-one women, who represented Queensland during this era.

The Book Launch. 3rd September 2021 during The Vintage Reds Annual Luncheon at The Caxton Hotel, Brisbane.
Pearl Palaialii, Vanessa Nooteboom, Shelley Handcock, Christine Gold, Debbie Grylls, Amanda Dinsdale, Tanya Osbourne, Bronwyn Laidlaw, Natalie Wanrooy, Bronwyn Calvert, Jodie Kairl, Lisa Dwan, Bronwyn Hart, Lee Anne Wilkes surround their coach and author Tasi Woodard.

These books were gifted to the inaugural playing members whose results may never be equalled let alone excelled, and in many quarters were acknowledged as perhaps the greatest provincial rugby team in the world. That claim can be supported by their outstanding and freakish scoring results and the team was never defeated during this period. They also became the first Australian team to beat an International team that was ranked number two in the world of women's rugby.

Twenty-five years previous these women were elder teenagers or in their early twenties. Sadly some have passed, many are mothers and some are now grandmothers.

—⁓—

THE FINALE 2022 *Suncorp Stadium* Brisbane, Australia

The Queensland Rugby Union (QRU) is the only state in Australia to cap its women's representative players and for the very first time, this ceremony occurred on Saturday 2nd April 2022.

This event took place at 2:00 PM before the late afternoon and evening Super Rugby matches. Being the inaugural coach of the Queensland Women's team in 1996, I was invited to attend and present the caps to the players from that era.

The occasion took place in front of a very large crowd at the function area. Standing on a rostrum, the ceremony was initiated by the introduction of the players being invited onto the stage and presenting them with their caps. The No 1 cap was presented to Bronwyn Calvert, who was the inaugural Queensland Captain of 1996. Bronwyn was then followed by the players in alphabetical order with some two hundred caps covering twenty-six years of representation, presented on the day.

**Coach Tasi Woodard presents the No 1 cap to Bronwyn Calvert
the inaugural Queensland Captain of 1996.**

It was a pleasant experience to be introduced to husbands, parents, family members, and the children of ex-players.

A circuit of Suncorp Stadium was applauded by the large spectator contingent before the commencement of the Super Rugby matches.

It is worth noting that Selena Worsley became the first woman to be inducted into the Queensland Rugby Union Hall of Fame, representing her state in thirty-four matches over nine years.

2021 saw the twenty-fifth anniversary and the release of the book 'Queensland Women in Rugby. The First Two Years – 1996/1997' with a distribution of the book to those players at a function held in Brisbane. Now with the completion of the same ladies being capped at Suncorp Stadium on the twenty-sixth anniversary in 2022, concludes the history of Australia's most successful sporting team, male or female in 1996/1997.

—ᨓ—

To enjoy this book please visit your favourite book website
And search by Title & Author or quote ISBN: 9781925707571

—ᨓ—

BIBLIOGRAPHY

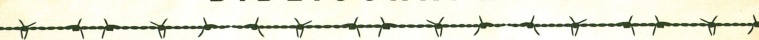

Farewell
Army HQ and *Defence Newspapers.* Silsby, Jason. imagery.copyright@defence.gov.au

Extract from The Army Newspaper 1982
Army HQ and Defence Newspapers. Mihaich, Richard. editorial@defencenews.gov.au

Barnes, Clifford Aubrey
Australian War Memorial. https://www.awm.gov.au/collection/C1017617

C.E.W. Bean
Bean, C.E.W. Official History of Australia in the War of 1914-1918 Vol VI - The AIF in France 1918 page 1043. Australia: Angus and Robertson Ltd, 1942.

Tragedy at King Cascade
Edwards, Hugh. Crocodile Attack in Australia. Australia: Swan Publishing, 1988.

Image of Fourex Brewery
Fearnley, Lachlan. https://en.wikipedia.org/wiki/Castlemaine_Perkins#/media/File:XXXX_Brewery_Milton.jpg.

King Island
https://www.freeworldmaps.net/australia/tasmania/map.html

Author's (C W Woodard) article
Ganey, Michael. Just One More Day: Their Stories. Montbrehain. Australia: Arramlu Publications Pty Ltd, 2019.

B' Company
Ganey, Michael. Just One More Day: Their Stories. Montbrehain. Australia: Arramlu Publications Pty Ltd, 2019.

Grange, Joy Winifred. Beyond Secrets - A Journey. Australia: Self-published, 2011.

King Island News 18 June 1919
King Island Courier. Smee, Holly. hollys@fontpr.com.au

King Island News 19 September 1917
King Island Courier. Smee, Holly. hollys@fontpr.com.au

Monash, John. Australian Victories in France in 1918 page 278. Great Britain: Naval & Military Press, 2009.

Citation Lt. Geaorge Ingram
McAleer, A J. Great Courage and Initiative: The Heroic Life of George Ingram VC, MM. Australia: Wandin & District Historical Museum Society Inc, 2015.

Queensland RSL News. Matilda-Editor editor@rslqld.org

Just a Common Soldier
Vaincourt, Lawrence. http://vaincourt.homestead.com/common_soldier.html

Death at Sea – Extract from the book Heroes at Sea by Don Wall.
Wall, Don. Heroes at Sea. Australia: Self-published, 1991.

Wikimedia Commons

Map of Phuoc Tuy Province
Anotherclown at Wikipedia. https://commons.wikimedia.org/wiki/File:Map_of_Phuoc_Tuy_Province_South_Vietnam.png

Image of Bungle Bungles
https://commons.wikimedia.org/wiki/File:183._Beehives_of_the_Bungle_bungles.jpg

Map of South East Asia
https://www.cia.gov/library/publications/the-world-factbook/docs/refmaps.html   https://cdn18.picryl.com/photo/2019/10/07/southeast-asia-d203ea-1024.jpg

Map of Malaysia
Fitzgerald, Peter. https://commons.wikimedia.org/wiki/File:Malaysia_regions_map.png

Map of Corps and 44 Provinces
George L. MacGarrigle, 'The United States Army in Vietnam: Combat Operations, Taking the Offensive, October 1966-October 1967'. Washington DC: Center of Military History, 1998. https://commons.wikimedia.org/wiki/File:South_Vietnam_Map.jpg

Image of Sydney Harbour, Sydney Olympics 2000

Shapinsky, David. Washington, D.C., United States, Public domain, Sydney Olympic Fireworks During Closing Ceremonies by Robert A. Whitehead, USAF, October 2000 https://commons. wikimedia.org/wiki/File:Fireworks,_Sydney_Harbour_Bridge,_2000_Summer_Olympics_closing_ ceremony.jpg

Image of Lake Te Anau
Shook, James. Wikimedia Commons. https://commons.wikimedia.org/wiki/File:On_Lake_Te_ Anau.jpg

Map of III Corp Tactical Zone
United States Army. https://commons.wikimedia.org/wiki/File:War_zone_C,_D,_Iron_Triangle_ Vietnam.jpg